D1472649

Also by Tim Mulligan

The Hudson River Valley: A History & Guide
Virginia: A History & Guide

The Traveler's Guide to
Western New England
and the Connecticut River Valley

The Traveler's Guide

TO

Western New England and the Connecticut River Valley

Vermont, New Hampshire, Western Massachusetts, and Connecticut

Tim Mulligan

Illustrations by Stan Skardinski

Random House New York

Library of Congress Cataloging-in-Publication Data

Mulligan, Tim
The traveler's guide to Western New England and the Connecticut River
Valley : Vermont, New Hampshire, Western Massachusetts, and
Connecticut / Tim Mulligan
p. cm.
Includes index.
ISBN 0-679-74413-4
1. New England—Guidebooks. 2. Connecticut River Valley—Guidebooks.
I. Title.
F2.3.M78 1944
917.404'43—dc20   93-44734

This book is dedicated—with equal affection—to
Ned and Grace
Sam and Susan

HOW TO USE THIS BOOK

When I write I like to think I'm writing to a friend, and therefore I have written only about things I enjoy—why should both of us be bored? Consequently, this guide makes no attempt to cover everything in the regions discussed.

In the *Where to Stay* sections I have not listed any motels, and unless they are exceptional or the only place to stay, I have also avoided listing hotels. After all, one of New England's most characteristic features is its inns, and that is where people want to stay. At the same time, many of the places listed have, to put it kindly, byzantine price structures that include—or don't include—a certain number of meals, require—or don't require—a stay of a specific number of nights, have—or don't have—seasonal rates, package offers, or midweek rates, and so forth. Therefore, I have developed a pricing key using the $ sign that can be translated as follows:

$	Up to $49
$$	$50 to $74
$$$	$75 to $99
$$$$	$100 to $149
$$$$$	$150 and up

This is only a guide, and when you call for reservations, *be sure* to ask what is included. In addition, if you plan to travel in the fall, *reserve as soon as possible.* In some cases, a year's lead time may not be enough.

In the *Where to Eat* sections I also use a $ key, which is based on the cost, for one person, of an entrée, a glass of wine or a drink, where available, and a dessert.

$	Up to $9
$$	$10 to $25
$$$	$25 and up

Again, this can serve only as a guide, not a guarantee. Please note: I urge you to make a reservation after you have selected a restaurant. I guarantee you that the time you don't reserve there will be an hour-long wait.

Important note: In addition, the hours and seasonal schedules of many of the smaller museums and places of interest can change faster than the leaves in autumn. It is always a good idea to call in advance.

Finally, I have learned from publishing other travel books that readers like to write and tell me of finds or disappointments that I can incorporate in later editions of the book. I hope you will do the same. Write: Tim Mulligan, c/o New England Books, 10 Montague Terrace, Brooklyn, N.Y. 11201.

CONTENTS

How to Use This Book   ix

Introduction: The Connecticut River Valley   xv

Vermont   1

  Map of Vermont   2

  Lake Champlain and Its Valley   8

    Burlington Area   8

    Middlebury   16

      A Drive   19

  Northern Vermont and the Northeast Kingdom   19

    Stowe   19

    The Northeast Kingdom   21

      Drives   21

      St. Johnsbury   23

  Central Vermont and the Upper Connecticut
  River Valley   24

    Woodstock   24

      A Drive   26

    Montpelier   28

    The Plymouth Notch Historic District   29

  Southern Vermont and the Upper Connecticut
  River Valley   31

    Bennington   31

    Grafton   35

      A Drive: Day 1   37

      A Drive: Day 2   39

Dorset	43
A Drive: Day 1	44
A Drive: Day 2	48
Where to Stay and Eat	49
New Hampshire	**65**
Map of New Hampshire	66
Northern New Hampshire—The White Mountains	71
The Kancamagus Highway	73
Franconia Notch	75
Pinkham Notch	78
Mount Washington	78
Crawford Notch	80
New Hampshire and the Upper Connecticut River Valley	82
Hanover	83
The River Villages North of Hanover	84
The River Villages South of Hanover	86
Central and Southern New Hampshire	90
The Lake Winnipesaukee Region	90
Nearby Excursion: Castle in the Clouds	92
A Special Drive	92
The Monadnock, Concord, and Manchester Regions	93
A Drive: The Monadnock Region	93
A Drive: The Concord Region	97
Manchester	100
Portsmouth and the Seacoast	104
What to See and Do	109
Nearby Excursions	114
Where to Stay and Eat	117

Western and Central Massachusetts   129

Map of Connecticut and Massachusetts   130

The Berkshires   133

   The Great Barrington Area   134

   The Lenox Area   139

   The Pittsfield Area   143

   The Stockbridge Area   150

     What to See and Do   151

   Tyringham Valley   159

   The Williamstown Area   162

     A Drive: The Mohawk Trail   164

The Connecticut River Valley   167

   Deerfield   167

   Amherst   172

   Northampton   173

   South Hadley   175

   Springfield   177

   Nearby Excursions   181

Where to Stay and Eat   187

Connecticut   199

Hartford and the Central Connecticut River Valley   204

   Hartford   204

   The Surrounding Area   212

     Farmington and Avon   212

     Granby   214

     Middletown   214

     New Britain   216

     Suffield   217

     Wethersfield   219

Windsor	222
Woodstock	224
The Connecticut Shore	225
Stonington and Mystic	225
New London	230
A Perfect Weekend: Essex, East Haddam,	
and Other Villages	232
New Haven	237
Western Connecticut	244
Litchfield	244
A Drive from Litchfield	248
A Drive from Litchfield That Includes the	
Housatonic Valley	251
Where to Stay and Eat	255
Index	271

INTRODUCTION
THE CONNECTICUT RIVER VALLEY

If there is one element that physically and culturally ties together the Western New England region of Vermont, New Hampshire, western Massachusetts, and Connecticut, it is the Connecticut River.

The Connecticut rises in New Hampshire, close to the Canadian border, and flows southward, eventually forming the border between Vermont and New Hampshire, then down through Massachusetts, meandering by Deerfield and Holyoke and Springfield, and on into Connecticut (named for the river), where it neatly bisects the state as it flows toward its exit into Long Island Sound.

The Connecticut is a peculiarly friendly river. Not for it the majestic course of the lower Hudson or the overwhelming power of the Mississippi, nor is it characterized by heavy river traffic and great industrial plants greedy for its waters. Instead, this is an intimate river, one bordered, generally, by broad fields and small towns; the few cities, such as Hartford and Springfield, are the exceptions. More typical of its banks are the glorious villages and towns of Essex and East Haddam, Wethersfield and Brattleboro, Hanover and Orford and Walpole. These are towns whose pasts still resonate in the present, giving the river and its valley a romantic nineteenth-century aspect.

I should also point out that this river valley has always supported a strong intellectual life, and that today it hosts an amazing number of great colleges, including Dartmouth, Amherst, the University of Massachusetts, Smith, Mount Holyoke, Wesleyan, and Trinity, as well as many secondary schools. In addition, in the seventeenth, eighteenth, and nineteenth centuries a distinctive culture developed here that has had a major influence on our country. To cite only one instance, the Connecticut River Valley drew the first westward-bound pioneers in our history when colonists from southeastern Massachusetts heard of its agricultural possibilities—it is the richest agricultural land in New England—and came to settle around Hartford. What they learned and how they developed would influence the entire westward movement.

In the nineteenth century, the painter Thomas Cole wrote about the Connecticut River in terms with which we can still identify. "Whether we see it at Haverhill, Northampton or Hartford," he wrote, "it still possesses that gentle aspect; and the imagination can scarcely conceive Arcadian vales more lovely or peaceful than the valley of the Connecticut—its villages are rural places where trees overspread every dwelling, and the fields upon its margin have the richest verdure." A quiet river, then, given to understatement, yet extremely influential, and bountiful in its gifts. It could be the description of a New England gentleman.

The River

The Connecticut—the word comes from the Indian word *Quenticut,* or one of its variations, which means "long tidal river"—is the longest river in New England, flowing 407 miles from its source in the Connecticut Lakes in northern New Hampshire to its exit into Long Island Sound, where it passes between Old Saybrook and Old Lyme. During its passage it drains over 11,000 square miles of Vermont, New Hampshire, Massachusetts, and Connecticut.

The history of the river after its European discovery in 1614 by the Dutchman Adrian Block (for whom Block Island in Long Island Sound is named) is woven throughout this book. Here let it suffice to say that the colonization of the valley, which began in Connecticut, then advanced to southern Massachusetts, and finally moved on to northern Massachusetts, New Hampshire, and Vermont, was undertaken by people united by the common bond of their Puritan ethic, and it was this that gave the entire region its homogeneity, not only in terms of religion and government but also in terms of its culture.

The Culture of the Valley

The first colonists were attracted by the rich soil and the consequent possibilities for agriculture. But what interests today's visitors to the region is the distinct yet thoroughly American culture these people created, a culture that is evident in their architecture, furniture, paintings, and other arts and crafts. For the traveler, these are the features that make the region so different from all others in New England and therefore so rewarding to visit.

For instance, in the eighteenth century Connecticut Valley architecture, although influenced by other regions of New England, developed the unique and instantly recognizable Connecticut Valley doorway, which can be seen today primarily in the region between Deerfield and Hartford. These richly carved, quirkily individualistic entranceways, characterized by pilasters supporting an entablature (upper section) and broken-scroll or swan's-neck pediment, have an exuberance more typical of folk art than of the sophisticated English baroque architecture from which they sprang. They are quintessentially American in their confidence and bold design.

The same individualism is seen in the furniture of the Connecticut Valley. There's even a cliché about valley furniture: "Odd + cherry = Connecticut." In the early colonial period, from about 1630 to 1730, the distinctive Hadley chests were crafted, with their handsome, stylized floral carvings. Today they can be seen in museums throughout the area, as well as in major American collections throughout the country. Later, in the period leading to the Revolution, Connecticut Valley cabinetmakers were creating many pieces as fine as those of their counterparts in Boston, Newport, New York, and Philadelphia, and the river carried their work to the households throughout the valley.

In painting, too, there is a distinctive valley personality, one that flowered primarily after the Revolution. In this book, the exemplar of valley painters is Ralph Earl (1751–1801), whose work is seen in almost every museum in the region and in major museums throughout the country, and who was the most influential artist in the valley.

Earl studied under Benjamin West in London and was perfectly adept at painting in the stylized English academic manner of the time, but his work in the valley is characterized by bright colors, patterned surfaces (floors and books, primarily), a linear brushwork that gives his sitters a certain shrewd angularity, and realism in the depiction of the sitters and the settings in which they actually lived, not the idealized settings so often used at this time. He expressed, in short, the values and beliefs of his patrons, and "reading" his portraits gives a unique insight into the character of the valley's citizens.

And so it goes throughout the valley. No matter what one looks at, from metalwork to ceramics and glass, from books and prints to clocks and textiles, there is a distinctive Connecticut River Valley stamp. As you travel through the valley, enjoying its scenery and its rich history—both its artistic development and its role in this country's life—you will become familiar with this Connecticut Valley style, and you will realize that what it really represents is a character we hear so much about—the old-fashioned Yankee.

Vermont

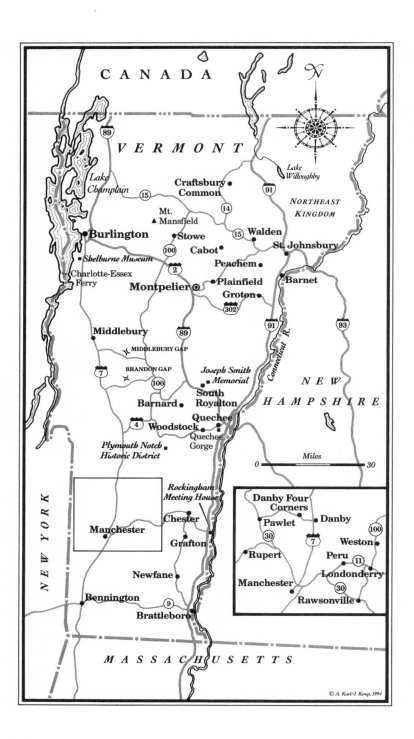

CANADA

VERMONT

89

Lake
Champlain

Lake
Willoughby

15

Craftsbury
Common

91

NORTHEAST
KINGDOM

Mt.
▲ Mansfield

14

Burlington

Stowe

15

Walden

St. Johnsbury

100

Cabot

■ Shelburne Museum

Peachem

2

Charlotte-Essex
Ferry

Montpelier ◉

Plainfield

Barnet

Groton

302

Middlebury

89

91

93

MIDDLEBURY GAP

7

BRANDON GAP

Joseph Smith
■ Memorial

NEW

100

Barnard

South
Royalton

HAMPSHIRE

4

Woodstock

Quechee

Plymouth Notch
Historic District

Quechee
Gorge

Miles

0   30

Rockingham
Meeting House

Danby Four
Corners

NEW YORK

Chester

Pawlet

Danby

100

Manchester

30

7

Weston

Grafton

Rupert

Peru

11

Londonderry

Newfane

Manchester

30

Bennington

9

Rawsonville

Brattleboro

MASSACHUSETTS

© A. Karl/J. Kemp, 1994

Area Code for Vermont: 802

Some general facts: Vermont is the third-smallest state in population (562,758 residents, according to the 1990 census) and is the most rural in the country. Its largest city, Burlington, has just under 38,000 people; its second-largest, Rutland, just over 18,000. I think it would be fair to say that to most Americans it epitomizes New England, eliciting in all of us the collective memory of a more innocent and idyllic past, a Currier and Ives Eden of green farms and white villages, welcoming church steeples in the distance, and riotous colors in the fall, deep snow and roaring fires in the winter, and rugged men and women who exemplify the American virtues of honesty, integrity, thrift, and charity. What is amazing is that so much of this is true.

As a result, Vermont has become a mecca for tourists; its appeal is reinforced by the fact that there are activities aplenty in every season. Consider: It is the skiing capital of the East, with such major ski resorts as Stowe, Stratton, Bromley, Killington, Sugarbush, and about twenty others, as well as fifty cross-country ski touring centers, all of which generate approximately $230 million a year. . . . It offers hundreds of lakes for water sports, including the 120-mile Lake Champlain. . . . It has some of the best bicycle touring routes in the country over untold miles of backcountry roads, which also make the more sedentary art of driving a pleasure (enhanced in both instances by the fact that outdoor advertising is forbidden throughout the state). . . . It is a hiker's paradise. . . . Why go on? You get the point.

What appeals most to me, and sets Vermont off from every other state in New England, is the villages. Simplicity is the keynote here. You will not see in Vermont the grand architecture that is found elsewhere in New England; splendid houses are the rare exception. But the villages throughout the state are extraordinary for their beauty, their diversity, their harmony with the landscape, and an architecture that could have inspired the aphorism "Less is more."

History

"Regardez les verts monts," Samuel de Champlain said as he sailed southward on the lake that bears his name, and he thereby named the state. It doesn't keep me up at night, but why, I wonder, was such an obvious—even banal—comment retained in the minds of future generations and then transposed into Vermont? In any case, it's a very pretty name.

It was the French who created the first settlement in Vermont, in 1666, on the Isle La Motte in Lake Champlain, but it did not survive. It wasn't until 1724, when the English established Fort Dummer on the Connecticut River, near the present site of Brattleboro, that permanent settlement took hold. The reason for the relatively late entry of settlers into the region was that the French and Indians constantly raided the territory, and it was only with the English victory at Quebec in 1759 that the area became relatively safe for colonization.

At this time, the land between the Connecticut River, today Vermont's eastern border, and Lake Champlain, a good part of today's western border, was claimed by both New Hampshire and New York and was known as the New Hampshire Grants.

In 1764, Governor Benning Wentworth, mentioned several times in this book, began making grants of townships west of the Connecticut, claiming New Hampshire's domain extended westward from the Atlantic Coast to Lake Champlain, and to a line twenty miles east of the Hudson. That intensely irritated the New Yorkers, and their authorities insisted with equal vehemence that their eastern border was the Connecticut River. Both groups made grants, and the result was chaos. (An interesting aside on Governor Wentworth: Throughout this period he managed to retain for himself the choicest part of his township grants, and he wound up accumulating 100,000 acres of land. Bennington is named after him.)

Back and forth, back and forth went the claims and counterclaims, and eventually the whole matter was laid before the king, George III. He, in 1770, decided that New York's was the valid claim, and New York, exhibiting total arrogance, promptly began to dispossess settlers who had received their grants from New Hampshire, or to make them pay for the land all over again.

In the best of circumstances this kind of approach will not make people happy. In this instance it provoked Ethan Allen (1738–1789), who, with his brother Ira and several other leaders, had organized the Green Mountain Boys in 1764. "Be it known," Allen wrote Governor Tryon of New York, "that we will not be fooled or frightened out of our property, and that persons are cowards indeed if they cannot as manfully fight for their liberty, property and life as villains do to deprive them thereof." At another time he sent an invitation to the New Yorkers to come up to Vermont and meet "as good a regiment of marksmen and scalpers as America can afford." New York, it would turn out, had bitten off more than it could chew.

Allen is best remembered now for his role in capturing Fort Ticonderoga from the British in the first engagement of the Revolution, in May 1775. But his chief significance is that he and his allies were the true founders of Vermont—although they did not accomplish this without a struggle.

In 1777 Vermont, getting nowhere with the Continental Congress in its struggle to escape the clutches of New York, declared itself an independent republic and drew up a constitution modeled on the liberal constitution of Pennsylvania, but with two significant additions: it outlawed slavery (Vermont was the first state in the country to do so) and it allowed universal male suffrage without property requirements (again, Vermont was the first to include this provision).

After the Revolution, New York still refused to abandon her claim, and Vermont continued in its independent-republic state for a total of fourteen years, coining its own money, running a postal service, and treating with such foreign nations as the United States. There even was talk of Vermont's rejoining Britain by allying herself with Canada if her claims to sovereign independence weren't recognized by the United States. Finally, after New York's claims were settled for the sum of $300,000, the way was cleared for Vermont to join the Union, and in 1791 President George Washington and Secretary of State Thomas Jefferson signed a bill passed by Congress making Vermont the fourteenth state of the United States.

To this day, though, Vermont retains its veneration for independence, expressed most obviously through its Town Meeting

One of the great joys of Vermont is its simplicity—a modest but well-designed white Congregational church, a lovely shaded green, a war memorial, clapboard houses, and quiet streets . . . you are truly away from it all.

Day, held on the first Tuesday in March, when many of the towns and villages discuss and vote on municipal and school budgets.

In the nineteenth century, much of the land that had been claimed and cleared as farmland at so much cost was abandoned when the more welcoming lands of the West were opened to settlement. As a result, forests have reclaimed a major portion of the farmland. Now dairy farming is the principal farm industry in the state, and the black-and-white Holsteins, Brown Swiss, and Jerseys sometimes seem to outnumber the two-footed population.

Vermont is the country's largest producer of maple sugar, and you see signs everywhere announcing that *real* maple sugar is sold here. Sheep raising is making a comeback—it was very important during part of the nineteenth century—and Morgan horse breeding (see page 18) also has a central place in Vermont. And, of course, Vermont granite and Vermont marble are famous, the former found in Barre, the latter in Proctor. Interestingly, this highly rural area ranks fourth in the nation

with respect to the percentage of its nonagricultural labor force
employed in high-technology industries.

Special Interest Sources

Sources of information on specialized interests are listed
below.

ANTIQUING

For a listing of over one hundred members of the Vermont
Antique Dealers Association, with a brief description of their
stock, send a stamped, self-addressed business-size envelope to
Muriel McKirryher, 55 Allen Street, Rutland 05701.

BOOKSTORES SPECIALIZING IN VERMONT

The Vermont Historical Society Shop in Montpelier has the
most complete stock of books on Vermont known to man, but
other favorites are the Johnny Appleseed (362-2458) in
Manchester, a dream of a bookshop with a large stock of out-of-
print books in many categories; and the Vermont Bookshop
(388-6991) in Middlebury, which also carries out-of-print ti-
tles. I also wouldn't skip Cold Hollow Cider Mill near Stowe
(see page 21).

MAPS

The official state map is available from the Vermont Travel
Division, 134 State Street, Montpelier 05602. Telephone: 828-
3236. The problem with it, though, is that it isn't very useful
for traveling on many of the glorious back roads that make
Vermont such a rewarding place to explore. For that you will
need "The Vermont Road Atlas and Guide," available from
Northern Cartographics, 4050 Williston Road, South Burlington 05403. Telephone 860-2886 for the exact cost. And remember—*always start out with a full tank of gas.* Shell, Mobil,
and Exxon are not readily found in state forests or on mountain
peaks and dirt roads.

LAKE CHAMPLAIN AND ITS VALLEY

This 120-mile-long body of water, shared by New York, Vermont, and Canada, takes its name from the French explorer Samuel de Champlain, who sailed down it from Canada in 1609.

For the French, the lake was an extremely important "highway" for the shipment of their furs, and it enabled them and their Indian allies to attack the English and the colonials with ease. As I mentioned earlier, this constant threat was a primary reason that Vermont was settled later than other areas of New England.

Then the English defeated the French at Quebec, and with the onset of the American Revolution, the English, too, saw the lake as the means of relatively easy entry into the colonies; they planned to send their invasion force west to the Hudson River, bring it under their control, and thereby neatly split the colonies in two. It was not a bad plan, but it didn't work. Nor did another plan work in the War of 1812, when the English once again tried to use the lake to send their troops on an invasion into the United States.

Burlington Area

The Shelburne Museum   This is one of the most extraordinary and original museums in this country and the most popular attraction in Vermont. You will need the better part of a day to do it full justice.

In 1947, Electra Havemeyer Webb (1888–1960) began developing plans to start a museum where she could display what she perfectly described as her "Collection of Collections." Currently there are thirty-seven exhibit buildings containing roughly eighty thousand artifacts, all spread out over forty-five acres and representing three hundred years of American history and art. It seems that everything is here: a covered bridge, a lighthouse, a 220-foot steamboat, a Victorian railroad station, paintings and decoys, weather vanes, magnificent carousel figures, glass canes and toys and cigar-store Indians. No one could walk away from this brilliant, joyous celebration of America and Americana dissatisfied.

This little covered bridge on a dirt road is so perfect that it brings a tug to the heartstrings.

It was a cigar-store Indian, in fact, that was the first American piece Mrs. Webb bought. She tells the story in a recorded talk she gave in Colonial Williamsburg in 1958, and you can hear her recount it yourself if you see the orientation film available to visitors at the museum's entrance.

"One day," Mrs. Webb says, "I was driving through our little town of Stamford, Connecticut, and what should I see but a cigar-store Indian. Well, she spoke to me; I just had to have her. So I went in and I said to the man, 'Will you sell me that cigar-store Indian?' Well, he looked me over and he said, 'Have you got fifteen dollars?' I said, 'No, but I'll get it.' So, at any rate, I took this man's word that he'd keep the Indian for me and I went home, got the fifteen dollars, came down with the old foreman of our place and the wagon, and brought her home to my mother. Ladies and gentlemen, if you could have seen my mother's face! She said, '*What* have you done?' And I said, 'I've bought a work of art.' She said, 'This is perfectly dreadful.'"

Not terribly surprising, as her parents were Henry Osborne Havemeyer (1847–1907) and Louisine Havemeyer (1855–1929), two of the most extraordinary collectors our country has ever produced and, among other things, the first Americans to buy Impressionist pictures. Louisine's bequest of the better part of her collection—1,972 objects ranging from paintings and Japanese prints to Oriental brocades and sculptures—to the Metropolitan Museum of Art ensured that institution's European paintings collection a place among the world's greatest. In fact, it's worthwhile telling you a bit about her.

In 1875, Mrs. Havemeyer, then Louisine Elder, met the great American Impressionist painter Mary Cassatt while on a visit to Paris. They immediately took a shine to each other, and Cassatt took Miss Elder to Degas's studio, where Miss Elder promptly bought *Ballet Rehearsal,* now in the Nelson-Atkins Museum of Art in Kansas City. (Mrs. Havemeyer later wrote of the experience, "It was so new and strange to me. I scarcely knew how to appreciate it or whether I liked it or not, for I believe it takes special brain cells to understand Degas. There was nothing the matter with Miss Cassatt's brain cells, however, and she left me in no doubt as to the desirability of the purchase, and I bought it upon her advice.") Thus began a lifelong relationship, later joined by her husband, who had accumulated a vast fortune in the sugar trade. The result was one of the greatest collections of art ever assembled in this country.

Electra was their second daughter, and in 1910 she married James Watson Webb, a descendent of Commodore Vanderbilt with, of course, a sizable fortune of his own. It was Webb who introduced her to Vermont, and it was here that she began collecting her American works with an appetite that can only be called voracious and with tastes years ahead of her time. "How can you, Electra," said her mother, "you who have been brought up with Rembrandts and Manets, live with such American trash?" Fortunately for us, Electra paid no attention.

In 1947, her brother-in-law, Vanderbilt Webb, gave her the superb Webb family collection of carriages and sleighs. This gave Electra the opportunity she had been looking for to start a museum, and she bought a red brick farmhouse (c. 1840) and eight acres of land in Shelburne. Quite soon after, her holdings would be expanded to twenty acres. To house the carriage collection she built a horseshoe-shaped barn, one of the handsomest buildings on the museum grounds, whose beams and 17,000 feet of boarding came from dismantling eleven old regional barns and two grist mills. This was the first building constructed at the museum; it was opened to the public, along with eleven other period buildings, in 1952. These and later period buildings were moved here from all over Vermont. Today, the oldest house on the site is the 1733 Prentis House from Hadley, Mass. That, the Shaker Shed, from East Canterbury, N.H., and the Stencil House, from Columbus, N.Y., are the only structures from outside the state.

I won't describe all the buildings, but I will tell you something of a few favorites to give you some idea of the richness of the place.

The visitor enters the museum grounds through the **Round Barn,** built in 1901 and 60 feet tall and 80 feet in diameter. The 9,000-pound silo, by the way, was moved here and placed in the center of the building by helicopter.

From there I like to go straight to the **Circus Parade Building,** where I am invariably awestruck by the glorious, 518-foot tableau of a circus parade with 450(!) individually carved horses. The ensemble is the embodiment of every child's fantasies of what the Greatest Show on Earth is all about. There are also circus posters and 40 carousel animals from the Gustav Denzel Company, the first American carousel manufacturer, some of which were carved by Daniel Muller, one of the greatest of all carousel artists. And I must mention the intriguing 3,500-piece circus you see as you enter the building. Created between 1916 and 1956 in Harrisburg, Pa., by a man named Edgar Decker Kirk, it is a tour de force of wit, joy, and artistry.

My favorite building—at least as of this moment—is the **Vermont House** because of the brilliant selection of furnishings, including eighteenth-century Philadelphia and Newport pieces and a particularly handsome Connecticut desk and bookcase, as well as the fine paneling and antique French wallpapers. But certainly no one should miss the **Stencil House,** with its perfectly preserved and extremely fine floor-to-ceiling stenciling dating from the first quarter of the nineteenth century; or the 1840 rose pink **Meeting House,** with its simple, dignified beauty that, when seen in conjunction with the **Vergennes Schoolhouse** (1830—and perfect, down to its books and charts and maps), is so evocative of earlier American values and priorities; or the **Tuckaway General Store and**

Apothecary Shop, which is crammed to the rafters with all the goods you would have seen one hundred years ago and also contains a post office, a barbershop, and dentist's and doctor's offices.

And then there's the **Stagecoach Inn,** which dates from just after the Revolution and has an outstanding and vast collection of American wood sculpture and weather vanes; the late-Victorian **Shelburne Depot,** with its railroad memorabilia, including, on a siding, a private railroad car that is the last word in luxury; or the **Dorset House,** with more than 1,000 decoys. . . . As you can see, the list goes on.

Special to me, too, are the SS *Ticonderoga* and the **Colchester Reef Lighthouse.**

The *Ti* operated on nearby Lake Champlain from 1906 until 1954, when it was finally moved overland to the museum grounds in a remarkable operation that included a sixty-eight-day journey over the two-mile distance. Along with the steam-engine train, steamboats seem to me incredibly romantic, and I find it intriguing to actually wander around one, reading old broadsides and examining old photos and getting as near as humanly possible to a bygone means of transportation.

As for the lighthouse, it served from 1871 to 1933 to warn sailors of one of the most treacherous reefs on Lake Champlain. It was built for the ages, or, rather, to withstand the devastating winds and storms that sweep across that part of Lake Champlain. The timbers, for example, are both pegged and bolted together, and the sills are anchored to the building's foundation by iron rods that are three feet long. It has real charm—snug bedrooms and pleasantly proportioned kitchen and living room—but even with a loving family around one, how desolate and lonely it must have been at times, with the wind howling around the tower, or the 1,600-pound bell tolling its warning through the clinging fog.

Finally, there are two other buildings you must visit, the **Webb Gallery** and the **Electra Havemeyer Webb Memorial Building.**

The Webb Gallery contains American paintings covering three centuries of American life and was the last project the Webbs undertook together, for it was opened in 1960, the year in which they both died. It is strongest in its examples of

American art from the first six decades or so of the nineteenth century. (Don't miss, though, the very fine Copley portrait *John Scollay*, with its subdued palette of silvery greens and whites and its remarkable insight into the sitter's character.)

I particularly like three seascapes from the nineteenth century: *The Burning Ship* (1869) by Albert Bierstadt, with its masterly and dramatic use of light; Fitz Hugh Lane's quietly glowing *Sunrise Through Mist* (1852); and Martin Johnson Heade's *Coastal Scene with Sinking Ship* (1863), with its ominous portent of doom rendered almost palpable by the angry black of an overarching storm, in sickening contrast to the shrinking pink-and-blue sky.

In addition, the Hudson River School is well represented—Cole, Cropsey, Church, and others—and there are some excellent genre pictures, as well as Winslow Homer's wonderful *Milking*; Erastus Salisbury Field's *Garden of Eden*, in which the serpent happily skitters away, tongue flashing, as Eve reaches for the apple; and a rather bizarre but fully realized picture by Charles Deas called *The Death Struggle,* in which a frontiersman and an Indian, on horseback and locked in mortal struggle, plunge over a precipice as the Indian's companion watches, horrified. Deas would die insane, and this picture is deeply disturbing but oddly compelling.

The Electra Havemeyer Webb Memorial Building was built by the children of the Webbs to hold what Mrs. Webb had kept of her portion of the Havemeyer art collection. Over a period of seven years, six rooms were removed from the Webbs' apartment at 740 Park Avenue, brought to this specially constructed Greek Revival building, and then reconstructed exactly as they had been in New York, including all furniture, paintings, and sculptures.

The rooms are fascinating, not only for the spectacular art they contain—Degas, Rembrandt, Cassatt, Whistler, Monet, Manet, Courbet, to name a few—and the superb examples of French, English, and American furnishings and English eighteenth-century paneling, but also for the vanished lifestyle they represent. The Webbs were members of the last generation of fabled American millionaires who could buy anything they wished—and did. Fortunately, as time passed, many came to see their vast wealth as a public responsibility, and it can be truly said that Electra Havemeyer Webb and her mother both accepted their responsibility and left their country richer in ways that are inestimable.

Shelburne Museum, on Route 7 five miles south of Burlington, is open daily, mid-May to mid-October, 9–5. Admission fee. Telephone: 985-3344. There is a cafeteria on the grounds.

Shelburne Farms   This was the estate of William Seward Webb and Lila Vanderbilt Webb, the parents of James Watson Webb. Now, I have learned that whenever you see the words "Vanderbilt house," you can expect something huge, and if you see "Vanderbilt cottage," it's even bigger. This 1,000-acre estate, with a 110-room "house" that is the largest in Vermont, is no exception. It is well worth a visit; both the landscape and the buildings are on the National Register of Historic Places. In fact, if you were to see only the **Farm Barn** the visit would be worth the time. This is the most spectacular and beautiful barn I've seen in this country. It is reputed to be the largest barn in the United States; the courtyard alone covers two acres, and the barn is five stories high.

The farm-estate was developed between 1886 and 1902 as a model farm. Frederick Law Olmstead, who designed Central Park in New York City, was the consulting landscape architect. Gifford Pinchot, this country's first chief forester and reforming conservationist, was the forester, and Robert Henderson Robertson was the architect of the Queen Anne Revival house. The Webb family continued to live there until 1976.

Today the estate is owned by an independent nonprofit educational organization known as Shelburne Farms Resources, whose mission is "to preserve, maintain and adapt [the estate's] historic buildings, landscape and productive farmland for teaching and demonstrating the stewardship of natural and agricultural resources."

You can now stay at the house; it has been converted into an inn with twenty-four bedrooms and would be my choice for this region. You can also just visit the farm and take the ninety-minute guided tour in an open wagon; it gives you a good introduction to the landscape and includes stops at the Dairy Barn (but not the Farm Barn) and the gardens at Shelburne House, beautiful in themselves, spectacular when you include the backdrop of Lake Champlain. In fact, the views of lake and mountains from the house rank among the best in Vermont.

If you don't wish to take the guided tour, there is a walking tour that begins at the Visitors' Center and meanders through field and woodlands for about one mile. This is my particular favorite because it includes both the Farm Barn and, from Lone Tree Hill, the single best view of the Adirondacks and Lake Champlain on the estate.

The Visitors' Center also has a Farm Store, where you can buy Shelburne Farms cheddar cheese made from the milk of their own Brown Swiss cows, as well as cob-smoked hams and delicious sourdough bread. There is also a free slide show on the history and evolution of the farm.

The Visitors' Center is open year-round and has a mail order catalogue. To order a copy, telephone: 985-8686. Shelburne Farms, about a mile south of Shelburne Museum on Route 7, is open every day, mid-May through mid-October, 9–5. Admission fee. Telephone: 985-8686.

The Vermont Wildflower Farm   Only about five miles south of the Shelburne Museum on Route 7, this is the largest wildflower seed center in the East. But another reason to make a visit here is to explore the six acres of meadow and forest, complete with a brook and pond, all awash with wildflowers, whose colors change with the seasons to form a continuing kaleidoscope. Asters and cornflowers, cosmos and black-eyed Susans, devil's paintbrush and lupine, poppies and dame's rocket . . . Go, see, enjoy, and learn—it is not only very beautiful but also very instructive, for the pathways are filled with informative plaques that describe what you are looking at and tell you some of the history and legends and interesting facts associated with it. You can easily spend a refreshing hour here.

You might want to see the film *Wildflowers Through the Seasons* before you set out because it is well done and sets the perfect mood. (A nice bit of trivia I learned here: Did you know that the only place in the world that has fall coloring as vibrant as New England's is a small area of China?) In addition, there is a gift shop that has everything from china and crystal in wildflower designs to wildflower potpourri. The seed shop is spectacular, as you might expect.

The Vermont Wildflower Farm is open every day, early May through October, 10–5. Admission fee. Telephone: 425-3500.

Charlotte–Essex Ferry   If you have the time, take this short (twenty minutes) trip across Lake Champlain to Essex, N.Y. The trip offers some spectacular scenery, and it's an excellent way to enjoy Lake Champlain.

The Charlotte–Essex Ferry is in operation from April through January and can take your car if you wish. Because the times can vary, telephone 864-9804 for the schedule and fares.

Middlebury

I've always had a soft spot for this town. It's very pretty, with an impressive falls right at its heart, which you can see from Frog Hollow (see below) or from the west side of the Main Street bridge, and lovely old houses that make wandering about particularly pleasant. If you want to take a more formal walking tour, contact the Information Center (388-7951) for a

No one ever claimed Vermont was flat, and this street in Middlebury, in the Frog Hollow section, is certainly no exception.

map and information. Middlebury is home to a good college, with all the attendant activities, and there is enough to do in the town and around the region to fill two very pleasant days.

Congregational Church The most prominent building in Middlebury, and almost exactly at its heart, is this magnificent church (1806–1809) by Lavius Fillmore, the architect of the Congregational church in Bennington. Some consider this to be his masterpiece, and while I prefer the slightly earlier Bennington church, it is true that this building does have a more refined exterior. Like the Bennington building, this one was inspired by Boston-based Asher Benjamin's *The Country Builder's Assistant,* one of seven pattern books he wrote that helped spread Georgian, Federal, and Greek Revival styles throughout New England. The original interior was reworked in 1854, and some restoration was done in 1925.

Frog Hollow and the Vermont State Craft Center Frog Hollow was once the heart of Middlebury's industrial life. Among other things, it was here that the Vermont marble industry began in 1802 with the development of a machine that could carve marble, which was quarried in the Hollow. John Deere apprenticed here between 1821 and 1825, before moving to Illinois and fame and fortune.

Today it is an attractive assemblage of old stone buildings housing various businesses that cater to the tourist trade; it also offers the best views of the Middlebury Falls. It is the home, too, of the Vermont State Craft Center. Located in a renovated mill, the Center displays a wide range of arts and crafts, including pottery, glass, textiles and fabrics, jewelry, and wooden ware. The quality, naturally, varies, but for the most part the material displayed is quite good, and it's interesting and instructive to see what these artists are producing.

The Vermont Craft Center is open: May through December, Monday–Saturday, 9:30–5:30, Sunday, 12–5; January through April, Monday–Saturday, 10–5. Telephone: 388–3177.

Middlebury College Founded in 1800, this small college (1,900 students) has a pretty campus that you should take time to drive through, visiting in particular Old Stone Row, which includes Painter Hall (1815), the oldest building in the college and now primarily a dormitory, and Old Chapel (1835–1836), now an administration building.

The Morgan Horse Farm   The farm, only 1 1/2 miles from the town, is owned by the University of Vermont. Morgan horses are named after Justin Morgan, who created the first American breed of horse, famous for its strength, speed, and endurance. The Morgan is now Vermont's official state animal.

This farm was founded in the nineteenth century to study and improve the Morgan breed, and students from the university care for the horses. Visitors are allowed to tour the barn, a handsome nineteenth-century structure, and watch the daily workouts and training. The last time I was there it was foaling time, and after a short, informative tour, I watched the mothers nursing and caring for the foals.

There are guided tours and slide shows at the Morgan Horse Farm May through October, 9–5. Admission fee. Telephone: 388-2011.

There is only one word for this church: jolly. Rarely have I seen a cozier, happier-looking place of worship, and for me it is always a joy to see on the drive through the Middlebury Gap.

A DRIVE

One of the nicest drives in Vermont is from Middlebury
through the Middlebury Gap, then down to Rochester, and return by the Brandon Gap. It is "all scenery," a description of
which would only take up your time. Trust me. It is perfection.
Take Route 125 through the Middlebury Gap to Hancock, go
south on Route 100 to Rochester, west on Route 73 through the
Brandon Gap to Brandon and Route 7, where you will go north
to East Middlebury and then back into Middlebury.

NORTHERN VERMONT AND THE NORTHEAST KINGDOM

Stowe

Famous as a skiing resort, Stowe is an attractive village at the
base of Mount Mansfield, Vermont's highest peak at 4,393 feet.
Less well known is that there are summer activities here, too;
swimming, horseback riding, mountain climbing, and hiking
are all available. Stop at the Stowe Area Association in the
heart of the village to receive full information about what is
going on during your visit or to ask about your particular interests. You also can write: The Stowe Area Association, Box
1320, Stowe, Vt. 05672, or telephone 253-7321.

WHAT TO SEE AND DO

Mount Mansfield From the summit you can enjoy one of
the most sweeping vistas in Vermont; on a clear day you see all
the way west to Lake Champlain, north to Canada, and east to
New Hampshire's White Mountains. There are two ways to approach the summit; neither actually goes to the summit because it is a protected area with fragile arctic-alpine flora.

The Mount Mansfield Toll Road, which is open every day
from 9:30 to 5:00 from late May to mid-October, weather permitting, costs $6.00 per car and is a 4 1/2-mile gravel road with

steep hairpin turns. It does not go all the way to the summit and you have to hike the last 1 1/2 miles. However, it has one advantage—about 1/2 mile north of the Toll Road's entrance you will see a parking area. On the right you will find a path that leads through the woods to **Bingham Falls,** a deep chasm with a lovely series of waterfalls.

The other way is by gondola, which operates on weekends from late May to late June, 9:30–5:00, and then on a daily basis until mid-October, weather permitting, of course. The cost for this is $6.00, too, and it lets you off at a point near the summit.

Smugglers Notch   Another killer of a road. Narrow and full of hairpin turns, it climbs rapidly upward through dense forest and between large boulders that have split from the notch walls. Needless to say, the road is closed in winter. Still, "no pain, no gain," and the rugged beauty of the scenery makes it all worthwhile. Just be sure your car is in good shape.

Ben & Jerry's   Ben & Jerry's ice-cream factory, south of Stowe on Route 100, and the Shelburne Museum are the most-visited attractions in Vermont. Why is Ben & Jerry's so popular? I thought to myself, and without much enthusiasm, I must admit, off I went. They converted me, and you should go, too. The tour is amusing and cleverly done.

First of all, it's not too long, only thirty minutes, for the first ten of which they show slides with a witty, upbeat narration that tells you how Ben and Jerry turned $5.00 into a highly successful business. Not only that, you'll also see the interesting ways they share that success with their employees and community and how important they have become to Vermont's dairy industry.

Next you go out to the mezzanine, where you can watch the action in the production room below and learn how the ice cream is made. You also get a sample of the Flavor of the Day. The factory is quite unlike any I've ever seen, and the tour is fun and informative. Now I can understand its popularity.

A word of caution: I was there early in the morning on a rainy June day, and there was only one busload of people. But in July and August, I understand, it can be a madhouse, with the tours filling up immediately, so plan ahead and try to get

there in the morning. Another note: There is no ice-cream production on Sundays, holidays, and what they call company
celebration days, and a video is substituted.

Finally, near Ben & Jerry's, on Route 100 in Waterbury, is
Cold Hollow Cider Mill. Here you can get apple cider doughnuts so delicious that any effort you have made to get there will
seem worthwhile. They also have excellent cider, an extensive
gift shop, and an excellent selection of books on Vermont.

Ben & Jerry's is open year-round. Admission fee. (Half of the
proceeds are given to nonprofit and community groups in
Vermont.) Tours begin every thirty minutes, September
through June; every fifteen minutes in July and August.
Telephone: 244-8687.

The Northeast Kingdom

This area, which was named by Vermont's late United States
senator George Aiken in the late 1940s, is very different from
the rest of the state because it is mostly undeveloped. It is also
very poor, in large part, and very beautiful, with miles of unspoiled scenery filled with forests, lakes, and mountains, farms
and tiny villages, valleys and streams, and is reminiscent of
what Vermont must have been like years ago. The fall coloring
here is considered by many to be the finest in New England,
and consequently in autumn it is full of visiting "leaf peepers."

Bordered on the north by Canada, on the east by the
Connecticut River, on the south by the little villages just below
St. Johnsbury, the region's "capital," and on the west by Jay
Peak, it shelters a world of its own. Spend a day or two driving
here, soaking up the scenery. Almost any drive in the area will
be beautiful, but I would suggest three as particularly representative.

DRIVES

First of all, I would suggest that you stay in **Craftsbury
Common** at the **Inn on the Common.** You will be comfortably and conveniently situated in a perfect setting, for the village, with its huge green, creates an atmosphere that could
define the word *pastoral.* From here, a drive in almost any di-

rection is rewarding, but be sure to travel **Route 14** between Irasburg and Hardwick, and then just set off to get lost. (North of Irasburg, by the way, you may wish to explore Newport and the 33-mile-long Lake Memphremagog.)

A second suggestion, for those who will be there in the fall: Six villages near St. Johnsbury (see page 23) participate in the Northeast Kingdom Fall Foliage Festival, and a day-long tour through them is extremely pleasant. Each day during the festival one of the villages hosts special activities—craft fairs, church suppers, special house tours, and so forth. In alphabetical order the participating villages are: **Barnet** (a view of which is on the cover of this book), **Cabot, Groton, Peacham, Plainfield** and **Walden.** Obviously, visiting at this time of the year can be great fun—remember, though, reservations are a must and have to be made months in advance—but these villages and the surrounding scenery are pretty enough to make a trip at any time of the year a memorable experience. Peacham, for instance, is on the crest of a hill where the sky seems endless and the simple Congregational church (1806) and lovely white frame houses are quintessential Vermont.

My third day-trip has **Lake Willoughby** as its goal. Wander as the mood moves you, but be sure to approach from the south on Route 5A because it offers a grand and beautiful view of the

This wonderful little house looks, as they used to say in New England, "as snug as a bug in a rug."

lake and the two mountains at the southeastern end, Mount Pisgah and Mount Hor. The lake's setting is particularly theatrical, for these mountains have cliffs that form an extraordinary backdrop as they rise for a thousand feet or so above the water.

St. Johnsbury

Two notable facts that I shall immediately pass on to you: St. Johnsbury, population about 8,000, claims to have the oldest continuing performing band in the nåtion (1830), and the art gallery (see below) is the oldest art gallery still exactly as it was when it first opened.

The principal reason for coming here is to see the **art gallery in the St. Johnsbury Athenaeum.** The Athenaeum was built in 1871, and in 1873 the art gallery was added. Both were the gift of Governor Horace Fairbanks, then head of St. Johnsbury's most important, influential, and philanthropic family.

It is a particularly pleasant experience to walk through the library and into the gallery, pretty much unchanged since it was built, because you can really step back for a peek into the nineteenth century. The room itself is good-looking, with black walnut walls and floor and an arched skylight in the high ceiling. The gilt-framed pictures are hung cheek by jowl, floor to ceiling; interspersed are cases filled with art books, all elaborately bound.

As was the custom then, copies of world-famous masterpieces by such artists as Van Dyck and Rembrandt are hung among original works, which can give you a disconcerting shock until you remember that these are, of course, copies.

But the real reason you are here is to see the American collection, most particularly pictures from the Hudson River School (Cropsey, Durand, Whittredge, Gifford, and others) and the focal point and star of the gallery, Albert Bierstadt's huge (10 feet by 15 feet) *Domes of the Yosemite,* which was such a favorite of the artist's that he came here every summer until his death to visit it. The gallery refers to its "wildly magnificent grandeur," and it is indeed an impressive and important picture.

And then there are the other paintings—there are about one
hundred in all—some with great period charm (W. M. Brown's
lovely little *Raspberries,* for instance), some of awful sentimen-
tality (William H. Beard's *Why, Puppy Looks Like Grandpa!*—
just the title says it all). As for the sculpture, John Quincy
Adams Ward (a portrait bust of Governor Fairbanks) is the
most prominent artist represented.

The Athenaeum and art gallery are open Monday and
Wednesday, 10–8; Tuesday, Thursday, Friday, 10:00–5:30;
Saturday, 9:30–4:00. Free admission. Telephone: 748-8291.

CENTRAL VERMONT AND THE UPPER
CONNECTICUT RIVER VALLEY

Woodstock

This village is home to Vermont's most sophisticated architecture and its most sophisticated citizens. One of the oldest stories about Woodstock relates that one native of the town, a U.S.
senator and friend of Abraham Lincoln's, said to a colleague,
"The good people of Woodstock have less incentive than others
to yearn for heaven." More recent, but told with equal relish, is
the tale of a visitor who, as he paid for his *New York Times,*
was informed it would cost him thirty-five cents. Why, he
asked, should this be so when the price of the paper was clearly
noted as being twenty-five cents in the city and thirty cents
elsewhere. "Woodstock," said the store owner, "is beyond 'elsewhere.' "

In addition to being a village of great beauty with handsome
and well-appointed shops, it is surrounded by stunning and
even dramatic countryside. For these reasons and others, including the nearby cross-country and downhill skiing (the first
ski tow went into operation near here in 1934), Woodstock is a
major tourist center.

The town, located in a valley carved by the Ottauquechee
River, was incorporated in 1761 by none other than our old

friend Benning Wentworth. In 1787 it became the county seat and thereby attracted a professional citizenry who had the money to build the very beautiful houses you see today surrounding the triangular green and along the side streets.

Several residents, including Justin Morgan (see page 18), became well known in the nineteenth century, but the man whose influence resonates to this day was Frederick Billings, whose farm, now open to the public, is described below.

Billings went to California during the 1849 gold rush and became one of the first—and one of the most successful—attorneys in San Francisco. He came back to Woodstock in 1866 and then became involved in the completion of the Northern Pacific Railroad, during which time Billings, Montana, was named after him. It was Billings who, to no small extent, made Woodstock the beautiful spot it is today, for he planted more than ten thousand trees in the area, and on the denuded Mount Tom, which had been entirely stripped by timbering. He was strongly influenced by another Woodstock citizen, George Perkins Marsh, who helped to found the Smithsonian and wrote *Man and Nature,* a pioneering and vastly important work on environmental conservation.

In more recent times, Billings's granddaughter, Mary French, married Laurance Rockefeller, and their contribution to the welfare of the town has included opening the Billings Farm and Museum to the public and ownership of the Woodstock Inn and Resort that sits off the green.

If you are visiting Woodstock between June and the end of October, the first thing to do is to go to the Chamber of Commerce booth on the green. (At other times, go to their office at 4 Central Street.) Here you can join a daily walking tour of the village, but if you prefer to strike off on your own, they will give you a marked map to help you explore. Then, of course, you should walk along the commercial streets, wandering in and out of the shops and generally orienting yourself to the village and its life.

The Billings Farm and Museum   Billings established his farm in 1871 and developed a prize herd of imported Jersey dairy cows that continue to win blue ribbons to this day.

Since 1983, this operating farm has been open to the public, and it is the single most popular attraction in Woodstock. It offers interesting and informative museum exhibitions of family farm life in the 1890s; a tour of the 1890 farm manager's house, which has been restored down to its Sears, Roebuck and Montgomery Ward furnishings; visits to the barns and a museum shop. There is a dairy bar with ice cream made from the very rich milk of the Jersey herd, and you will have to search far and wide for its peer.

The Billings Farm and Museum is open: Daily, 10–5, May–October. Winter hours are limited. Admission fee. Telephone: 457-2355.

Woodstock Historical Society This occupies the 1807 Dana House at 26 Elm Street. The Dana family lived here until 1943, and the collection consists of decorative arts dating from the period of their occupancy and including silver, glass, paintings, furniture, china, and fabrics, in nine rooms. The adjacent barn has tools and other equipment plus a very handsome sleigh once owned by the Billings family. There is a gift shop.

The Woodstock Historical Society is open: Daily, 10–5, mid-May–late October; late November and December 10–5. Admission fee. Telephone: 457-1822.

A DRIVE

From Woodstock, take one of my favorite drives, and plan to arrive in Quechee for lunch. I would say this drive should take, at the outside, no longer than two to three hours.

Leave the village at Route 12, and turn right at the sign for South Pomfret. You will pass Suicide Six, a skiing area, and as you travel farther, the road will become a dirt one that eventually will come out in **Barnard,** once the summer home of Sinclair Lewis and Dorothy Thompson and now distinguished by a sky-blue mountain lake and a columned church. (If your time is very limited, turn left here and head back into Woodstock. You will have had a lovely drive.)

Turn right here, on Route 12. Go north to Route 107, and turn right, eventually going through Bethel. Continue east to Route 14, past the Fox Stand Inn (1818), made distinctive by its ten fireplaces, and through Royalton. Continue on to **South Royalton,** where you should cross the bridge over the White River in order to take a little tour of this interesting village, home of Vermont's only law school.

Back on Route 14, follow it one mile south to the sign for the **Joseph Smith Memorial and Birthplace,** built by the Mormons to honor their founder, who was born there in 1805. It is worth a visit. In the first place, the drive to it, up a long hill, is very pretty, but in addition, the monument and grounds are not only interesting but moving in their sincerity. The approach to the monument is tree-lined and rather formal. The monument itself is an impressive 38.6-foot granite obelisk, erected in 1908 to mark the site of the farmhouse in which Joseph Smith was born. Flower beds surround the obelisk, which is set on a slight hill. Speakers have been placed in the outlying trees, and quiet music surrounds you. Inside the buildings below the monument are exhibitions concerning Smith's life, and the 360 surrounding acres include campgrounds and picnic sites.

The Joseph Smith Memorial and Birthplace is open: Year-round during daylight hours. No admission fee.

Back to Route 14 south, and you soon will pass through Sharon, where you will see a large Greek Revival building that is home to a country store. Next door is Brooksie's Family Restaurant, a real family restaurant that has developed a devoted following, but eyes straight ahead and save yourself for Quechee.

Continue south on Route 14 until you cross over the White River and see a sign identifying West Hartford Road. Turn onto this road, which will take you through some particularly appealing farmland and then into the village of **Quechee,** where you will have lunch at the **Simon Pearce Restaurant,** enjoying the delicious food in a superb setting, a converted mill overlooking a waterfall. Afterward, you will surely wish to visit the Simon Pearce Store, where the renowned glassmaker offers his beautiful wares as well as the wares of other local craftsmen. It is one of the most attractive and appealing shopping sites in Vermont.

After lunch, continue on this road, passing the covered bridge and following the sign for the Inn at Marshland Farms.

Gingerbread, stone, Gothic elements . . . it's a confectioner's delight of a house. It is this kind of "find" that makes drives in New England so pleasurable.

Eventually the road will bring you out on Route 4, very near **Quechee Gorge,** one of the more spectacular natural sites in Vermont, being 165 feet deep and a mile long. The site is well marked, and it is an easy walk to the falls at the head of the gorge. Then, when you are through here, you can head back into Woodstock by going west on Route 4.

Montpelier

Montpelier, the capital of Vermont, is a small town of about 8,000 souls, but for its size it has an interesting array of buildings and an excellent inn, the Inn at Montpelier. Its small **State House** (1859) has the shiniest gold-leaf dome you could ever hope to see, and that rather large figure at the summit is Ceres, the Roman goddess of agriculture, whose intervention, I have always thought, must be much needed, given the rocky quality of Vermont soil. The very handsome Tuscan-order columns are from an earlier (1838) state house destroyed by fire. If you wish to see the interior, it's open: Monday through Friday, 10–3, in summer and fall for guided tours. If you wish to just look in on your own, which is the way I like to do it, that can be done 8–4, and there's a helpful brochure available. No admission fee. Telephone: 828-2228.

You also might wish to stop in at the **Vermont Historical**

Society, 109 State Street, to see the museum and library. The former traces with considerable imagination the history, traditions, and economy of Vermont. The façade of the building, by the way, is a replica of the nineteenth-century Pavilion Hotel that used to stand in Montpelier, and the lobby of the hotel has been reconstructed inside the building, with the display rooms located beyond.

The Vermont Historical Society is open: Daily, except Monday, 8:00–4:30 (10–4 on Saturday and Sunday in July and August). Closed: Major holidays. Free admission.

The Plymouth Notch Historic District

Located on Route 100A, not far north of Weston (see page 42), this was the birthplace and childhood home of Calvin Coolidge, and the entire community and the surrounding hilltops are listed on the National Register of Historic Places. Even so, I long thought to myself, how interesting could this be? Who cares where Calvin Coolidge was born? So for many years I never bothered to stop by. Then one day I had some extra time and I decided to see it. I loved it.

It's like stepping back into history when you enter this tiny little village, in which all the buildings are open to the public. The Visitors' Center is in perfect keeping with the other buildings and has a gift shop and little museum that tells you, through pictures, as much as you will need to know about Coolidge. The pleasures come in the other buildings, which really have not very much to do with Coolidge but everything to do with a vanished and nostalgic era.

There is the Wilder Barn, for instance, which is a museum devoted to farming in the nineteenth century. Across the street is the yellow clapboard Wilder House (c. 1830), the home of Coolidge's mother. The Coolidge Homestead, up the road, is furnished exactly as it was when Calvin received the oath of office from his father, a notary public, in August 1923. (One of the reasons little has changed is that the housekeeper, who died in 1956, could never bring herself to accept electricity or plumbing.)

Then you can see the Plymouth Cheese Factory (and buy some of the delicious product), and the exterior of the one-room schoolhouse, examine the Carrie Brown Coolidge garden—she was the president's stepmother—and the 1840 Union Christian Church, and see the Calvin Coolidge Birthplace, where he was born on July 4 (naturally), 1872.

There are other buildings, and there is the cemetery where he is buried, but my favorite stop of all, and what you must visit if you see nothing else, is the General Store, which Coolidge's father once owned. It still has wonderfully old-fashioned things for sale. The day I was there the old lady behind the counter zapped a fly into kingdom come with her deadly accurate fly swatter. And then she nailed a bee on the backswing. "Can't stand that buzzing," she said.

Upstairs is the large but extremely modest room that the president used for his summer White House office in 1924. My, how times have changed. And please note the old gas pump outside.

This is a wonderful memorial to a president who was not known for his words but who did wax eloquent on the subject of Vermont, particularly in a speech he delivered in 1928 at Bennington. It's worth quoting because it sums up so well the character of Vermonters and the way they look at their state and compatriots.

"I could not look upon the peaks of Ascutney, Killington, Mansfield and Equinox," he said, "without being moved in a way that no other scene could move me. It was here that I first saw the light of day; here I received my bride; here my dead lie pillowed on the loving breast of our everlasting hills. I love Vermont because of her hills and valleys, her scenery and invigorating climate, but most of all, because of her indomitable people. They are a race of pioneers who have almost beggared themselves to serve others. If the spirit of liberty should vanish in other parts of the union and support of our institutions should languish, it could all be replenished from the generous store held by the people of this brave little state of Vermont."

The Plymouth Notch Historic District is open: Daily, 9:30–5:30, late-May through mid-October. Admission fee. Telephone: 672-3773.

SOUTHERN VERMONT AND THE UPPER CONNECTICUT RIVER VALLEY

No one can claim to know Vermont if he or she hasn't seen Bennington and Manchester and the southern villages and taken some of the drives between and around them. I must admit, this area to me is quintessential Vermont, the section I most love to visit, perhaps because it was the first part of Vermont that I came to know well and to love.

A visit of four days here would be desirable, and I would spend two nights in Grafton and two nights in Dorset. However, I have divided the suggestions below in such a way that you can select what sounds most appealing to you and get a real flavor of the joys and beauty of southern Vermont even if you spend only one day in the area. In the same manner, although I suggest staying in Grafton and Dorset, you can accomplish the same day trips from anywhere in the region. In any case, try to include Bennington in your plans; it's a wonderful village.

Bennington

The Bennington Museum   What an appealing museum, small, relaxed, and charming. I overheard a woman remark to her husband on one of my visits, "This is a real people's museum." She couldn't have been more right. A highly intelligent effort has been made to display attractively the life and history of the area. In addition, there are some fine things to examine.

For example, the paintings collection includes Ralph Earl's *Landscape View of Old Bennington* (1798), one of the earliest American landscapes and an extremely fine painting on its artistic merits. Note the figure in the foreground; it's Earl himself, and the child he's sketching may be his son. (And also note the nearby high chest of drawers, made by Samuel Dunlap, with its exuberant latticework pediment and wonderful surface decoration.)

Earl (1751–1801) is a painter of more than passing interest and is represented in the Metropolitan Museum of Art in New York and the National Gallery in Washington, D.C., by others of his masterpieces. He also appears several times in this book.

Doors, I think, are often the key to the soul of a house. In this instance, the elegant, almost humorous decoration says to me that this house is welcoming in its comforts and hopes to please.

He was born in Worcester, Mass. As a Loyalist during the Revolution he fled to London, where he studied with another American, Benjamin West, and painted some very sophisticated portraits. However, on his return to this country he chose to paint in a simplified style, closer to what is now called the folk art tradition.

There are three other paintings by Earl here, including portraits of Captain Elijah Dewey and Mary Schenck Dewey. Dewey, among other things, operated a tavern that still stands in Bennington and is now known as the Walloomsac Inn. It's across from the Old First Church (see page 34) and is sadly run-down, but it's still a handsome building; if you had the money, you could make it one of the great New England inns.

I'll mention only one other painting, a portrait by Frederick W. MacMonnies (1863–1937), from early in his career and probably done at Giverny. MacMonnies is far better remembered as a sculptor and is not one of my favorites. If you wish to know why, take a look at the insipid *Bacchante with Infant Faun* in this collection (the much larger original is at the Metropolitan). In the portrait, however, he has painted another artist, May Suydam Palmer, with, as he describes it, "sunset on her red hair—and blown around in her best Chinese gown, toss't by the winds on the alley walk to Monet's boathouse." And he's pulled it off; the colors are wonderful, May Palmer quite dashing, and all in all this picture is a charmer.

The most famous painter in residence, though, is Grandma Moses. There are about two dozen of her pictures here, some of which you will recognize from innumerable reproductions. But my favorite of the Grandma Moses works is not a painting but the eighteenth-century tilt-top table she used as her easel, whose base she painted with six different landscapes.

The museum also has a beautiful collection of American glassware and, not surprisingly, has a first-rate collection of nineteenth-century Bennington pottery and porcelain. Not to be missed here is the fantastic, it-could-only-be-Victorian assemblage created by the United States Pottery Company of Bennington for the Crystal Palace Exhibition in New York City in 1853. The centerpiece is a ten-foot Monument—the capital *M* is well deserved—whose description I will quote from the excellent little handbook *Highlights from the Bennington Museum*. (The "Fenton" mentioned is Christopher Webber Fenton, founder of the U.S. Pottery Company.)

"The Monument . . . was the focal point of Fenton's exhibit and is made in four sections, illustrating a variety of clays and glazes; the base was of scroddled ware, or mixed clays, resembling variegated marble; the second section was of yellowware showing Fenton's famous flint enamel glaze; the third section featured a parian bust of Fenton . . . surrounded by Corinthian columns of scroddled ware with a flint enamel glaze. Finally, the Monument was crowned with a parian statue of a woman draped in robes, who held a bible toward the child in her arms."

There is a good collection of Vermont and New England furniture, too, but the museum's more eclectic pieces are the most fun. For instance, the collection holds the Bennington Battle Flag (1776), which is recognized as the oldest known Stars and Stripes in existence and is thought to have flown at the battle itself. One of the women who made it was the grandmother of Millard Fillmore, and it descended in the Fillmore family.

And to top it all off, there's an absolutely magnificent Wasp Touring Car, made in 1925. Manufactured in Bennington, only sixteen were completed, and no car buff worth the name can afford to miss this example, whose custom woodwork and body-work—note the steel hood—combine to create a vehicle the likes of which we will never see again. Douglas Fairbanks, Sr., bought one on sight—the car has all that rakish power and elegance and glamour associated with the twenties.

The Bennington Museum is open: Daily except Christmas and New Year's Day, 9–5. Admission fee. Telephone: 447-1571.

Old First Church   The aggregate of church, graveyard, and spectacular fence, all placed on a lovely hillside and surrounded by handsome houses, makes for one of the defining images of New England. In fact, the fence, swagged pickets with ends "held up" by elegant posts topped with boldly proportioned urns, is among the most beautiful in New England.

The graveyard, known as the Old Burying Ground, is full of splendid examples of the stone carver's art from the eighteenth and nineteenth centuries. It is well worth wandering here, visiting the grave of Robert Frost (he wrote his own epitaph: "I had a lover's quarrel with the world"), noting the last resting spots of those who died in the Battle of Bennington, and generally enjoying this lovely setting.

The church, formally known as the First Congregational Church of Bennington, was built between 1804 and 1806 and is, to me, the most beautiful in Vermont. As he did in Middlebury, the architect, Lavius Fillmore, based his plans on Asher Benjamin's *The Country Builder's Assistant,* and herein lies the structure's only weakness—it smacks a little of the workbook. But that's minor, and the influence of two of England's greatest builders, Christopher Wren and Inigo Jones, is very much a happy one.

What I particularly love is how the details—arches, ovals, triangles, pilasters, Palladian windows, beautifully designed and executed window tracery in the false oval "windows" (they are actually painted wooden panels) of the spire—combine to create a unified whole.

The interior, complete with box pews, was restored in 1937 and has the quiet dignity and beauty associated with the best of our church architecture of this period. Incidentally, each of the six tall columns was carved from a single pine tree.

Bennington Battle Monument   It stands 306 feet high
and—praise the Lord—has elevator service to the lookout floor,
from which you have an excellent view that includes the
Berkshires and the Green Mountains as well as New York
State. (The last time I was there, what seemed like two hundred motorcyclists zoomed up—a first, I'm sure, at the monument. For a moment I felt like one of the citizens in that old
Marlon Brando film about motorcyclists terrorizing a town,
The Wild Ones. As it turned out, they were perfectly pleasant
and were on a rather sedate tour of New England.)

The Battle of Bennington was fought in 1777. In it, the
American forces under Brigadier General John Stark defeated
two detachments of British General John Burgoyne's army.
(The battle, by the way, took place not in Bennington but a few
miles west in North Hoosick, N.Y.) This defeat was of no little
significance, for combined with the later and much more serious defeat of the British at the Battle of Saratoga, it ensured
that the British would not achieve their goal of dividing the
colonies by controlling the Hudson River.

On the grounds surrounding the monument are several
other monuments, creating a handsome effect. Approach it by
using Monument Avenue, which you can enter from the hill on
which Old First Church stands, so that you can admire the
houses.

The Bennington Battle Monument is open: Daily, April 1
through November 1, 9–5. Admission fee. Telephone: 447-0550.

Grafton

Grafton is my favorite village and the location of my favorite
inn in this section of New England, **The Old Tavern,** built in
1801, and a place where Emerson, Thoreau, Kipling, and
Teddy Roosevelt all stayed. This village is Vermont's answer to
Brigadoon—each approach to it is more beautiful than the last,
and each seems to take you farther and farther away from the
twentieth century (to which you can return, however, at any
time). I urge you to stay in Grafton. It is an ideal place to stay
while exploring southern Vermont.

The village was founded before the Revolution and became
prosperous as a mill town in the early nineteenth century when

The Old Tavern at Grafton, my favorite inn in Vermont and one of New England's loveliest. The barn in the rear has been made into an attractive lounge, where you can have drinks in the utmost comfort.

wool from its ten thousand Merino sheep was turned into cloth here. That accounts for the handsome Greek Revival buildings. But its prosperity rested on waterpower, and when steam began to take over, the village went into a long decline.

Then, some years ago, two cousins, Matthew Hall and Dean Mathey, began to summer here and fell deeply in love with the village, as did their aunt, Pauline Fiske.

When Pauline died, she left her considerable fortune to her two nephews, requesting that the money be used for a cause of their choice, but one that she herself would have enjoyed. It took them some time to come up with what they agreed would be the perfect project—the restoration and preservation of Grafton.

To that end, they set up the Windham Foundation, which now owns 1,400 acres in and around the town and has restored more than half the village buildings. The foundation also owns the village store, the village garage, the Grafton Cheese Factory, the North Star Gallery, and the nursery. Last, but hardly least, it owns and operates the inn and several buildings that are available for rent to the public, all of which are filled with splendid antique furniture, paintings, and prints. In short, it seems that the entire village is geared to making you comfortable in an idyllic New England setting that also includes two covered bridges, a Baptist church with Sandwich glass chandeliers, and a coronet band that has played on the green every Sunday evening in the summer since 1867. I should tell you that some people have criticized it as too perfect. Not me. I think the restoration has been exquisitely done and is in perfect taste. I wish I were there right now.

Using Grafton as home base, then, I would suggest two days of drives.

A Drive: Day 1

Leave Grafton on Route 35, going south toward **Newfane.** The scenery is perfection—woods and streams, open farmland, meadows, and hills. You will pass first through the village of **Townshend,** with a large open green and a c. 1790 building that is now the Congregational church but was originally the town meeting house. Leaving the green you will pass some interesting Victorian architecture, and between here and Newfane you will have a view of the 277-foot-long Scott Bridge, no longer in use but still one of the most beautiful covered bridges in the area.

And then you're coming into Newfane. Note on your right the red-brick 1884 Vermont National Bank, which looks as if it had escaped from a Western film set. The bricks, brought in by oxcart, cost five cents each for the front, three cents each for the side walls, and two cents each for the back. But it's the green that you're here for, the prettiest green in Vermont, in my opinion, and one of the prettiest in New England. But the whole village is lovely; it is said to contain forty buildings that are more than two hundred years old.

Newfane, first settled in 1774, is the Windham county seat, and the 1825 Greek Revival courthouse, white and green-shuttered, is the most beautiful building on the green, with four Tuscan-order columns and an attention to proportion and detail that make it a first-rate example of its period. Two other handsome buildings, also white with green shutters, are the Congregational church (1839) and the Union Hall (1832).

This serenely handsome Greek Revival building, just off the common in Newfane, is home to my favorite restaurant in Vermont, the Four Columns Inn.

The surrounding buildings—in particular the Four Columns Inn, home of my favorite Vermont restaurant, where you must have dinner, and the equally pretty Newfane Inn—together with a handsome Civil War Memorial and a fountain, all shaded by glorious old trees, make this as harmonious a setting as you could hope to find anywhere.

Spend some time wandering about, particularly noting the town jail directly across the street from the courthouse. At one point this was a "hotel-jail"; to avoid the need for two sets of kitchens, one for the hotel and one for the jail, a hotel wing was attached to the jail so that inmates, attorneys, visitors, and jurors all could be conveniently served.

On that side of the street, too, is the Newfane Country Store, where you will find a display of dozens of handmade quilts as well as jams and jellies, condiments, housewares, and much of the other paraphernalia one expects in an authentic New England country store.

When you are ready to leave Newfane, return to Townshend but at the green go north on Route 30 to East Jamaica. Here I suggest you turn left on Route 100 and enjoy Green Mountain scenery until you come in to the overdeveloped ski areas of Mount Snow. On this route you will pass through West Dover, which is not terribly interesting in itself, but the Inn at Sawmill Farm here is one of the most attractive inns in the area and the dining room is well worth a visit.

In any case, when you reach Route 9, go east, and as you climb Hogback Mountain, watch for the Skyline Restaurant, which will be on your left. Don't be put off by its roadhouse appearance. The food is delicious, and it makes an excellent spot to break for lunch. And, because it is located at about 2,300 feet, the views are wonderful, stretching out and away for one hundred miles. There is a stone fireplace, pine paneling, and considerate, friendly service. Breakfast foods—waffles and griddle cakes served with melted butter and real maple syrup, country sausage, doughnuts and so forth—are all homemade and are absolutely delicious, as are the generous sandwiches and more substantial meals, and the desserts are well worth a detour.

Waddle back to your car and continue east on Route 9. You soon will come to a sign for **Marlboro,** which you may wish to drive through to see the views from the pretty campus of Marlboro College or even just to visit the site of the world-renowned Marlboro Music Festival, which presents chamber music performances every summer from mid-July to mid-August.

You now can continue to **Brattleboro** and wander about there, perhaps stopping in at the Brattleboro Museum and Art Center (Canal and Bridge Streets; telephone 257-0124 for times and information) to see one of their changing exhibitions in what once was the Union Railroad Station, or enjoying the interesting architecture of Main Street.

From Brattleboro, go north on Route 30; in West Dummerston, you will pass the longest covered bridge in the state that is still in use. (Vermont, you may be interested to know, has 110 covered bridges.) And soon you will be back in Grafton.

A DRIVE: DAY 2

Today, leave Grafton on Route 121 south, taking it to Saxton's River, where you will go north on Route 5 to Rockingham. Go north here on Route 103 to see the **Rockingham Meeting House,** built in 1787 as a steeple-less church, and one of my fa-

The 1787 Rockingham Meeting House, set in lonely splendor on a hill, is, both on the interior and exterior, as beautiful as New England architecture gets.

vorite buildings in Vermont. Its setting—high on a hill and to-tally rural—is as idyllic as it was when the church was built, and the exterior structure is in near-pristine condition.

As noted, it was originally built as a church, but as early as 1792 it was decided that it would function not only as a church (for Baptists, Congregationalists, and Universalists) but also as a meeting house for the community. In 1829, it became solely a meeting house, which it remained until 1869, when the last meeting was held here. It was restored to its original condition in 1906–1907.

The white exterior is plain almost to the point of severity, the only relief being the pedimented center door. But the propor-tions and window placement are so just, so exquisite, as to give the whole a feel of dignified—even elegant—repose, which is underlined by the rural beauty of the setting and the old grave-yard behind it. In many ways, it is the quintessence of Vermont architecture.

The interior, you will find it hard to believe, can hold nearly a thousand people. The elements that make up the interior are in perfect harmony: a high, narrow pulpit with a sounding board, simple but beautifully carved enclosed pews. Much of the glass of the forty-eight windows is antique, creating a wavy, slightly tipsy landscape as you look through. (A bizarre note: Since the last time I was there—and I have yet to check it out—I've been told that some of the ancient gravestones dotting the hill have been arranged in alphabetical order because an overzealous caretaker decided it would be neater that way. Fortunately, he was stopped before he completed the job.)

I have been here many times over the years, and rarely have I found anyone else visiting the building. That, definitely, is part of its charm, for you feel drawn back into time and can admire and explore and enjoy at your leisure.

Continue on Route 103 to **Chester.** This is not what people think of as the usual Vermont village. It has a wide, tree-lined main street bordered by an eclectic group of buildings from, roughly, the late nineteenth century to the 1930s, but with an overall flavor that is distinctly Victorian, the predominant styles being Italianate, Shingle, Gothic, and Queen Anne. Not, as I said, your classic New England villagescape but a pleasing mix that makes a walk here and on the side streets a charming experience.

I also like the name of the inn on Main Street—the Inn at Long Last. It is owned by Jack Coleman, a former president of Haverford College, who gained some notoriety working anonymously as a garbage man and ditch digger and then writing about his experiences in a book entitled *Blue Collar Journal.* Across the street is the Historical Society and Art Guild, where there are changing exhibitions and displays on the history of the village. The churches here are interesting, too, particularly the 1829 Congregational church with its five-tiered tower.

The most interesting aspect of Chester, though, is the **Stone Village,** which you reach by turning onto Church Street by the Congregational church. You will immediately notice the architectural unity of the stone buildings, which came about for a very simple reason: Most of them, including the church, were built by two brothers named Clark. They had learned the stonemason's trade in Canada, from Scottish experts, and were known for both their skill and their speed. Their first house was built in 1834 (for one Ptolemy Edison, a name worth passing on); eventually they erected more than seventy buildings, some of which contain secret rooms to shelter runaway slaves, for this was a stop on the pre–Civil War Underground Railway that ferried slaves into Canada.

When you leave here, go west on Route 11 to Route 100 in Londonderry and then north to **Weston.** This town has a beautiful deeply shaded green with a nineteenth-century bandstand. In fall it becomes one of the prettier greens in the state and a favorite site for photographers because of the brilliant coloring. But the real reason to come here, even to make a detour if necessary, is the **Vermont Country Store,** just off the green on Route 100.

I like to plan my visit here so that I can have lunch in the Country Store's Bryant House Restaurant, where you can get honest homemade soups and delicious sandwiches and pies. They even have ice-cream sodas. Then, fortified, it's off to the store. It has everything, including things you thought were no longer made but wished were. You want some handsome table mats? They've got a great selection. Soaps? Dozens of kinds. There are foodstuffs and bathrobes, towels and kitchen implements (the last time I was there I bought a beautiful olive-wood kitchen spoon), creams for tired feet and a natural herb insect

In Weston, home of the Vermont Country Store, you will also find this little shop that specializes in weather vanes.

repellent, vinyl bowl covers and women's cotton ankle socks, curtains and hanging baskets . . . talk about a cornucopia. The store has a branch, farther south in Rockingham, but I don't know . . . there's nothing like the original.

The Vermont Country Store is open: Daily except Sunday and major holidays, 9–5. There is a wonderful mail order catalogue. Write for it to: The Vermont Country Store, Mail Order Office, P.O. Box 3000, Manchester Center, Vt. 05255-3000. Credit cards. Telephone: 362-2400.

Other attractive shops in Weston have sprung up around the Country Store, and you should leave yourself enough time to explore them. Just north of the green, for instance, again on Route 100, is something called the Weston Bowl Mill, which has an amazing array of wooden bowls and household products that are made there. They have seconds, too, and at reasonable prices. Open: Every day, 9–5, except for major holidays. Credit cards. Telephone: 824-6219.

If you have time, consider going farther north on Route 100—almost always a pleasure to drive—to the Plymouth Notch Historic District on Route 100A (see page 29).

Dorset

Another picture-perfect village, this time with three lovely inns to choose from. Like Grafton, it is surrounded by beautiful countryside with a host of sights and scenery to enjoy. While here, I like to stay at the **Barrows House,** although the **Dorset Inn** is also very comfortable.

Dorset has been a popular summer resort for many years. It has a long and rather interesting history. In 1777, for instance, Vermont's leaders gathered here and proclaimed the "Free and Independent State of Vermont." In 1785, the first marble quarry in this country was opened here, and the Dorset Inn is supposed to be the oldest inn in continuous operation in the state. There also are some handsome eighteenth-century landmarks, among which the Memorial Library (1790), originally a tavern, and the United Church of Dorset and East Rupert are noteworthy, as are the clapboard homes in and near the town. With Dorset as your very comfortable base, you can now set out on your drives from here.

A Drive: Day 1

Go south on Route 30 to **Manchester,** a popular summer resort since before the Civil War when the Equinox first opened
its doors in Manchester Village. Today it is an area of con-
trasts. Manchester Village, for instance, is one of the prettiest
villages in New England; its side streets are a compact study in
New England vernacular architecture, and the main thoroughfare, Route 7A, becomes a wide, tree-lined avenue filled with
elegant, exquisitely maintained houses.

At the same time, Route 7A in Manchester Center is one long
shopping mall, with store after store in dreary succession.
Admittedly, it can be a shopper's paradise, for many of these
places are factory outlet stores, and there are bargains galore,
but appealing it is not.

In any case, the area taken as a whole is lovely, and there is
enough to do here to easily fill a day. As I wrote above, I like to
stay in nearby Dorset, out of the fray, but the **Equinox** or **The
Reluctant Panther** would be my choices if I were to stay in
Manchester.

Hildene   One doesn't go to Vermont to tour houses; it's the
overall blend that is so lovely here, the grouping around the
common or even entire villages, such as Grafton or Newfane or
Dorset. Hildene is the exception and the only house I suggest
you visit. But even here, although the house is very pleasant,
it's the garden and view that make it special.

Hildene—the name in Old English means "hill and valley"—
was completed in 1905 for Robert Todd Lincoln (1843–1926),
eldest son of Abraham and Mary Todd Lincoln. The family
lived there until 1975, when Mary Lincoln Beckwith, Robert's
granddaughter, died. A group of area residents soon formed to
buy the estate, and they succeeded in 1978 with the purchase
of all 412 acres and twenty-seven buildings from the Christian
Science Church, the organization that had inherited it.

Robert Lincoln had been familiar with Manchester and the
surrounding area for many years before he actually bought
land here. In fact, he and his mother were guests at the
Equinox in both 1863 and 1864. They even registered with the
hotel to return with the president in 1865, a date they were
never able to keep because of the assassination.

Hildene, Robert Todd Lincoln's home, the only house worth visiting in Vermont, also offers lovely gardens and a spectacular view.

Following the Civil War, in 1868, Robert married Mary Harlan, daughter of a United States senator. He became a highly successful attorney in Chicago and later served both as secretary of war to President Garfield and as ambassador to the Court of St. James's under President Harrison. At the end of his career he was chairman of the board of the Pullman Company and a very rich man.

In 1903, after buying the land, he retained the Boston firm of Shepley, Rutan, and Coolidge to design and build his house. And because he seems to have kept every scrap of paper connected with the building and furnishing of Hildene, the restoration is considered to be extremely accurate.

The house, in the Georgian Revival style, is good-looking in a restrained way. The interior is spacious, with a graceful entrance hall and staircase. In 1908 an Aeolian pipe organ was installed here; it is in working order and is accompanied by 242 player rolls of music, from which a sample is played on the tour—fortunately or unfortunately, depending on your point of view. The furnishings are comfortable but undistinguished. It is, in short, a large, pleasant house, typical of its time.

The gardens and view, though, are special, as I said. The collection of peonies, in particular, is spectacular, but all the plantings, now completely restored, are well worth exploring for half an hour or so.

As for the striking view, it is found at the end of the garden, on a promontory that looks out over a sweeping panorama of the Green and Taconic mountains, including Mount Equinox.

Hildene, off Route 7A and two miles south of the intersection of Routes 11 and 30 is open from mid-May through October, 9:30 to 4:00 (grounds close at 5:30), and offers a video introduction to the estate and a guided tour. Admission fee. Telephone: 362-1788.

Southern Vermont Art Center   What a gratifying surprise it is to make a visit to this very pleasant regional arts center.

First of all, the site is an old, beautifully maintained 450-acre estate on the eastern slope of Mount Equinox and very close to Manchester Village. The house, a large, comfortably proportioned Georgian Colonial called Yester House, was built in 1917 and now houses special exhibitions as well as the permanent collection, gift shop, and library. In 1956, the Louise Arkell Performing Arts Pavilion was added for dance and theater performances, and there is also a sculpture garden, the Boswell Botany Trail, and an old carriage house that is now used for artists' studios and classrooms.

Second, a little background on the center and its mission. The area has long been a popular summer resort for artists, and in 1921 a small group of them organized a joint exhibition. This became an annual tradition, and the number of contributing artists increased each year. Eventually they formalized their mission this way: "To serve the arts and the community by furthering art in all its aspects, with a foremost goal of education for artists, art students and young people. To encourage community interest as a cultural center in the visual and performing arts through opportunities for participation, and by offering presentations and programs in all the arts. To provide facilities for artists by which their work may be presented and promoted, to develop interest and understanding in the visual and performing arts, and to assure all necessary support for the attainment of these objectives."

And now to what you can see and do while you're here.

The house is the heart of the operation, so I like to start there and see what special exhibitions they are offering in the sunlight-filled rooms before going up to see the permanent collection, which now holds more than 700 works of art. Of course, only a small number of these can be seen at any given time, but the artists represented range from Peter Max to Grandma Moses, Reginald Marsh, and James McNeill Whistler. Individually, no work is a spectacular representation of the artist in question, but the collection taken as a whole has a very comfortable "feel" and personality.

I think, though, what I usually enjoy best here is the Boswell Botany Trail, whose three-quarter-mile walk takes no more than thirty minutes at the most leisurely pace. I like it so much because it has such a feeling of naturalness and peace, and because what you see, in such a small area, is so varied, from rock formations to luxuriant ferns and wildflowers to a small pool and lovely old trees. It is sponsored by the Garden Club of Manchester as a conservation and education center, and there are excellent signs to tell you what you are looking at, as well as a little folder that lists all the fern and wildflower varieties found here. On a hot day in particular, this shaded trail makes a lovely break, and at any time the center is an oasis of welcoming beauty.

The Southern Vermont Art Center is two miles north of Manchester Village's green and is on West Road. Open: May through mid-October, every day but Monday, 10–5; Sunday, 12–5; December through April, Monday–Saturday, 10–4. Admission: Contribution. Telephone: 362-1405.

American Museum of Fly Fishing Anyone interested in fishing in even a tangential way will want to visit this museum, which was established in 1968 to house the history and lore of fly fishing. There are early books on the subject, fishing memorabilia, including rods, reels, and flies from an amazing variety of famous Americans (Dwight Eisenhower, Winslow Homer, Bing Crosby, Daniel Webster, Herbert Hoover, and Ernest Hemingway, among others), and an inclusive display of brilliantly colored artificial flies. On second thought, even if you've never dropped a hook into water, there probably will be something here to interest you.

Fishermen should also be aware that the 8,000-square-foot

home of **Orvis** is on Route 7A in Manchester Center; there you can buy everything from classic country clothing to custom shotguns and hunting gear to a superb selection of fly-fishing gear and more. The basement has a sale room where savings can reach as much as 70 percent. It is open every day, 9–6. Credit cards: American Express, MasterCard, Visa. Telephone: 362-3750.

The American Museum of Fly Fishing is on Seminary Avenue and Route 7A in Manchester Village. Open: May through October, daily, 10–4; November through April, Monday through Friday, 10–4. Closed: Major holidays. Contributions welcome. Telephone: 362-3300.

A DRIVE: DAY 2

This is as pretty as a drive gets in Vermont. Leave Dorset by going to the end of Church Street, the main street of the village, and turn right on Dorset West Road. This will end at Route 315. Turn left and go over Antone Mountain—lovely views and countryside—into **Rupert.** Here you can visit the Merck Forest Farmland Center and take some time wandering the foot trails on the 2,800-acre site.

Now go north on Route 153 to Route 30 and then south a bit to **Pawlet,** a little village with some attractive buildings. (My favorite pieces of lore about Pawlet are that it once was home to five distilleries, and that it also had the first cheese factory in Vermont, which was built in the 1860s.) Be sure to visit Johnny Mack's General Store, where there is a glass-topped counter through which you can look down into the gorge below and see the rushing waters of Flower Brook—a rather disconcerting experience if you don't know in advance what's down there.

From Pawlet, turn right off Route 30 and go to **Danby Four Corners.** When you first turn from Route 30, you'll see enormous piles of slate along the roadside. These are "leftovers" from the days when Pawlet was a slate-manufacturing center. The rest of the road to Danby Four Corners offers pleasant views and attractive farms, and in the Corners there is a splendid perspective of the two Dorset Peaks.

Here you will turn right to go to **Danby.** The scenery

changes almost immediately, for you go through a glen and woods until you reach the village. Danby was home to Vermont's first millionaire, a man named Silas Griffith, who made his pile in lumber in the 1850s. More recently, in the 1960s, Pearl Buck lived here—in a building built by Silas Griffith, as it happens; she bought seven buildings and worked on their renovation until her death. Quarries are found here, and their marble has been used in Washington in the Supreme Court Building.

From Danby, get on Route 7 south, where you will have wonderful views of the Green Mountains. In Manchester Center, take Route 30 and then Route 11 toward **Peru.** You are now in the Green Mountains. Be sure to see Peru, which is just off Route 11 and is charming. Its 1827 country store, J. J. Hapgood, has such delights as penny candy, cheese and maple syrup.

This is one of my favorite drives in the Green Mountains, for some of the more spectacular views of the mountains are here, from Bromley in particular, and the drive in general is extremely pleasant.

Next you will come into Londonderry, where you will go south on Route 100 on a very pleasant drive to Rawsonville, where you will get on Route 30 north. This is the Stratton Ski Area, but once past that, the road again passes through rural and largely undeveloped land. You're on your way back to Manchester Center and then to Dorset.

WHERE TO STAY AND EAT

It sometimes seems to me there are more inns in Vermont than maple trees; there isn't a self-respecting village in the entire state without at least one inn. Fortunately, a large portion of them also maintain high standards, and one of the best parts of a trip to this state is that you always have a pleasant place to stay at the end of the day.

The list that follows is not meant to be exhaustive. Instead, it is meant to give you my favorite inns, with a broad enough geographic distribution to suit most needs. Remember,

Vermont is not a big state, and an inn listed, say, in southern Vermont can adequately serve as your headquarters to visit the middle part of the state and even some of the north.

For fall foliage season you must reserve months in advance. The ski season can be difficult in many places, too. It is important to reserve as early as possible for those periods in order to get what you want.

As for dining, there are two outstanding restaurants that can hold their own against any in the country. They are the **Four Columns Inn** in Newfane and the **Inn at Sawmill Farm** in West Dover. In addition, when I feel an inn or restaurant is truly outstanding, I list it at the head of the section as Best in the Region.

Where to Stay

Area Code: 802

LAKE CHAMPLAIN AND ITS VALLEY

Best in the Region: Inn at Shelburne Farms, Shelburne; Vermont Marble Inn, Fair Haven

Burlington area—Shelburne

Inn at Shelburne Farms, Shelburne Farms, Shelburne 05482.

This is far and away the most elegant inn in northern Vermont and has one of the loveliest settings in the entire state. (For a full description, see page 14.) The inn is expensive, but the beauty of its setting and the quality of its service make it well worth the cost. The food is good and reasonably priced, and the dining room, with its black-and-white marble floor and fireplace, is the most handsome public room in the house. In season, there are concerts and other special events, and there is a tennis court, a croquet court, a game room, walking trails, and lake fishing and swimming. Double room with private bath, $$$$$. Open: Late May to mid-October. Telephone: 985-8498, late May to mid-October; 985-8686, mid-October to late May. Credit cards.

Middlebury

I have three recommendations here, listed alphabetically; all
are more than adequate.

Middlebury Inn, Box 798, Court Square, Middlebury 05753.
This is my personal favorite. Perhaps it's because I've known
it so many years, or maybe it's because it's so quietly old-fashioned, but for whatever reason, I always enjoy my stay here.
However, there are motel accommodations behind the inn that
have no appeal. Be sure you're not booked there. The inn itself
is old (1827) and has a wonderful porch from which you can
enjoy a view of the green. Double room: $$$–$$$$. Open: All
year. Telephone: 388-4961; reservations, 800-842-4666. Credit
cards.

Swift House, 25 Stewart Lane, Middlebury 05753.
Many now consider this the most elegant hostelry in the
area. I find that it leans a little too much toward the precious,
but there is no doubt that great care and attention have been
paid to the refurbishing of the three buildings (a carriage
house, a gate house and the main house, which was built in
1814) that make up the inn. Some rooms have fireplaces, and
the inn has an attractive dining room. Double room: $$$–$$$$.
Open: All year. Telephone: 388-9925. Credit cards.

Waybury Inn, Route 125, East Middlebury, 05740.
The exterior of this inn is known across the nation because it
was used for the exterior of the inn in *The Bob Newhart Show.*
About six miles from Middlebury, this is an attractive inn with
stenciled wallpapers and fireplaces. Double room: $$$$. Open:
All year. Telephone: 388-4015; reservations, 800-348-1810.
Credit cards.

Rutland area—Fair Haven

Vermont Marble Inn, 12 West Park Place, Fair Haven
05743. (Fair Haven is very near the New York border and is
minutes from Rutland.)
The innkeepers here, Shirley Stein and Bea and Richard

Taube, are among my favorite people. I first stayed here right after they had restored the building and opened this lovely 1867 Victorian built of locally quarried marble and situated right on the green. I was truly impressed by the quality of what they had achieved in furnishing and decorating the rooms and the excellent food they served, but even more by the love they had lavished on this building. This is the "homiest" inn I know of, and friends I have sent are in complete agreement. If you want to be coddled and treated like family, this is it. In addition, the dining room is superb and worth a detour. Double room: $$$$$. Open: All year except two weeks in November. Telephone: 265-8383; reservations, 800-535-2814. Credit cards.

NORTHERN VERMONT AND THE NORTHEAST KINGDOM

Northern Vermont

Stowe

Because of its enormous popularity as a ski resort, Stowe and the surrounding area are filled with attractive places to stay. I have listed four, the most famous (Trapp Family Lodge), an inn in the village (Green Mountain), a luxurious resort (Topnotch at Stowe), and, my personal choice, an inn with an excellent dining room (Ten Acres Lodge). Should you want other recommendations, I suggest you call the excellent Stowe Area Association, 253-7321.

Trapp Family Lodge, Trapp Hill Road, Stowe 05672.
   The hills are alive, all right, but it's with skiers, not music. The original lodge burned in 1980, Baroness Maria Von Trapp died in 1987, and the rebuilt main lodge (1983) subsequently lost some of its personal touch. Nevertheless, the service is all one could ask for, people still flock to it, and even if you don't stay here, you should see what it's all about by going to the Austrian Tea Room, which offers tea, pastries and sandwiches, and one of Stowe's loveliest views. Double room: $$$$$. Open: All year. Telephone: 253-8511; reservations, 800-826-7000. Credit cards.

Green Mountain Inn, Box 60, Main Street, Stowe 05672.

If you want to be in the village, this brick-and-clapboard building, part of which goes back to 1833, is the place for you. There is an annex at the back. The inn was completely modernized and redecorated with antique reproductions in 1983 and has several fireplaces in the public rooms and a fully equipped health club. It is a good deal more reasonable than the other two suggestions. Double room: $$$$. Open: All year. Telephone: 253-7301; reservations, 800-445-6629. Credit cards.

Topnotch at Stowe Resort and Spa, Box 1458, Mountain Road, Stowe 05672.

Where to begin? There is a health-and-fitness spa with a special spa menu. There is a cross-country ski center. There is a riding stable and a skating rink. There are four indoor and ten outdoor tennis courts and an indoor and an outdoor swimming pool. And believe me, there is much more. In fact, there is so much more that one ski magazine selected Topnotch as one of the twelve most luxurious ski hotels in the world. Rooms, suites, townhouses with kitchens and fireplaces, studios—all are available, and the variety of housing makes rates vary widely, too. Open: All year. Telephone: 253-8585; reservations, 800-451-8686. Credit cards.

Ten Acres Lodge, RR 3, Stowe 05672.

The old red farmhouse that is the main structure has only eight rooms, but there are two guest cottages and a separate unit, Hill House, that has eight guest rooms with fireplaces. All in all, this is a luxurious choice made special by the quality of its dining room. Double room: $$$–$$$$$. Open: All year. Telephone: 253-7638; reservations, 800-327-7357. Credit cards.

Northeast Kingdom

Craftsbury Common

Inn on the Common, Main Street, Craftsbury Common, 05827.

The main building is near a wonderful old cemetery, another building is across the street, and the third is on the common. In bad weather you can entertain yourself with one of the films from the inn's collection of several hundred. There are fireplaces—some bedrooms also have them—and attractively decorated and furnished rooms. The inn also has a dining room, a godsend, as there is no other place of any quality to eat here. In addition, there's a 140-acre sports complex nearby, where you can cross-country ski in winter, swim and canoe in summer, or just take nature walks. But you really are here because the area is so beautiful, and after a day of enjoying the Northeast Kingdom, this is the place to which you will wish to return. Double room: $$$$. Open: All year. Telephone: 586-9619; reservations, 800-521-2233. Credit cards.

St. Johnsbury area—Lower Waterford

Rabbit Hill Inn, Route 18, Box 55, Lower Waterford, 05848.
A very good, comfortable inn if a little on the cute side. It's conveniently located for touring the Northeast Kingdom. Double room: $$$$$. Open: All year except the month of April and early November. Telephone: 748-5168. Credit cards.

CENTRAL VERMONT AND THE UPPER CONNECTICUT RIVER VALLEY

Montpelier

Inn at Montpelier, 147 Main Street, Montpelier 05602.
Montpelier is an excellent location from which to explore central Vermont because it is almost at the center of the state. If that's what you want to do, this is the place to hang your hat. The two Federal buildings that compose the inn were built in the early 1800s; more recent additions include a wonderful wraparound porch that is extremely inviting. It is comfortable and well furnished and decorated, and some bedrooms have fireplaces. The inn is just outside the center of town, so it is a

comfortable walk to anyplace in the town. Double room: $$$$.
Open: All year. Telephone: 223-2727. Credit cards.

Woodstock area and Quechee

Woodstock Inn & Resort, Woodstock 05091.
This inn, the finest resort in the area and just off the green,
is owned by Laurance Rockefeller. It opened in 1969 and
currently has 146 rooms, 23 with fireplaces, and also offers—
either on the premises or nearby—meeting rooms, a gift shop,
indoor and outdoor tennis facilities, an 18-hole golf course, an
exercise room and pool, whirlpool, sauna, squash courts . . . in
short, every facility you could conceivably want. And I
shouldn't forget to mention the 10-foot fireplace in the lobby. It
is a splendid resort, one of the finest in New England, but it's
almost too smooth (there's even a concierge) for Vermont. The
inn is open all year and offers a wide variety of prices and packages. For complete information, telephone 800-448-7900.
Credit cards.

Quechee Inn at Marshland Farm, Box 747, Clubhouse
Road, Quechee 05059.
An extremely attractive and appealing inn with a good dining room whose core is an eighteenth-century farmhouse. It
once was the home of conservationist George Perkins Marsh's
family. However, the last time I was there my room was rather
small and spartan. When you reserve, then, be sure to ask
about what you are getting. Double room: $$$$$. Open: All
year. Telephone: 800-235-3133. Credit cards.

Kedron Valley Inn, P.O. Box 145, South Woodstock 05071.
Route 106 going south of Woodstock is very pretty indeed,
and Kedron Valley Inn therefore wins the Best Setting award
from me. Some of the rooms in this handsome old building have
fireplaces or woodstoves, and the dining room is good too.
Double room: $$$$. Open: All year except the month of April
and a few days before Thanksgiving. Telephone: 457-1473.
Credit cards.

SOUTHERN VERMONT AND THE UPPER CONNECTICUT RIVER
VALLEY

*Best in the Region: The Old Tavern, Grafton; The Inn at Sawmill
Farm, West Dover*

Dorset

Barrows House, Dorset, 05251.
This is my first choice of the inns in Dorset. It is composed of
eight buildings on a surprising 12 acres of land; I say "surprising" because the inn is in the village, and these expansive
grounds are not what you would expect. I think it is this
space—which is filled with a particularly attractive   garden, a
swimming pool, a gazebo, and tennis, croquet, and badminton
courts—that, for me, gives the inn an edge over the others.
Each of the seven cottages near the inn has its own sitting room
and porch or terrace. Double room: $$$$$. Open: All year.
Telephone: 867-4455; reservations, 800-639-1620. Credit cards.

Dorset Inn, Dorset, 05251.
Built in 1796, this inn lays claim to be the oldest in Vermont
and is listed on the National Register of Historic Places.
Completely restored, and in the heart of the village facing the
green, it is a charming and beautifully run inn. One of the
owners, by the way, was formerly a chef at the Barrows House.
Double room: $$$$. Open: All year, except for the first three
weeks of April. Telephone: 867-5500. Credit cards.

Grafton

The Old Tavern, Main Street, Grafton 05146.
In a state famous for its inns, this is my favorite of all. The
perfect setting doesn't hurt, and the inn is at the center of village life, as inns often were in the eighteenth and nineteenth
centuries, when they brought news and excitement from the
outside world. The inn is flawlessly decorated and furnished
and no expense has been spared. The family (see page 36),
through the foundation, obviously decided that they would
make every effort to create a living memorial their aunt would

have loved. They have succeeded, and now, whether we stay at the inn or across the street in the annex or take one of the six available village houses, we all can enjoy a particularly wonderful experience. Double room: $$$$. Open: All year except for the month of April. Telephone: 843-2231. Credit cards.

Manchester Village

The Equinox, Manchester Village 05254.

This grand old resort, now owned by Guinness Enterprises, which has poured a fortune into it, is both attractive and comfortable. And right next to it is one of my favorite bookshops in Vermont, The Johnny Appleseed. If you want a relatively formal setting, a fitness center, a golf course, and all the other amenities, this is the place. Rates cover a broad range. Check for full information. Open: All year. Telephone: 800-362-4747. Credit cards.

The Reluctant Panther, Box 678, Manchester Village, 05254.

Don't be startled by the rather violent purple paint of this inn. It's really very comfortable—several rooms and all the suites have fireplaces and Jacuzzis, for example—and the restaurant has excellent food. This is a No Smoking inn. Double room: $$$$–$$$$$. Open: All year. Telephone: 362-2568; reservations, 800-822-2331. Credit cards.

Newfane

The Four Columns Inn, West Street, Newfane 05345.

There are many reasons to choose this inn, not the least of which is that it is on a spectacular green (see page 37). The restaurant is my particular favorite in Vermont. A No Smoking inn. Double room: $$$$. Open: All year, except for two weeks after Thanksgiving and two weeks in April. Telephone: 365-7713. Credit cards.

West Dover

The Inn at Sawmill Farm, P. O. Box 367, West Dover 05356.

This is one of the most luxurious and best-run inns in the

state, and its dining room is absolutely superb. The problem, as far as I am concerned, is that although the inn grounds are lovely, West Dover and the immediate surroundings are not. I also think it's too expensive, given what else is available in this region. Double room: $$$$$. Open: All year. Telephone: 464-8131. Credit cards.

Where to Eat

Area Code: 802

LAKE CHAMPLAIN AND ITS VALLEY

Best in the Region: The Vermont Marble Inn, Fair Haven

Burlington area—Shelburne

The Inn at Shelburne Farms   Open: Dinner, late May to mid-October. $$$. Phone: 985-8498. Credit cards.

The dining room is the most handsome room in this magnificent house, and the food is the best in the Burlington area. If you don't stay here, you certainly should treat yourself to a dinner here and enjoy the glorious view over Lake Champlain and the gardens.

Middlebury

The Swift House Inn, 25 Stewart Lane. Open: Dinner, Thursday–Monday. $$$. Phone: 388-9925. Credit cards: MasterCard, Visa.

This is the favorite of many, but I find the food a little too "planned elegant."

The Dog Team Tavern   A few miles north of Middlebury and off Route 7. Open: Lunch, late spring to October, dinner, all year. $$. Phone: 388-7651. Credit cards.

Like sticky buns? Relish trays? Fritters with real maple syrup? Old-fashioned desserts? Me, too. If you are in the mood for a reasonably priced, good New England dinner, this is the place for you.

Rutland area—Fair Haven

The Vermont Marble Inn, Fair Haven Green. Open: Dinner.
$$$. Phone: 265-8383. Credit cards.

Now we're into serious dining. In fact, this is the best restaurant in the Lake Champlain valley and is worth a detour. I recommend you make a reservation as there aren't many tables.

NORTHERN VERMONT AND THE NORTHEAST KINGDOM

Northern Vermont

Stowe

The Whip Bar and Grill Open: Breakfast, lunch, dinner.
$$. Phone: 253-7301. Credit cards.

Good for simple food (grilled meats and fish) and conveniently located in the center of Stowe at the Green Mountain Inn. It also has a lovely big fireplace.

Stowehof Inn, Edson Hill Road. Open: Breakfast, Sunday brunch, dinner. $$$. Phone: 253-9722. Credit cards.

The food is good. Not great, just good. Still, it's a reasonable alternative if you've already eaten at Ten Acres Lodge.

Ten Acres Lodge Open: Dinner. $$$. Phone: 253-7638. Credit cards.

This offers the best, most innovative and distinctive food in Stowe. The menu changes regularly, but I guarantee that whenever you eat there you will have a memorable experience—and don't omit the desserts; they are glorious.

Topnotch at Stowe, Mountain Road. Open: Breakfast, lunch, Sunday brunch, dinner. $$$. Phone: 253-8585. Credit cards.

I think this has the best food of the hotels here.

Northeast Kingdom

Craftsbury Common

Inn on the Common Open: Only to guests of the inn, which is unfortunate as the food is quite good.

St. Johnsbury area—Lower Waterford

Rabbit Hill Inn, Lower Waterford. Open: Dinner. $$$. Phone: 748-5168. Credit cards.

Very pleasant atmosphere and good food in an area where the latter can be hard to find.

CENTRAL VERMONT AND THE UPPER CONNECTICUT RIVER VALLEY

Montpelier

Elm Street Café, 38 Elm Street. Open: Breakfast, lunch, dinner. $$. Phone: 223-3188. Credit cards.

Reasonable prices for good food. This, like Tubbs (see below), is owned by the New England Culinary Institute, whose student chefs do the food preparation.

Tubbs, 24 Elm Street. Open: Lunch, Monday–Friday; dinner, Monday–Saturday. $$–$$$. Phone: 229-9202. Credit cards.

Another New England Culinary Institute operation, and the best restaurant in Montpelier. The food can sometimes go a bit far out on a limb, but it still is worth a visit.

The Inn at Montpelier, 147 Main Street. Open: Dinner, except Monday. $$$. Phone: 223-2727. Credit cards.

The food here is consistently good, more than many restaurants can claim, so this is an excellent alternative if you can't get a reservation at Tubbs.

Woodstock area and Quechee

Simon Pearce, Main Street, Quechee. Open: Lunch, dinner. $$–$$$. Phone: 295-1470. Credit cards.

This is my favorite spot in the Woodstock area because of its spectacular setting overlooking the waterfall and because of the really very good food. In addition, the prices are reasonable. It's hard to ask for more than all that.

Bentley's, 3 Elm Street, Woodstock. Open: Lunch, dinner. $$–$$$. Phone: 457-3232. Credit cards.

Meat-and-potatoes-type food, but well prepared and conveniently located.

Kedron Valley Inn, Route 106, South Woodstock. Open: Dinner. $$$. Phone: 457-1473. Credit cards.
French cuisine is the specialty here, and the atmosphere is casual. Because the food is good and the drive here and the setting are so pretty, this is a place to consider carefully.

Quechee Inn at Marshland Farm, Club House Road, Quechee. Open: Dinner. $$$$. Phone: 295-3133. Credit cards.
The dining room is attractive and the food good, although not quite as imaginative as the food at Kedron Valley.

SOUTHERN VERMONT AND THE UPPER CONNECTICUT VALLEY

Best in the Region: The Four Columns Inn, Newfane; The Inn at Sawmill Farm, West Dover

Bennington

The Four Chimneys, 21 West Road (Route 9). Open: Lunch, dinner. $$$. Phone: 447-3500. Credit cards.
The best food in Bennington, and the building is handsome. However, I'm never entirely satisfied here; it always seems to miss its potential.

Bennington Station, 150 Depot Street. Open: Lunch, dinner. $$-$$$. Phone: 447-1080. Credit cards.
This wonderful converted 1897 Romanesque railroad station is worth a visit in itself. That it also offers good, plain food can only be a plus.

Dorset

The Barrows House Open: Dinner. $$$. Phone: 867-4455. Credit cards.
The food here is respectable, if not really memorable.

Chantecleer, Route 7A, East Dorset. Open: dinner. $$$. Phone: 362-1616. Credit cards.
Attractively set in an old dairy barn, this establishment offers quite good food.

The Dorset Inn   Open: Breakfast, lunch, dinner. $$$. Phone: 867-5500. Credit cards.
American food with a New England bias is offered here, and I find it consistently good.

Grafton

The Old Tavern   Open: Lunch, dinner. $$$. Phone: 843-2231. Credit cards.
It has always irritated me that this inn, my favorite in Vermont, offers only passably good food. It's perfectly okay, mind you, but it should be so much better.

Manchester Village

The Reluctant Panther   Open: Dinner. $$$. Phone: 362-2568. Credit cards.
After the extraordinary choice of colors, both inside and out, the other great—and very pleasant—surprise is the food; it's good enough to merit a special effort to dine here.

Newfane

The Four Columns Inn   Open: Dinner. $$$. Phone: 365-7713. Credit cards.
Overall, this remains my favorite restaurant in Vermont. The food is fresh, delicious, and prepared with exquisite care, the dining room comfortable and attractive, the service knowledgeable and friendly.

Old Newfane Inn   Open: Dinner. $$$. Phone: 365-4427. No credit cards.
Also very good, with a Swiss accent, and more formal in its decor than the Four Columns. The dining room is quite lovely,

but I wish they would light the candles on empty tables to cheer things up.

West Dover

The Inn at Sawmill Farm   Open: Dinner. $$$. Phone: 464-8131. Credit cards.

You really should make every effort to dine here. The wine list is superb. The ambiance is superb. The food is superb. The service is superb. The prices are superb.

Weston

The Bryant House   Open: Lunch. $. Phone: 824-6287. Credit cards.

Good, solid sandwiches and soups and desserts that make you sigh with pleasure before you take off to shop at the Vermont Country Store, which owns this plain and excellent eatery.

The Inn at Weston   Open: Dinner. $$–$$$. Phone: 824-5804. Credit cards.

Very good food prepared with care and thought. You won't find the clever dish here—thank God.

New Hampshire

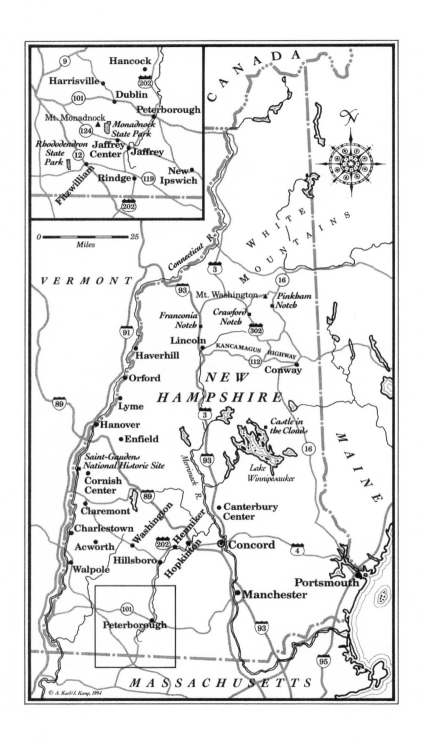

© A. Karl/J. Kemp, 1994

T HE Granite State. That's New Hampshire's nickname, but it really refers largely to the part of the state most people immediately think of when they hear the words *New Hampshire*— the White Mountains. In actuality, this is a complex state offering a wide range of landscapes, activities, and pleasures.

New Hampshire, 168 miles long and 90 miles wide at its widest, has almost twice the population of Vermont, with 1,109,252 residents living on its 8,992 square miles. The city of Manchester, New Hampshire's largest, has a population hovering around 100,000, and the southern part of the state has a strongly developed manufacturing tradition that now includes electronic products, machinery, plastics, and leather goods.

Yet about 86 percent of the state is forested, small villages abound in settings that embody rural New England, and tourism is vital to the good health of the state. In the winter, skiing—some of the best in the East—dominates the scene, and the blindingly white mountains are alive with brilliantly colored figures flying down the slopes. In the summer, it's the turn of the lakes—Sunapee, Winnipesaukee, Ossipee, and hundreds of others—and the seacoast around Portsmouth, not to mention the notches, where thousands come to enjoy the spectacular scenery.

New Hampshire has a very different feeling from Vermont. Once you cross the Connecticut River, the border between the two states, you rather quickly sense a change. Is it that the villages seem slightly larger and slightly more sophisticated in their architecture? That the lakes are more frequent, the landscape more dotted with stone outcroppings, the whole more subtly austere—the Granite State and the White Mountains versus the Green Mountains?

In any case, it is a fascinating state that includes the spectacular eighteenth- and nineteenth-century buildings of Portsmouth; some of the most beautiful drives in New England; the Connecticut River villages, one after the other, forming a chain

This house could only be in New England, and if you should try to copy it in another area of the country it would never look at home.

that exemplifies the New England look made famous through an infinite number of photographs; and the Monadnock region, a place overlooked by the twentieth century, to mention a few.

History

During the Ice Age, at least four cycles of glacial encroachment and retreat created the landscape you see today. Glaciers left the boulders strewn about on Mount Washington and at Crawford Notch, and glaciers rounded and smoothed the mountain peaks and gouged out the ponds and lakes and defined the lakeshores and riverbanks. It is no understatement to say that everywhere you go you witness the evidence of their work.

The glaciers left some thousands of years ago. Several hundred years ago, Europeans arrived to stay. There is some evidence and even more speculation that Basque and Portuguese fishermen and Vikings visited here, but in 1623 a permanent settlement was established when a man named David Thomson and a small band of colonists came for the purpose of fishing and trading with the Indians. That was the group whose arrival led to the founding of Portsmouth. The next town to be settled, also a coastal settlement, was Dover, in 1623.

After that, the coast developed relatively quickly until by 1641 there were four "centers"—Portsmouth, Dover, Exeter, and Hampton. (Settlements would remain confined to the coastal region until 1673, when Nashua was founded.) It was also in 1641 that the four applied to Massachusetts to be placed under that colony's jurisdiction, a situation that lasted until 1679, when they became a separate royal province under Charles II.

The colonial period was dominated by the Wentworth family. The first, John, appeared in 1717 and was lieutenant-governor of the province until his death in 1730. A wealthy Portsmouth merchant, he was an excellent administrator who, among other things, concluded a peace treaty with the Indians and encouraged the settling of the interior.

His son, Benning, was appointed governor by George II in 1741, and he quite literally ruled the province for the next twenty-five years, a period of extraordinary growth and prosperity. By the time he retired in 1766, the population had increased to 52,000 and Portsmouth was the cosmopolitan colonial seaport whose remnants so entrance us today. As I point out in the Vermont section of this book, Benning Wentworth always took care of number one, and while he was making the 124 township grants in New Hampshire and Vermont created during his administration, he never failed to skim off a large amount of the best acreage in each township for himself; eventually he owned 100,000 acres of prime land.

It was his greed that forced him into retirement in 1766, and his situation would have been far more serious if his nephew, another Wentworth named John, hadn't interceded on Benning's behalf and convinced the authorities not to undertake further action against him. (For a description of Benning Wentworth's house, one of my favorites in Portsmouth, see page 116.)

This John Wentworth became the last colonial governor of New Hampshire. He was a brilliant administrator, and it was he who developed a route between Portsmouth and Hanover, with its newly created college of Dartmouth, thereby linking the seacoast to the interior. But along came the Revolution and John, a loyalist, fled New Hampshire in 1775, never to return.

New Hampshire was the only one of the original thirteen colonies not to be invaded by the British during the Revolution. It also was the first to have a written constitution, adopted in January 1776. In June 1788 it became the ninth state to ratify the Constitution, casting the deciding vote to meet the two-thirds requirement.

The new state prospered to such an extent that it was estimated that exports quadrupled over the next three decades, while the population went from roughly 185,000 in 1800 to almost 250,000 in 1820. But during this period attention also began to turn toward the interior, and although in the early 1830s over 80 percent of New Hampshire residents were farmers, the real news was that there were forty cotton mills and several shoe factories. Soon the mills and factories were drawing the youth from the farms and attracting increasing numbers of immigrants. By the end of the century, one out of five New Hampshire residents were foreign-born—many of these were French Canadians—and Manchester was the world's largest producer of cotton cloth. It was during the second part of the nineteenth century, too, that the development of the railroad, and particularly its entrance into the White Mountains in the 1870s, allowed for the creation and growth of the tourist industry.

The twentieth century brought rapid change. By 1935 Manchester's huge Amoskeag Manufacturing Company was bankrupt and 11,000 of its workers were jobless. The shoe factories, too, were in decline, and the economy of southern New Hampshire faced serious trouble. Now, at the end of the century, the area has managed to diversify and generally prosper, but the northern part of the state is largely dependent on the tourists and the seasonal employment they bring.

Special Interest Sources

ANTIQUING

The best source is the New Hampshire Antiques Dealers Association, RFD 1, Box 305C, Tilton 03276. Write for their listing of 170 dealers and 20 antique centers with multiple dealer membership.

MAPS

The best map is the Official New Hampshire Highway Map and Parklands Guide. It and a vacation package are available free from the New Hampshire Department of Resources and Economic Development, Office of Travel and Tourism. Telephone: 800-FUN-IN-NH The map contains information on everything from covered bridges and golf courses and scenic drives to state park facilities, general lodgings, shopping, and New Hampshire State Liquor Store locations.

NORTHERN NEW HAMPSHIRE – THE WHITE MOUNTAINS

As I have noted, New Hampshire's nickname, the Granite State, comes from its most famous natural feature, the White Mountains—the northern terminus of the Appalachian chain—which range across central and northern New Hampshire and into western Maine. For scenic grandeur, it is the peer of any region in New England.

The White Mountains are composed of three principal ranges: the Presidential, which is the tallest and includes Mount Washington, the highest point in the northeast (6,288 feet) as well as peaks named after Jefferson, Adams, Madison, and Monroe; the Carter-Moriah; and the Franconia, where you can see the Old Man of the Mountain, a rock formation that has come to symbolize New Hampshire (its fascination has always eluded me).

In all, there are 86 mountain peaks and nine "notches," which are known as gaps or passes in other parts of the United States. The most famous notches, all of which are described in this section, are Crawford, in the center; Franconia, to the west; and, to the east, Pinkham.

The mountains were formed during the last Ice Age as the huge glacier embracing the earth withdrew. In the valleys, meanwhile, smaller glaciers left the record of their retreat by creating the notches.

Because of the difficulty of the terrain and the harsh weather for a good part of the year, the area was settled more slowly than the southern part of the state or the benign Connecticut River Valley region. But then the Romantic Movement arrived, and by the mid-nineteenth century northern New Hampshire had become a favorite source of material for painters and writers, beginning with Thomas Cole and Nathaniel Hawthorne, who often visited the area. And, as is always the case, as soon as the artists began broadcasting the beauties of the region through their splendid canvases and words—and with accessibility made easier by the advent of the railroad in the region— the tourists arrived en masse.

This was the age of the grand hotel, great wooden edifices that strode the land with haughty pride, their seemingly endless verandas offering views of the mountains beyond, and their rooms accommodating as many as five hundred people. Almost all are gone now, burned down and torn down, ultimately defeated by the arrival of the automobile and the cabin colonies designed for more transient visitors. The colonies, in turn, were succeeded by the motel, and it sometimes seems today that if there's a spot that can take a motel, there you will indeed find one.

One of the reasons tens of thousands of people visit the area each year is to enjoy the splendors of White Mountain National Forest, the largest in the East, covering 772,108 acres. In the nineteenth century, powerful logging interests ravaged the landscape—one lumber mill processed 7 1/2 *miles* of lumber each day. Clear cutting was the standard order, and by the beginning of the twentieth century parts of this great area looked like a moonscape, the slopes denuded of trees, the earth eroded and barren.

Fortunately, the problem was addressed through the Federal Weeks Act of 1911. The spectacular wilderness you see today is a direct result of that act, and although timber harvesting continues, it is now sensibly controlled, and hikers, campers, fishermen, and others have full use of miles and miles of unspoiled territory.

For information about activities such as camping and fish-

Have a pumpkin. Have three hundred. In this case, excess is completely appropriate.

ing, write White Mountain National Forest, Box 638, 719 Main Street, Laconia 03247, or telephone 528-8721. For information on hiking the 1,128 miles of trails, contact the Appalachian Mountain Club, 5 Joy Street, Boston, Mass. 02108, or telephone 617-523-0636 and ask for the *White Mountain Guide.* For general tourist information on attractions and lodging, contact the White Mountain Association at 800-FIND-MTS.

I like to stay at an inn named the **Christmas Farm Inn** because it is centrally located at the southern end of Pinkham Notch in a very pretty spot, and because I particularly like the choice of accommodations.

There is a great deal to see here, and a visit of four days is necessary to take in the highlights. In my opinion, the Kancamagus Highway offers the most beautiful drive in the region, while Franconia Notch is the most spectacular of the notches, so if your time is limited, at least be sure to explore these two. After that, I would visit Pinkham Notch and Mount Washington and, last but certainly not least, Crawford Notch.

The Kancamagus Highway

The highway is named for an Indian chief who, in the 1690s, was driven from the area by the English. The construction of the present road was begun in 1939 and continued for twenty years. It wasn't completely paved until 1964, and it was opened year-round only in 1968. Hard to believe when you realize that now almost 800,000 vehicles make this 34 1/2-mile trip between Lincoln at the western end and North Conway at the eastern each year.

At the Kancamagus Pass, an elevation of about 2,850 feet, you will be at the very heart of the White Mountains, which from here stretch out in a radius of 35 miles. You will not, I hope, simply drive over this route; plan to take time to enjoy the scenic overlooks and picnic areas and even some of the shorter hiking trails (trails ranging from 1/2 mile to a hike of several days are accessible from the highway). Here are descriptions of a few of the pleasures (and the sheer variety of them) that you can explore.

Certainly not to be missed is **Sabbaday Falls.** It's an easy fifteen-minute walk from the highway along Sabbaday Brook Trail, and it's exhilarating as well as beautiful to see the water tumbling down over ledges and into glacier-created potholes and finally racing through a flume.

Another easy, informative, and pleasant hike begins at the **Passaconaway Historic Site,** a few miles east of Sabbaday Falls. This is an information and nature center, and from here you can follow the **Rail 'n' River Trail,** a 1/2-mile loop nicknamed for the old railbed it follows, which is designed to introduce you in an informal and interesting way to the amazingly varied trees and shrubs in the area.

Even closer to North Conway is **Covered Bridge Campground,** from which you can take the **Boulder Loop Trail,** about 2 1/2 miles; you should allow two to three hours at least to enjoy the sweeping views up and down the river valley. Across the valley, by the way, is Mount Chocorua, with mounts Paugus and Passaconaway to the right. Passaconaway was the grandfather of Kancamagus, mentioned above, and in 1627 he created the great Penacook Confederacy of seventeen Indian tribes. It is this confederacy that was destroyed and scattered in the 1690s. It is said that when Passaconaway died, twenty-four huge wolves bore him on a sled to the top of Mount Washington, from whence they ascended to heaven in a cloud of fire.

Chocorua, on the other hand, died at the hands of a white man in the mid-eighteenth century, but not without first hurling a curse at the white man and all his creations and progeny and all he might use or profit by. For some years after that the people of the area did indeed suffer losses of crops and cattle, and they believed it was the result of Chocorua's bitter curse. The curse, however, brought him lasting fame, but what caused it is forgotten. There is a trail to the summit of Mount Chocorua—it's a full day's hike—and the view from there is one of the great vistas of this region.

Finally, there are Lincoln and **North Conway** themselves, at the western and eastern ends respectively of the highway. Lincoln can be skipped, but North Conway is of more than passing interest. It has been a resort center since the area began developing in the nineteenth century and consequently has a great variety of shops and restaurants along Main Street, which is crowned by the delightful old **Boston & Maine Railroad Station** (1874). This Victorian interpretation of early Russian architecture is a confectionery delight, the sort that the witch in Hansel and Gretel would have built if she had been into railroad stations. Today it is home to a steam excursion railroad that will take you on an hour's round-trip tour of the Saco River Valley. There's also a railroad museum here. For information, telephone 356-5251.

What also draws people to this area is the factory outlets outside the village and stretching endlessly to the horizon. There are more than 200, ranging from L. L. Bean and Ralph Lauren to bath shops and kitchen shops and shoe shops and you-name-it shops. It looks awful, but I must admit you can find some great bargains.

Franconia Notch

It is said that more people visit here each year than there are residents of New Hampshire. Not surprising, for this western-most of the notches is home to two of the most famous natural features in the state, the Old Man of the Mountain and the Flume.

The **Old Man of the Mountain** was discovered in 1805, when two surveyors who were planning the first road through the notch stopped to wash in what now is called Profile Lake. Looking up, they immediately identified the now famous granite profile, 40 feet from chin to forehead, which has been protected by stabilizing but unobtrusive cables and anchors. This great stone face inspired Nathaniel Hawthorne to write a short story, "The Great Stone Face," and P. T. Barnum was so impressed he wanted to buy it for his show. (In fact, Barnum loved the whole area and said Mount Washington and its surroundings made up the second-greatest show on earth.)

It is viewed to best advantage from Profile Lake. Once there was a famous hotel, the 400-room Profile House, that offered its guests a splendid view of the Old Man; only certain spots make good vantage points from which to see the profile, which is one reason it was discovered as late as 1805. In any case, for the life of me I can't see what all the excitement is about. It must be a general flaw in my character, but my first view was a huge disappointment, and my opinion has not improved with time and subsequent viewings. I don't even like the Hawthorne short story.

On the other hand, a visit to **Franconia Notch State Park** is one of the highlights of a trip to New Hampshire.

You first go to the Gilman Visitors' Center. Because this is the flagship of the state park system, the Visitors' Center is particularly complete and provides not only brochures and maps but also films of the area, a snack bar, and a gift shop.

The most famous site here is the **Flume,** a racing, deep, and narrow falling stream 7/10 of a mile from the Visitors' Center. The most commonly accepted version of its discovery is that in 1808, "Aunt" Jess Guernsey, in her nineties at the time, came upon it while looking for some good trout fishing, and that it took her some time to convince others it really existed. One of the most impressive features of the Flume at that time was an enormous (10 feet high by 12 feet long) boulder suspended between its walls. Then, in 1883, a landslide swept the boulder away, and it was never found. The same storm that started the landslide also created Table Rock Cascades off Ridge Path and the 45-foot Avalanche Falls (see page 77).

At first, your walk to the Flume is mostly downhill, passing a mammoth 300-ton boulder—the many boulders were left here by the great mile-thick ice sheet as it retreated north—

and then crossing over the Pemigewasset River on a covered bridge which, as it happens, is one of the oldest in the state.

Next you will reach Boulder Cabin, and from there you will pass Table Rock and then enter the Flume gorge and follow its length on a system of staircases and boardwalks alongside the rushing water, between towering (70–90 feet) moss-covered granite walls. It is unique and awesomely impressive. For me, it demonstrates the power and grandeur of nature in a Wagnerian manner . . . warm and welcoming it is not; brooding and massively indifferent to the tiny human creatures toiling through it is.

After viewing the 45-foot Avalanche Falls you can return to the Visitors' Center if you wish, but I would urge you to continue to the Pool by following Ridge Path through the forest to the turnoff for Liberty Gorge and the Cascades and then, slightly farther on, to Sentinel Pine Bridge, which overlooks the Pool. You can then return to the Visitors' Center on Wildwood Path. The entire loop will take you about an hour and fifteen minutes to an hour and a half.

The Flume is open: Mid-May to late October, 9–4. Admission fee. Telephone: 745-8391.

While in the vicinity you may also wish to visit the **Basin,** a deep glacial pothole almost 30 feet in diameter, and **Cannon Mountain,** a popular ski area and the site of the first aerial tramway in this country. The present one will take you to the summit, from which you will have a splendid view of the notch. Open: Ski season and mid-May to late October, 9–4. Admission fee.

You also should consider visiting **Lost River Gorge,** about 8 miles from Lincoln, in Kinsman Notch, on Route 112W. Less popular than the Flume and some of the other features of this notch, the gorge is therefore less visited and can provide a more relaxed experience. It is slightly more strenuous—the entrance trail is steep in spots, and you descend about 300 feet—but there are benches on which you can rest, and it is a fascinating experience to visit the caves (some of which are of easy access and some of which are difficult to navigate) and observe the potholes and waterfalls along the system of boardwalks and staircases. Open: Mid-May to late October. Admission fee. Telephone: 745-8031.

Pinkham Notch

Pinkham Notch is a 5,600-acre section of the White Mountains National Forest that begins just north of Jackson and is bordered on the west by Mount Washington, Mount Franklin, and Mount Eisenhower, and on the east by Carter Dome and North, South, and Middle Carter Mountains. Named for Joseph Pinkham, who settled here in 1790, the notch is less developed and visited than Franconia Notch, but it offers its own special rewards.

Going north from Jackson on Route 16, the road that takes you through the notch, I always make an effort to see **Glen Ellis Falls.** A brief walk along a comfortable trail will take you to the base of the falls. The Glen Ellis Falls and pools may lack the grandeur of some of the others, but the gentle tranquillity of this spot is particularly delightful.

North of the falls is **Wildcat Mountain.** There is a gondola lift here that will take you to the summit, from which you will have one of the great views of the White Mountains. Mount Washington is to your left, and other peaks of the Presidential Range march by your gazing eyes in a dignified and splendid procession. The gondola operates: Weekends, late May to mid-October, 9:30–4:30; daily, late June to Labor Day, 9:00–4:30. Admission fee. Telephone: 466-3326.

As you travel north you will pass the entrance to the road to the summit of Mount Washington on your left; on your right will be the entrance to the Glen House, from where you can take a van to the summit. See below for full details. As you continue north, the scenery remains ravishing. Before you return, take Route 2 East where it joins Route 16, to enjoy the Shelburne birches, an extensive stand of beautiful birches along the road, which seem so fragile against the rugged mountain landscape surrounding them.

Mount Washington

Some facts: 250,000 people visit it annually . . . it rises 6,288 feet above sea level and is the highest peak in the Northeast . . . it was first climbed in 1642 by a gentleman named Darby Field . . . its weather, often a brutal combination of bitter cold, wind, and ice,

The famous cog railway that takes you up Mount Washington. It always reminds me of the children's story "The Little Engine That Could."

is comparable to the subarctic climate of northern Labrador . . . winds of 231 miles per hour, the strongest ever recorded in the world, sped across the summit on April 12, 1934, while winds of over 100 miles per hour are relatively common . . . there is fog for at least part of the day more than 300 days each year. . . . After all that, you will not be surprised to hear that many people say that the weather here, all in all, is the worst on earth. So how can you not join those 250,000 visitors and go to the summit?

As I mentioned above, you can drive or take a van on Mount Washington Auto Road. Of these two choices, I would strongly urge the latter. (You also can take a cog railway, my preferred method, which is described on page 80.) If you do go by car, be sure that it is in prime condition—particularly the brakes. The narrow road was originally opened in 1861, and its 8-mile length maneuvers treacherous curves on an average grade of 12 percent. It has a remarkable safety record, but I've seen enough white-knuckled drivers to know that taking the van saves a lot of wear on the psyche. And anyway, the guides on the one-and-a-half hour guided tour are extremely well informed about all aspects of the mountain.

But, as I mentioned, I think the most pleasant way to reach the summit is to take the **Mount Washington Cog Railway,** which operates from Crawford Notch on the other side of Mount Washington. The engines and passenger cars appear to be right out of the nineteenth century which, in essence, they are. This 3 1/2-mile railway was built in 1869 and operates over grades steeper than 37 percent, something no ordinary train could possibly accomplish.

To solve the problem, a notched track was laid down between the rails, while the steam-powered engine operates a cog (toothed gear) that fits into the notches, allowing the train to move forward on the grade. At rest at the base, the engines look particularly odd because they are fitted with boilers at an angle to compensate for the grade. All in all, a brilliant technological feat for its time, and still a marvel. But, of course, it's the ride that counts most, and this slow approach to the summit—about an hour and fifteen minutes—allows you to see and absorb at leisure the changes in the landscape and vegetation. In addition, much of the trip is over trestles, and the part over Jacob's Ladder is better than any ride I've ever had on a fairgrounds.

You also might be interested in knowing about **Tuckerman Ravine,** accessible only by the Tuckerman Ravine Trail, which ascends to the summit of Mount Washington and is the hiker's favorite route. Here, where snow can build to a depth of 75 feet or more, skiing is possible as late as June, but particularly in April you will see skiers walking the trail—there are no lifts—to reach the slopes.

Mount Washington Auto Road is open: Daily (weather permitting), mid-May to mid-October, 7:30–6:00. Admission fee. Telephone: 466-3988.

Mount Washington Cog Railway is open: Weekends in May, daily (weather permitting), June to mid-October. Admission fee. Telephone: 846-5404. Reservations suggested.

Crawford Notch

This is the least-developed notch, but its history goes back to 1771, when it was first discovered by the white man. The Crawford family, who gave the notch their name, settled here in 1792 and opened the Mount Crawford House for travelers, the first "hotel" in the notch and one that would become famous throughout New England.

The Crawfords dominated the area for years. It was on a trail blazed by Ethan Allen Crawford, son of the founding settlers, Abel and Hannah, that the cog railway would eventually run, and Ethan Allen gave the mountains of the Presidential Range their names. But the Crawfords particularly excelled in the tourist business, and the last Crawford House, a huge building that could accommodate 400 guests, operated until 1977, when it was destroyed by fire.

This notch is still the home of one of the very rare grand survivors from the era of great hotels. I refer, of course, to the famous Mount Washington Hotel at Bretton Woods. This great five-story white building, with its red roof and two large octagonal towers, has a particularly spectacular setting, for you see it from the highway at a dramatic distance, with Mount Washington its breathtaking backdrop.

Built in 1902, it is at the center of a complex offering all the amenities of a resort, including tennis, swimming, golf, skiing,

The great appeal of this brick house arises from its elegant proportions, its situation on several levels, and its many, varied windows.

and horseback riding. Its most famous moment, of course, was when it served as the site of the International Monetary and Financial Conference, better known as the Bretton Woods Conference, in 1944, at which the gold standard was established at $35 an ounce, plans for the World Bank and the International Monetary Fund were developed, and the American dollar was selected as the unit of international exchange. This area, too, is where, in 1826, Samuel Willey, his family of six, and two hired hands rushed from their house to reach a nearby shelter when they heard the rumbling of an approaching landslide. Unfortunately, the landslide divided at the house but destroyed the shelter and swept the occupants to their deaths. Nathaniel Hawthorne wrote about this, too, in "The Ambitious Guest," a much more successful story, I might add, than "The Great Stone Face."

There is not much to do in this notch other than enjoy the scenery as you drive—with one exception, **Arethusa Falls.** It is a relatively easy 1 1/2-mile walk to the falls from the highway, and at the end is the highest and loveliest falls in a state famous for them. And take the time, too, to travel the 8 miles through Bear Notch, which lies between Bartlett, at the eastern end of the notch, and the Kancamagus Highway. The road is marked in Bartlett, and it offers a series of exquisite views.

NEW HAMPSHIRE AND THE UPPER CONNECTICUT RIVER VALLEY

This special grouping combines rural valley scenery and towns made particularly appealing by their interesting and beautiful buildings and commons; the sophistication of Hanover, the home of Dartmouth College and, to me, one of the most special places in New Hampshire; and the estate of Augustus Saint-Gaudens, my candidate for the greatest American sculptor of the nineteenth century. To see it all comfortably, I would plan on three days.

Because the most convenient place to stay in the area is in Hanover at the Hanover Inn, I will begin there and then, after a brief excursion to the north, will move south down the valley.

Hanover

Dartmouth and Hanover have been inextricably entwined since 1769, when the Reverend Eleazar Wheelock founded the school "for the instruction of the Youth of Indian tribes and others." Wheelock chose Hanover because the town offered him 3,000 acres, as well as free labor and a cash gift. Then the Earl of Dartmouth made a generous contribution—hence the name—and Governor John Wentworth officially established the school by granting it a royal charter.

Classes began in 1770, and today, with 4,000 current students and an illustrious group of alumni, from Daniel Webster to Nelson Rockefeller, this Ivy League college has a national reputation for academic excellence. It dominates the town's and the region's economy (through its educational institutions, including the Amos Tuck School of Business Administration and medical and research facilities) and cultural life (with the Hood Museum of Art and the Hopkins Center for the Arts, which contains two theaters and a concert hall).

Dartmouth Row, on the east side of the expansive green, consists of four striking white Greek Revival buildings; you have seen them reproduced many times. Until 1845, they were the complete college, and when the central and largest building, the 1791 Dartmouth Hall, burned, it was immediately replicated by the 1904 building you see now.

Also worth noting is what has been called the state's finest example of Romanesque architecture, the 1886 **Rollins Chapel** with its octagonal corner tower, at the north end of Dartmouth Row, and the 1928 **Baker Memorial Library,** placed at the north end of the green and clearly modeled after Independence Hall in Philadelphia. Make every effort to go to the basement of Baker to see the brilliant and deeply moving frescoes *The Epic of American Civilization,* painted by the great Mexican artist José Clemente Orozco between 1932 and 1934. As Jacquelynn Baas, chief curator of the Hood Museum, has written, Orozco's magnificent vision "re-enacts the chronicles of human suffering within a vision of invincible promise."

Next visit the **Hood Art Museum,** at the southeast corner of the green. This eclectic, smallish collection (splendid Assyrian bas-reliefs, African art, Italian and Dutch pictures, works of American artists ranging from Ralph Earl through Frank Stella) will offer you a pleasant hour or so with works of art attractively displayed in a well-designed setting. (By the way, if you have seen any of the Ralph Earl paintings mentioned elsewhere in this book, please note the early portrait in this museum, for it is painted in a highly sophisticated manner, quite unlike his later, often more "primitive" pictures; he consciously modified his style on his return to America.) The Hood Museum is open: Tuesday–Saturday, 10–5, Sunday, 12–5. Closed: Mondays and major holidays. Free admission. Telephone: 646-2808.

You will, of course, want to take some time to drive and walk about the town and campus. If you are interested in contemporary architecture, you may wish to visit the two buildings here that were designed by Pier Luigi Nervi, the Leverone Field House and the Rupert C. Thompson Ice Arena and Auditorium.

The River Villages North of Hanover

A drive north of Hanover on Route 10, through Lyme, Orford, and Haverhill Corner, offers some of the best river scenery in this part of the valley, as well as towns that are interesting not only for their beauty but for unusual features that make them distinctive.

Lyme has a particularly good grouping of buildings, both homes and shops, crowned by the Lyme Congregational Church (1812), a well-proportioned wood-frame Federal building with an unusual tower composed of three cubical stages capped by a small octagonal dome. Also unusual are the twenty-seven numbered horse stalls for the parishioners, built by John Thompson, Jr., the same master builder responsible for the church.

In **Orford** you will need to get out of your car to see the seven Ridge Row houses, built between 1773 and 1839. While they were built by local master builders, these Federal-style houses were clearly influenced by the designs found in the architectural handbooks of such architects as Asher Benjamin.

The houses are set, obviously, along a ridge, with deep, slop-

This is the quintessential New Hampshire house—symmetrical, long, and roomy, and as solid and handsome as a house can be. And please note the gingerbread trim on its next-door neighbor.

ing lawns flowing down to the road. They are all quite beautiful, but one bears a little more description and history. I refer to the middle house, the Morey House.

The first part of the structure, now the middle section, was built by Orford's first minister in 1773. In 1799 it was purchased with all the Ridge land by Samuel Morey, who added the back portion in 1800 and the part facing the road in 1804. The house is open by appointment, June to Columbus Day, with tours by its owner. Telephone: 353-4815. But before going on I should tell you that Morey was an inventor who designed and developed the first steamboat, in 1797. Unfortunately, he told an old friend, Robert Fulton, all about it, and the next thing he knew, Mr. Fulton was moving full steam ahead (I couldn't resist). In 1826, he also invented a gas-powered internal combustion engine.

Orford has two interesting churches, the Gothic Revival Congregational and Universalist churches, both on Route 10, where the Ridge is found.

Continuing north to Haverhill Corner you will pass a 16-sided barn in Piermont. It was built in 1906 and is the only one of its kind in New Hampshire. And then you come to **Haverhill Corner,** with its roomy common surrounded by an absolutely first-rate grouping of nineteenth-century buildings; on Court Street, which bisects the common, are two eighteenth-century buildings that formerly were taverns. You also should go east from the common on Court Street, where you will find another grouping of handsome buildings. Haverhill Corner is not to be missed.

The River Villages South of Hanover

Now you will head south, first on Route 12A and then on Route 12, through another group of uniquely beautiful towns, but before you go, if you have time and if you are interested in the Shakers, you might wish to visit **Enfield,** which was an active Shaker community from 1793 to 1923, and where you still can see thirteen Shaker buildings, including the Great Stone Dwelling (1841), the largest building ever built by the Shakers and the home of 150 adults. There is a small museum. Open: June to mid-October, Monday–Saturday, 10–5; Sunday, 12–5. From October 15 to May 31 closing time is 4. Admission fee.

Saint-Gaudens National Historic Site   You will arrive first in **Cornish,** where you will visit the elegantly beautiful Saint-Gaudens National Historic Site. Leave some time to explore Route 12A, where the Saint-Gaudens property is found, and see some of the homes of the old Cornish Colony of friends and companions of Saint-Gaudens who summered here, including Maxfield Parrish, Everett Shinn, and other well-known artists, writers, musicians, composers, and theater people. More prosaically, the Cornish–Windsor Covered Bridge (1866), the longest wooden bridge in the country, is also here.

Among the most famous works of Augustus Saint-Gaudens (1848–1907) are his *Diana,* which once topped the old Madison Square Garden, designed by Stanford White (and where White was murdered) in New York; the great masterpiece *Memorial to Robert Gould Shaw and the 54th Regiment of Black Volunteers* on the Boston Common opposite the State House; the *Sherman Monument* on Grand Army Plaza in New York City, and the *Adams Memorial* in Rock Creek Church Cemetery in Washington, considered by many to be among the finest works of sculpture of the nineteenth century.

Saint-Gaudens was born in Dublin, Ireland, of an Irish mother, Mary McGuinness, and a French father, Bernard Paul Ernest Saint-Gaudens, who had emigrated from a tiny village in the foothills of the Pyrenees called Aspet (after which Augustus would name his house). Six months after his birth the family left for the United States, where they settled in New York.

By the age of thirteen, his talent already recognized, he was apprenticed to a cameo cutter, an apprenticeship that would last until he was nineteen. During this period, too, he attended both the art school at Cooper Union and the National Academy of Design.

In 1867, at 19, his father offered him the opportunity to go to Paris; there he eventually attended the École des Beaux-Arts while supporting himself by cutting cameo portraits. In 1870 he went to Rome, where he stayed for five years, and where he met his future wife, Augusta.

In 1875, now twenty-seven years old, he returned to New York and in 1876 received his first great commission, the *Farragut Monument,* which he completed in 1880 (with a base designed by Stanford White) and which can still be seen in New York's Madison Square Park.

From that time on he went from triumph to triumph, both here and abroad. Then, in 1900, after winning the Grand Prix in the Paris Salon for his statue of General Sherman, he discovered he had cancer. He returned to this country and moved permanently to the house in Cornish, where he died on August 13, 1907. From his deathbed, while watching a sunset behind Mount Ascutney, he said, "It's very beautiful, but I want to go farther away."

Saint-Gaudens discovered Cornish and the property that would become Aspet in 1885. The house had originally been built as an inn around 1800. Saint-Gaudens remodeled it extensively, painting the brick white and adding a wing and the lovely columned porch in order to take advantage of the view of Mount Ascutney, putting in roof dormers and so forth.

Visitors are allowed to tour the downstairs, which has original furnishings and is moderately interesting. But the real interest here is the ensemble of gardens, walks, sculpture, and outbuildings that creates, in the end, a deeply moving experience.

I like to go first to the Little Studio, painted green, white, and Pompeian red, not allowing myself to be tempted by the garden and reflecting pool, passing under the trellis supported by columns and thick with grape vines, then through the doorway topped by a copy of a portion of the Parthenon frieze. Inside is Saint-Gaudens's studio, which contains many of his works—a wonderful way to begin exploring his world.

Go through the door at the end of the studio (there's a very pleasant little gift shop here), turn right, and you quickly are back outside, where you can now stop to enjoy the pool and then enter the formal garden, which is small but perfect; sit on the bench and enjoy it. From there, move on to the copy of the *Adams Memorial,* set by itself in the garden, and so extraordinarily mysterious and still and poignant.

Then pass into the path lined with birches, one of the loveliest lanes imaginable, the leaves flickering in the light breeze and an open field off to your left, and turn into the Old Bowling Green. Here you will find a copy of the *Shaw Memorial,* on the original of which Saint-Gaudens worked for fourteen years, creating the brilliantly modeled portraits of Shaw and his black volunteer regiment, the Fifty-fourth Massachusetts, and forming perhaps the greatest memorial to have been inspired by the Civil War.

Back out to the birch path and now head for the gallery, which is built around an atrium and pool, of whose water-spouting turtles I am particularly enamored. Changing displays of Saint-Gaudens's work can be seen here—on my last visit I saw some of his exquisite bronze relief portraits and an exhibition of his designs for $10 and $20 gold coins, created at the request of Teddy Roosevelt. On permanent display is a copy of *The Puritan,* my least-favorite work of his. Just outside the gallery, in a covered ellipse, is the original Stanford White base for the *Farragut Monument,* moved here because the bluestone was being eroded by the pollution of New York City. And beyond that is a picture gallery where you can see works by other artists.

Before you leave, take a stroll through the meadow to the small Greek temple where the sculptor is buried. Originally, this was a plaster stage set, designed for a masque (*The Gods and the Golden Bowl*) presented in 1905 by seventy members of the Cornish Colony to honor the twentieth anniversary of the arrival in Cornish of Saint-Gaudens. After his death it was replicated in marble, and somehow it seems absolutely right in its classic simplicity as the last resting place for this magnificent artist.

Saint-Gaudens National Historic Site buildings are open: Daily, last weekend in May through October 31, 8:30–4:30; the grounds from 8 to dark. Admission fee. Telephone: 675-2175.

From Cornish continue on to **Claremont,** a town large enough to include an opera house in its 1897 Renaissance Revival city hall, which you will pass. The architect, Charles A. Rich, also designed many buildings at Dartmouth, and if you can get into the auditorium of the opera house, do; it has never been "updated" or "improved," and now has been carefully restored. Just consider this very partial description: "At the front of the stage, the proscenium arch is adorned with a combination of basswood painted cream and stereoreliefs called 'Haut Relief Friezes.' These friezes are colored with more rich cream and are decorated with gold. At the top of the arch the frieze work is capped with a smiling Janus face. This face has a beard and wears the crown of a court jester. On the top of the crown rests a classic Greek theater lyre, symbol of the performing arts. Framing the Janus face is more relief work in the form of a leaf wreath. This entire decorative work is gilded." So much for New England simplicity and puritanism.

You also will see one of the best-preserved small mills in New Hampshire, the Monadnock Mills, and three identical Greek Revival houses on Central Street known as the Dutton, Ide, and Russell Houses (1836).

Charlestown is next on the drive south on Route 12. The town is one of the more interesting in this part of the valley from a historical point of view. In 1745 it was known simply as No. 4, the settlement farthest north on the New Hampshire side of the river, and it was fortified against the Indians in that year. Indeed, there were Indian attacks in the summer of that year, and with the onset of winter, the settlers withdrew for their safety.

Two years later they returned, but hardly had they arrived when the Indians attacked, and for five days the fort barely managed to hold out. Trouble broke out again in the 1750s, and this time No. 4, which had now assumed its present name of Charlestown, became the home of Major Robert Rogers and his Rangers as well as the colonial militia. It was Rogers and his men who would eventually break the back of the Indian movement and thereby make the Connecticut River Valley completely safe for habitation.

Today, Main Street is a splendid 200 feet wide and a mile long and is bordered by just under 70 buildings, some of which are of the eighteenth century. The harmonious whole is now a National Historic District. One of the buildings you should be sure to see is the small wooden **St. Luke's Episcopal Church,** designed by the famous American architect Richard Upjohn (1802–1878) and completed in 1863. It is the only wooden church by Upjohn in New Hampshire. Later, in 1869, his son enlarged it.

From Charlestown it is a short drive to the village of **Walpole,** which could be the Hollywood version of an American hometown come to life. Louisa May Alcott was a summer visitor, and James Michener has written of its "midsummer perfection." Because of its beauty it has attracted many rich residents, but it is still the home of merchants and farmers and just plain New England folks.

The large green is surrounded by a grouping of extremely attractive buildings, and the Greek Revival houses are of particular interest because many of them were built by the gifted master builder Aaron P. Howland. See, for example, the 1831 Walpole Academy, the 1843 Howland-Schofield House at Elm and Pleasant streets, and the 1833 Louisa Bellows Hayward House at the north end of Main Street.

During the summer, this village perfection is enhanced by band concerts on Sunday nights that draw people all the way from Keene, a good 15 miles to the south.

CENTRAL AND SOUTHERN NEW HAMPSHIRE

The Lake Winnipesaukee Region

Lake Winnipesaukee, the largest and best-known lake in New Hampshire, covers 72 square miles and has almost 300 miles

The best way to see the beauty of Lake Winnipesaukee is from a boat, and the Mount Washington *is the most famous and popular of all that ply the lake.*

of shoreline. But there's a problem—unless you are staying near the western part of the lake, you will find that views of it are few and far between, and much of the western part is too heavily developed and commercial for comfort.

The first true summer house in this country, some claim, was built here in 1763 by Governor Benning Wentworth's nephew, Governor John Wentworth, described elsewhere in this book. That was about it for "summer people" until the arrival of the railroad on the western shore in the nineteenth century, when that part of the lake quickly developed. By the late nineteenth century, Lake Winnipesaukee had become the major resort area that it remains to this day, the crown jewel of New Hampshire's Lakes Region, where more than 30 lakes cover at least 100 acres each, and dozens of smaller lakes dot the landscape.

If you are not planning to stay in the area but want to get a taste of its beauty, go to **Weirs Beach** or **Wolfeboro** (my choice because it's a pleasant village to visit, and Weirs Beach is much more commercial) and board the *M/S Mount Washington,* the most famous and popular boat plying the lake. The first *Mount Washington,* an old side-wheeler, operated from 1888 to 1939, when she was destroyed by fire. The present boat originally operated on Lake Champlain. It was extended in 1983 to a length of 230 feet, creating a passenger capacity of 1,250. The cruise takes 3 1/4 hours. The *M/S Mount Washington* operates: Late May to mid-October, daily. Admission fee. Food is available on board. For excursion times and special cruise information, telephone 366-5531.

Shorter cruises also are available. One boat, the *M/V Doris E.*, leaves from Meredith and offers one- or two-hour excursions. Operates: July to Labor Day, daily. Admission fee. For excursion times and other information, telephone 366-5531.

NEARBY EXCURSION: CASTLE IN THE CLOUDS

In Moultonborough, to the north, there is an extravaganza of a house, **Castle in the Clouds,** which was built in the early 1900s at a staggering cost for the time—$7 million—by a man named Thomas Plant. His hero was Napoleon, and he wanted to astound the world with his own drive and vision. He chose to do it by building this house. Norman, Swiss, and even Norwegian and Japanese influences can be seen here, while inside every gadget then known to man—and many that weren't—was installed, creating a truly extraordinary environment.

Now it is part of a privately owned complex called Castle Spring, a 5,000-acre site offering spectacular views of the lake, horseback riding on 85 miles of trails, hiking, picnic areas, and a tour of the house.

For information, times, and dates, telephone 800-729-2468 or 476-2352. Admission fee.

A SPECIAL DRIVE

Of even greater interest is the drive farther north, through increasingly beautiful scenery, to **Center Sandwich,** as pretty a village as you can find in New Hampshire, with three lovely churches and two handsome Federal houses. It is, indeed, an idyllic spot. While you're here, be sure to stop in at Sandwich House Industries, from which the League of New Hampshire Arts and Crafts sprang, and where you will see many examples of the crafts the state has to offer—pottery, lamps, glass, furniture, textiles. I've even bought some delicious homemade preserves here.

If you have some extra exploring time, when you leave here continue north on Route 113 to North Sandwich, then take 113A north to Wonalancet to enjoy some particularly ravishing scenery.

The Monadnock, Concord, and Manchester Regions

Some of the prettiest scenery in New Hampshire—as opposed to grand and formidable and magnificent—is here, and spending a leisurely three or even four days driving through the lovely villages and enjoying the farmland and forest scenery is extremely pleasant. In addition, both Manchester and Concord have points of interest you will wish to consider.

As for a place to stay, I would recommend **The John Hancock Inn** in Hancock. I also would urge you to use the excellent New Hampshire highway map (see page 71) and set your own itinerary to cover the sites that follow.

As a matter of interest, Mount Monadnock, the 3,165-foot peak that is at the heart of this region, is one of the most climbed mountains in the world, each year hosting well over 125,000 persons struggling to the summit. The word *monadnock* is derived from the Algonquin for "mountain that stands alone." Today it is used by geographers to describe a hill or mountain that has evolved through many geological periods and become a residual mountain that stands alone.

A DRIVE: THE MONADNOCK REGION

For the first day, you will go from Hancock in the north to Fitzwilliam in the south, with short detours to see some of the more special sites.

Hancock is a village with an extremely good collection of late eighteenth- and nineteenth-century architecture: an attractive old meeting house (1820) and other lovely old buildings in an exquisite rural setting. Once it was one of New Hampshire's cotton-manufacturing centers, which explains where the money came from for those handsome houses. To complete the picture: Each year, on July 4, the bells in the church toll from midnight to one in the morning, in celebration of our independence.

Nearby is **Harrisville,** an early nineteenth-century mill village and one of my favorite villages in New Hampshire. Harrisville, it is said, is the only unaltered industrial community of its period to survive in this country. It is superbly placed

Tiny red-brick Harrisville and its glittering pond, right in the middle of the exquisite Monadnock region, is worth a trip in itself.

at the southern end of Harrisville Pond, which reflects back to the visitor a grouping of houses, a pretty little Congregational church, and other buildings. This is as tranquil and pretty a setting as can be imagined. It should be pointed out that the residents of the village took over and restored these buildings themselves when the old textile industry, started in the early nineteenth century by Bethnal Harris, finally closed in 1970. He had three sons, Cyrus, Milan, and Almon, and their houses as well as their father's are still there.

Next, go to **Peterboro,** home of the world-renowned MacDowell Colony, which was founded by the American composer Edward MacDowell (1861–1908) and his wife, Marion, a concert pianist, and which began operating in 1908. Here famous and not-so-famous writers, composers, and painters have come to work and be inspired in the glorious New Hampshire countryside. Peterboro itself is a pleasant town and has a Carpenter's Gothic cottage (c. 1855) at 22 Pine Street that is a delight.

When you leave here, go to **Dublin,** set on a hilltop and with a lovely pond. Gold was discovered here in 1875, causing a brief flurry of excitement until it was realized that extracting it would cost more than would be realized from the sale of the gold. Then Dublin became an artists' colony, and today it is the headquarters of *Yankee* magazine and *The Old Farmer's*

Almanac. A particularly beautiful brick-and-frame Federal house is here, the Dr. Asa Heald House (1827) on Main Street, and the surrounding scenery makes it eloquently clear why artists loved the town so much.

Now visit **Jaffrey** and **Jaffrey Center.** In Jaffrey Center make a point of seeing the Old Meeting House (1775–1799). According to tradition, the frame of the building went up on the day of the Battle of Bunker Hill, and the men working on it could hear the cannon fire. In the graveyard Willa Cather is buried. I also like to stop to see the First Congregational Church (1830–1831), a wonderful hodgepodge of architectural styles, and the old Stone Brothers and Curtis Mill (1872, with an 1897 addition), and to drive out on Thorndike Pond Road to look at the handsome old houses.

From Jaffrey you can go to **Monadnock State Park** and, if you wish, become one of those who go on the roughly two-hour climb to the summit, which is bald and windswept, but from there, on a clear day, you can see Mount Washington to the north and the Berkshires to the west.

Monadnock State Park is open: Daily. Admission fee. Telephone: 532-8862.

Next I would go to **New Ipswich,** by either of two routes. The first would take you off Route 119 to the **Cathedral of the Pines.** (The road is well marked.) This is an outdoor "cathedral" dedicated by his parents to the memory of a son killed in World War II. Set on the pine-filled crest of a hill, the altar, called the Altar of the Nations, looks out to Mount Monadnock. It now is a national memorial, recognized by Congress, to all Americans who lost their lives in wartime. There is a memorial bell tower at the entrance to the pine grove honoring American women war dead, and the four bronze bas-reliefs above the tower arches were designed by Norman Rockwell. Nondenominational services are held here, as are weddings. The Cathedral of the Pines is open: May to late October, 9:00–4:30.

If you do not wish to visit the "cathedral," stay on Route 119 and pass through **Rindge,** which has one of the largest meeting houses in the state (1796), a glorious Victorian house (the Rice House, 1880) and, next door, an interesting Romanesque library (c. 1894).

New Ipswich is particularly worth visiting to see the

"What goes up must come down" is apparently true for just about everything. A very practical solution to a wind problem.

Barrett House (c. 1800), an exceptional and splendid Federal house. The façade is graceful and open, with many windows and elegant proportions. Inside, the house is brilliantly furnished with many objects that belonged to the family—they lived here until 1948—and includes superb examples of Queen Anne and Federal furniture, as well as Empire and Victorian pieces; Chinese export porcelain; and, in the marvelous third-floor ballroom with its tiled fireplaces, barrel ceiling, and deep window seats, a collection of musical instruments. And if you're wondering about the lovely house next door, that's the Bullard-Baer House (c. 1780), a good example of late Georgian architecture. You may also be interested in knowing that the Barrett House was used by the team of Merchant and Ivory for their film *The Europeans,* based on the Henry James novel. Open: June 1–October 15, Thursday–Sunday. Tours on the hour beginning at 12, last tour at 4. Telephone: 878-2517.

And finally, you will arrive in **Fitzwilliam,** with its Federal houses and, on the green, its old meeting house, known as the Fitzwilliam Town House (1818). This is another of those villages impossible to drive through, so give in, get out of your car, and stroll the tree-lined streets. From there, if it's mid-July and therefore the season, visit the **Rhododendron State Park,** set 1 1/2 miles off Route 119 East, with 16 acres of rhododendrons.

A DRIVE: THE CONCORD REGION

For the second day, I would take in this region. First, the city of **Concord** itself. The **State House** is the oldest state capitol in the country in which the legislature still meets in its original chambers. (It also houses the largest state legislature in the country, with over 400 representatives—this in a state with only a little more than 1,000,000 residents. By comparison, New York State has 211 legislators.) The building as you see it, though, evolved over three periods. From 1816 to 1819, the original building went up. Then, from 1864 to 1866, a third story was added, along with the two-story portico and the cupola and dome. Finally, from 1910 to 1911, the three-story rear extension was added, nearly doubling the size of the building, and a new third story was constructed. Inside, a Hall of Flags on the ground floor displays regimental colors, and the Senate Chamber has murals that depict events in New Hampshire's history.

The State House, 107 North Main Street, is open: 8:00–4:30, Monday–Friday. Closed: Major holidays. Free admission. Telephone: 271-2154.

The New Hampshire Historical Society and Library is housed in a particularly good-looking Neoclassical building of granite and marble. Over the doorway is a sculptural grouping by Daniel Chester French (see page 155), and inside is a genealogical research library and a museum that offers changing exhibitions, all related to New Hampshire history. On permanent display on the ground floor is a Concord coach, made by the once-famous company of Abbot, Downing, who built coaches between 1813 and 1900. Pulled by four to six horses, they were noted for their comfort and durability; it is said they conquered the West, and they are the familiar coaches that you see in movies about the Old West. They were exported as far as Australia and South Africa.

The New Hampshire Historical Society, 30 Park Street, is open: 9:00–4:30, Monday–Friday; 12:00–4:30, Saturday and

Sunday. The Library is not open Sunday. Free admission to the Historical Society, fee for the library. Telephone: 225-3381.

From Concord you should take the time to travel to **Hopkinton, Henniker, Hillsborough** (reminds me of *My Fair Lady*—just add "hurricanes hardly ever happen"), **Washington,** and **Acworth,** for these five villages form an exquisite composite.

Hopkinton has several fine antique shops and enough handsome buildings to warrant getting out of your car. Henniker, a college town, also boasts a covered bridge; north of the town on Route 114, and worth seeing, is a Congregational church and, to its right, the old Henniker Academy School building, both built in the 1830s. Hillsborough has a splendid—and rare—wooden textile mill and many fine colonial, Federal, and Greek Revival houses, among which is the Franklin Pierce Homestead, about 3 miles west of the center of town and near the juncture of Routes 9 and 31. Pierce, our fourteenth president and the only one from New Hampshire, spent his childhood here. It now is owned by the state and can be visited from May through September. Telephone first, however, to make sure it's open when you wish to be there: 478-3165 or 464-5858. You also should go to Hillsborough Center while you are here. Turn west at the blinking light in Hillsborough—you'll see a sign—onto School Street, and soon you will pass some of the most beautiful stone walls—I mean it—in New England, as well as those lovely white houses that fit so beautifully into the landscape.

Now on to Washington, whose common is crowned on the north end by a splendid grouping of meeting house, school, and church, and finally to Acworth, where the magnificent meeting house is worth a special effort.

Another especially rewarding trip is a visit to **Canterbury Shaker Village,** 15 miles north of Concord. (Take Exit 18 from I93 and follow the signs for about seven miles.) This Shaker village consists of 24 buildings set on a hilltop and surrounded by 694 acres. (At its height in the 1850s, the community was home to 300 people and there were 100 buildings on 4,000 acres. For more on the Shakers, see page 143.) One thing I've learned: The Shakers invariably chose settings of unusual beauty for their villages. Canterbury is no exception; it is a joy to visit.

It sometimes seems that stone defines New England, both its landscape and its character. Here a particularly solemn and massive stone wall protects an ancient burial ground.

A few years after Mother Ann Lee arrived in the Hudson Valley from England in the 1780s, two of her followers came to this site to found the sixth of an eventual nineteen Shaker communities.

The Shakers were noted throughout the nineteenth century for the quality of their produce; their herbs and seeds were valued as far away as Europe. Today you can still get tins of Shaker herbs and they are the peer of any others. Even so, the Shakers probably are best remembered for the beauty of their furniture and architecture, both of which are notable for meticulous workmanship and simplicity of form. This village has excellent examples of their work, and informative tours of the village are available, but I prefer to wander off on my own, lingering to look at the buildings as I please, and enjoying the tranquillity and beauty of the setting.

The oldest building, and my particular favorite because of its sense of intimacy and natural simplicity, is the **Meeting House,** which was erected in 1792 and has the typical two-door entrance, one for the brethren and one for the sisters. It now is used as a museum of Shaker history and artifacts. However, I must admit that the most handsome building is the main one, the **Dwelling House,** erected in 1793 with the later additions of a domed cupola, slender and elegant chimneys, a row of dormers that give it distinction, and a beautiful porch.

Once I have wandered to my heart's content—sometimes walking north to visit the cemetery—I very much enjoy lunching at the **Creamery Restaurant,** where the food is delicious and the cost is minimal. There is a gift shop, where you can pick up some of those excellent herbs, among other things.

Canterbury Shaker Village was incorporated as a nonprofit museum in 1969 by the Shakers then living there. It is open: May–October, Monday–Saturday 10–5, Sunday 12–5; April, November, December, Friday and Saturday 10–5, Sunday 12–5. Admission fee. The 90-minute guided tour is on the hour, 10–4, except from June through October, when it takes place on the half hour.

The Creamery Restaurant is open: April–December, daily for lunch and for Sunday brunch. Candlelight dinners with entertainment are offered April through December, Friday and Saturday nights, by reservation.

The Village also hosts many special events. For detailed information on what will be going on during your visit, write: Canterbury Shaker Village, Canterbury, N.H. 03224, or telephone 783-9511.

MANCHESTER

Finally, on the third day, I would visit Manchester, which, with about 100,000 people, is New Hampshire's largest city. It is located on the Merrimack River, and in 1800 a canal was built around the Amoskeag Falls to connect the town by water with Boston. Textile manufacturing had been going on here since the late eighteenth century but became extremely important only in the 1830s, when the Amoskeag Manufacturing Company was formed by investors in Boston and New York. The company wound up owning 15,000 acres of land, essentially the entire city, and created a master plan for developing streets, housing, parks, churches . . . in short, all that made up a nineteenth-century city.

Between 1838 and 1910, the company built its red-brick buildings, which stretched for more than a mile along the

Merrimack, and at its height employed 17,000 people. It laid
claim to being the largest textile mill in the world, and as it
prospered, so did the city. But in this century, cotton began to
lose out to rayon, there were labor disputes, management
seemed to lose its touch, and nonunionized mills in the South,
offering cheap labor, began to draw away business. In 1935
Amoskeag went bankrupt. But the citizens of Manchester
bought the old mill buildings for $5 million and since then have
leased and sold the space to a highly diversified group of more
than 200 industries making everything from electronic equipment to shoes.

Thanks to its early prosperity, Manchester has some interesting buildings that make it an attractive town. **Grace
Episcopal Church** (1860) at Lowell and Pine streets, for example, was designed by Richard Upjohn, whose most famous
building is New York's Trinity Church; and there are two
houses designed by Frank Lloyd Wright, in particular the
Isadore J. and Lucille Zimmerman House (1950), which was
given to the Currier Gallery of Art (see below) and can be visited. And, of course, you should see what remains of the great
mill complex on either side of the river. Despite the destruction
of many of the buildings and the fact that some of the canals
have been filled in, this remains one of the greatest examples of
a nineteenth-century industrial complex that can be found in
this country.

The Currier Gallery of Art   Interestingly enough, the
founders of this gallery, Moody and Hannah A. Currier, were
not connoisseurs, so when the building opened to the public
in 1929, the "permanent collection" was small and of minor
interest.

From the beginning, though, the trustees decided to use
their acquisition funds to "gradually assemble, through careful
selection, a collection of paintings, bronzes, and decorative
arts, that shall be worthy of the generous gift of ex-Governor
and Mrs. Currier." This policy has been followed to the present
day, to the great benefit of the institution, and the small collection holds some first-rate examples of artworks that range
from the thirteenth century to the contemporary period. It is a

delightful museum. The building and grounds are handsome, as is the 1982 north entrance and addition designed by the New York firm of Hardy Holzman Pfeiffer Associates, and the collection, for the most part chosen with superb judgment, is small enough to be comfortably seen in one visit.

From the main entrance, you are aware of the trustees' specific interest in New Hampshire, as well as a general desire to collect the best in whatever category, for downstairs is a weather vane from the Amoskeag Mills and on the second floor is a first-rate fifteenth-century Flemish tapestry, *The Visit of the Gypsies.*

The first-floor west galleries contain the European paintings and sculpture, while the west wing has the twentieth-century American pieces. The east galleries hold special exhibitions, which change every three months. The remainder of this floor houses a gift shop, small but with attractive items, and a display case with examples from the Currier's extensive collection of American and European glass.

I will give you an idea of the range and quality of the collection by mentioning some of my favorite works. There is a small German sculpture by an unknown artist, *Saint Martin on Horseback* (c. 1400), that exemplifies grace, gentleness, and sweetness. The *Banquet of Anthony and Cleopatra* (1669), by the Dutch artist Jan de Bray, depicts the moment when Cleopatra removed her pearl earring to dissolve it in a glass of wine; the two look at each other with a mixture of sensuousness and what can be called imperious bravura that gives the painting an extraordinary sense of sexual tension. A Tintoretto portrait, *Pietro Capello* (c. 1586), is painted with almost insolent insouciance—"The colors of Titian and the drawing of Michelangelo," Tintoretto proclaimed on a sign in his studio. A probable *Self-Portrait* by Jan Gossaert, called Mabuse, would be a crown jewel in any collection; and the Ruisdael *View of Egmond-on-the-Sea* (1648) depicts a tree trunk in the foreground that has more expressive power than most portraits.

From later European periods there are excellent examples of Corot, Monet, Constable, Greuze, Tiepolo, Romney, Degas, Matisse, Rouault, and Picasso, while in the twentieth-century American collection, Wyeth, Nevelson, Calder, O'Keeffe, Kuhn, Sheeler, and Albers are all represented.

The second floor is dedicated to American paintings, sculpture, and decorative arts from the seventeenth through the nineteenth centuries, with emphasis given to New Hampshire subject matter and artists. Bierstadt, Heade, Hassam, Homer, Cole, Church, Eakins, Durand, Copley, Stuart . . . all here, as are such great folk artists as Ammi Phillips. And there are interesting examples of lesser-known artists—Henry Bacon, Elihu Vedder, and John Neagle, for example.

I always like to compare three portraits in this section of the gallery that are nicely representative of their painters: Thomas Eakins's *Miss Florence Einstein* (1905), the sitter in profile, gazing intently to the left, her eyes deep with the knowledge of sorrow; John Singer Sargent's *Portrait of Marchioness Curzon of Kedleston* (1925), in which the sitter looks at us almost defiantly, but also with a slight lack of assurance that gives her an appealing vulnerability and saves the portrait from vulgarity; and finally, Robert Henri's *Mary Anne with Her Basket* (c.1910), a portrait of a pretty child, assured and curious and completely American.

The examples of furniture in these galleries are especially interesting to anyone attracted to American decorative arts, particularly the rare and beautiful New Hampshire pieces such as the desk (c. 1785) attributed to the Dunlap family of New Hampshire, with its series of shell carvings; the elegant card table (c. 1800), also from New Hampshire; or the absolutely perfect sewing table (c. 1825) attributed to the Shaker colony in Canterbury (see page 98).

The Currier Gallery of Art, 192 Orange Street, is open: 10–4, Tuesday–Saturday (to 9 P.M. on Thursday), Sunday, 1–5. Closed: Monday and most holidays. Admission by donation. Telephone: 669-6144.

The **Zimmerman House** is one of only five houses in the Northeast designed by Frank Lloyd Wright and is the only one open to the public, having been bequeathed to the Currier Gallery in 1988. Wright also designed the furniture, fabrics, and gardens for the house, and the Zimmerman's collection of pre-Columbian, African, and Chinese sculpture is on display.

Admission to the Zimmerman House is by reservation only. Tours are scheduled Thursday–Sunday. Admission fee. Children under seven not allowed. Transportation to the house is from the

Currier, and tickets should be purchased in advance at the Currier admissions desk. Reservations can be made by phone: 626-4158, and MasterCard and Visa are accepted.

You may wish to take some time to see **America's Stonehenge,** off Route 111 in North Salem. This 30-acre site 19 miles southeast of Manchester and near North Salem, dates back to 2000 B.C. and is one of the oldest man-made complexes on the continent.

The large free-standing stone slabs are astronomically aligned so that on March 22, June 21, September 22, and December 21 they indicate the summer and winter solstices and equinoxes. There are chambers and tunnels as well. One slab is known as the sacrificial table because it is scored with grooves that might have carried off the blood of victims. It was obviously created by an advanced civilization, and guesses as to who the builders were have ranged from the ancient Greeks to those notorious Visitors from Another Planet.

PORTSMOUTH AND THE SEACOAST

Portsmouth, New Hampshire's only seaport and a town of about 25,000, was first settled in 1623, and is therefore one of the three oldest towns in New England. (The other two are Plymouth, settled in 1620, and Salem, settled in 1628.) It is a treasure-house of some of the best Georgian and Federal architecture in the country and is worth at least a two- to three-day visit.

From the very beginning Portsmouth was distinguished from the first towns in its neighbor, Massachusetts, for one very good reason: Plymouth and Salem were settled by Puritans, not, as we all know, a fun-loving bunch. Portsmouth, on the other hand, was settled by colonists interested in trade and fishing, not religion, and they were much more liberal in their approach to life. More than that, these first settlers were known for being as feisty and tough as any in New England; there's more than one reason that New Hampshire came to be known as the Granite State.

The town, located at the mouth of the Piscataqua River, one

of the world's fastest-flowing navigable rivers, was permanently settled in 1630 by Captain Walter Neal and a small group of Englishmen. Two miles upriver from the mouth of the Piscataqua, they noticed a luxurious growth of wild berries along the west bank. Seeing this as a good omen, they decided to settle there, calling the site Strawbery Banke.

They immediately constructed a Great House, which served not only for living, cooking, and storage space but also for defense. By 1640, some 170 people were living in the community. By that time, too, they had moved away from the Great House and were primarily settled on the Isles of Shoals (see page 114) and at the river's mouth on Great Island, which today is the community of New Castle (see page 116). In 1653, the Strawbery Banke community changed its name to the much more prosaic Portsmouth because "we are at the river's mouth and our port is as good as any in the land."

Growth was hindered in the remaining half of the century and through the early eighteenth century because of the resistance by the Indians to the Europeans' extending their settlements. Then the provincial government instituted a particularly grim and brutal policy of offering a high bounty to every man who presented a scalp as proof he had killed an Indian. By 1730 the Indians were no longer a threat.

But even during this period Portsmouth prospered enough to become the capital of the colony and the most important port north of Boston, trading south along the coast to Virginia, east as far as Spain and Portugal, and north to Newfoundland. The most important items of trade were lumber products, and in particular masts for the British navy, made from pines as much as 1,000 years old, whose height could reach 200 feet.

After 1730, Portsmouth entered its greatest period of growth and development, when the profits from trade created a sophisticated merchant class with the means to build splendid dwellings for themselves. After all, living in a port of international consequence, many of these men not only knew London and English society but were familiar with other European cultures as well.

By the time of the Revolution, Portsmouth was one of the major cities in the colonies. Then, in 1774, Paul Revere dashed into town to warn that a British ship was on its way to take Fort William and Mary at the harbor's mouth and to seize the arms and ammunition stored there. The citizens of the town got there first, though, and kept the fort and its cache for the rebels. No other military action was seen in New Hampshire, much less Portsmouth, for the duration of the war, but even so, the capital was moved to a safer spot inland.

By the last decade of the century, trade was not only back to normal but booming, a situation that would continue until 1807, when President Jefferson's embargo on trade would wreak havoc on the shipping from American ports. Then came the War of 1812, and although Portsmouth merchants profited from privateer raids on the enemy's commercial shipping— the most successful brought in more than $300,000, a huge sum in those days—the port would never recover its former stature. In 1800, for instance, Portsmouth ranked twelfth in population in the United States. By 1850 it was not even the largest city in New Hampshire.

Portsmouth then turned to shipbuilding. The Navy Yard, still in existence, was established by the federal government in 1800, and commercial shipbuilding was soon to follow. Clippers built in Portsmouth set new records for speed and became famous around the world, but because they were sailing for the merchants of Boston and New York, the commercial glory went to those cities.

The city continued its gentle decline throughout the century until, by 1900, there was very little maritime activity outside the Navy Yard, which remained the primary industry through the better part of this century. The first submarine was launched here in 1917, and during World War II the yard built a total of 75 subs. But the town itself was only a shadow of what it once had been. Then, seemingly out of the blue, it was galvanized into action and entered into the renaissance that continues to this day.

The event that started the ball rolling was a federal urban renewal project in the late 1950s. Urban renewal was well meant but managed to destroy some of our best urban architecture. In Portsmouth, the urban renewal officials announced that they had decided to tear down and replace what they called substandard housing in the oldest section of Portsmouth, Strawbery

People generally associate Portsmouth with great houses of the 18th and 19th centuries, but I take special pleasure in the charms of the harbor, such as this delightful row of tugs.

Banke. Some of this housing was 250 years old, and the citizens of Portsmouth, to their everlasting credit, rallied and decided to save what was, after all, their heritage.

In 1958, they set up Strawbery Banke, Inc., as the umbrella group. At that time, New Hampshire law required that all buildings in a renewal area had to be demolished, and one of the organization's first and most important actions was to convince their legislature to change the law to include restoration in the concept of renewal.

The next step was to have the Portsmouth Housing Authority purchase the buildings originally scheduled for demolition, relocate the remaining residents, and then get rid of those structures of no merit or historic value. What was left was deeded to Strawbery Banke, Inc., and today the 10-acre museum site continues to grow and develop. It is well worth making a special effort to see it. (For a description of Strawbery Banke see page 110.) Equally important, this project sparked the revival and restoration of other areas of Portsmouth, bringing new vitality and vigor to the city and making it one of the more interesting destinations in New England.

The Architecture of Portsmouth Because architecture plays such a prominent role in the enjoyment of Portsmouth, and because there are such magnificent examples of Georgian and Federal buildings here, it might be helpful to provide brief descriptions of these two styles.

The *Georgian* period covers roughly the years between 1715 and 1785. It derives from the work of that greatest of architects, the Italian Andrea Palladio, who lived from 1518 to 1580. Palladio's influence was slow in reaching England, but when it did, in the early eighteenth century, it swept all before it, resulting, among other things, in the production of many architectural guidebooks to the style. It was not long before these reached the colonies, where they had an immediate effect upon our architecture.

Georgian-style architecture, commonly—and incorrectly—called colonial, is characterized, on the façade, by corner quoins (dressed stones that are set into the corners of a building, usually with large and small stones alternating), symmetry, window pediments, classical moldings, and elaborate doorways with impressive pediments, which can be triangular or scrolled or segmented, and with pilasters (flat, ornamental piers that project only slightly from a wall and are decorated, like a column, with a capital, shaft, and base) to either side. The effect is one of solidity and dignified importance.

Interiors continue this impression. There is often a central hall with a grand staircase displaying beautifully carved balustrades, classical moldings, paneled walls, and lavish detail.

The *Federal* period began about 1785 and continued well into the nineteenth century, until about 1830. Once again, the style arrived in this country via architectural books, but now the influence was that of British architects, in particular the delicate and highly refined neoclassical work of Robert Adam (1728–1792). As they had done with the Georgian style, American builders amended the Federal style, making their own innovations and giving it a distinctly American tone.

On the exterior, Federal houses are usually rectangular and have hipped roofs that slope upward from all four elevations of the building and are sometimes hidden by a balustrade. Façade detailing has a delicacy and grace characterized, for example, by elongated pilasters. Front doorways are still very important but now are more open than their Georgian predecessors and usually have a fanlight above them, with delicate wooden tracery and side windows. In fact, windows are larger in general, which gives these buildings an open, airy feeling of refinement and welcome.

Inside, too, one notices a desire to open up the space. Chimneys are usually placed against the outer wall. The stairways, often spiral or elliptical, are in a central, elaborately decorated hall.

What to See and Do

For complete information on events in the area while you are there, stop in at the excellent Chamber of Commerce at 500 Market Street.

Portsmouth is an extremely pleasant town to walk in—almost any street will take you through an attractive urban landscape. After all, although Georgian and Federal styles are the ones Portsmouth is most famous for, good examples of other styles are also here. Some of my favorite streets follow.

Market Street is filled with shops and good-looking buildings including the Moffatt Ladd House, one of the great dwellings of Portsmouth. **Ceres Street,** my favorite of all, will take you along the old wharfs, where tugboats are neatly tied up, and past many restaurants, including some with open-air decks; the **Blue Strawbery,** the best restaurant in Portsmouth, is on Ceres Street.

Bow Street will lead you to **St. John's Episcopal Church,** built in 1807 to the designs of Alexander Parris. Within its lovely interior you can view a rare Vinegar Bible (1717), so called because of a misprint of "vinegar" for "vineyard," and see some original box pews, the oldest operative organ (before 1708) in this country, and shadow painting that was done in 1848. In the churchyard, known as "God's little acre," is buried Benning Wentworth, who appears so many times in this book.

Hay Market Square, whose Congregational church (1854) sports the highest spire in Portsmouth, also has, I think, the most beautiful example of Federal architecture in Portsmouth—and one of my favorite buildings—the 1804 **Portsmouth**

Athenaeum, which can be toured on Tuesday and Thursday, 1–4, and Saturday, 10–4. If you're there on an appropriate day, it's well worth taking in, if only for the ships' models on view.

Strawbery Banke Museum   I've already described how Strawbery Banke came to be, and now it's time to tell you what you will see there.

First of all, the setting: Strawbery Banke is separated from the Piscataqua River by Prescott Park, a relaxing spot in which to rest, with well-maintained flower gardens and strategically located seats.

Before you enter the museum grounds, note the liberty pole across the way. Before the Revolution, these poles were set up on village greens in market squares to serve as symbols of protest against the British, and anti-British rallies were often held around them. When you enter the grounds, be sure you get the excellent Visitors' Map; it will give you succinctly all the basic information about what the buildings and grounds contain.

Strawbery Banke, as the organizers themselves say, is a work in progress. That means that of the thirty-seven buildings that make up this 10-acre museum, nine have been completely restored and furnished, six have been renovated to house topical exhibits, three contain crafts workshops, and one is usually in the process of restoration (and the public can see the fascinating process and methods of restoration). The remainder are in the planning stage. It should be noted that most of these structures stand where they were built and are on their original foundations. Four houses, off in a corner by themselves, were saved and moved here from other parts of the city.

In essence, the museum traces the neighborhood's development over the past 350 years. The oldest dwelling, the Sherburne House (c. 1695–1703), with its central chimney, seems even older than its dates would indicate; it is an almost medieval building with subtle decorative elements like ornamental gables and diamond-paned windows. Inside is an exhibit on house construction in the seventeenth century. And let me tell you at the outset that all the exhibits here are ex-

tremely well done, with clear, detailed, and interesting signage
that is a pleasure to read. The guides in the furnished houses,
I should add, are friendly and informative and basically let you
proceed at your own pace.

It isn't necessary to tell you in detail about all the houses,
but I will mention my two favorites, the Georgian **Chase
House,** built about 1762 and notable for its beautiful carving,
in particular the rococo frieze of flowers, fruit, foliage, and rib-
bon over the parlor fireplace; and the **Walsh House,** from
about 1796, which has a stairway with yellow marbleized
stairs and beautifully painted wood graining on the pine doors
of the lower hallway, and whose early Federal style works extremely well. Additional furnished houses take the neighborhood through the Victorian period, the World War II era, and
down to the 1950s.

Strawbery Banke is more than just an assemblage of houses,
though. As I've already suggested, there are exhibits on construction techniques from different periods. In addition there
are archeological exhibits, lovely gardens re-creating, for example, a vegetable and herb garden of about 1720, or a 1908
Colonial Revival flower garden, or a garden, now being reconstructed, that harks back to the 1830s. And there are exhibits
of early craftsmen's tools, a craft shop where you can watch a
cooper as he makes barrels and casks . . . even a boat builder
and a potter.

In short, the museum is a small fascinating neighborhood,
unique in its presentations. Particularly interesting to me is
the fact that so much more is still to come, that it is in a constant state of highly visible change and growth. For example,
they plan to restore and furnish one of the houses as it was in
the early twentieth century when a Russian Jewish family
lived there. In that time, this neighborhood's population was
about half immigrant, and this aspect will be presented and
explained with the same care and attention as is given to the
earlier, more prosperous periods. With this kind of imagination
and care devoted to it, Strawbery Banke will continue to grow
and be recognized as one of the most fascinating and dynamic
museums in New England.

Strawbery Banke also operates a store that is well worth visiting for its stock shows the same imagination that has been devoted to the museum itself.

Strawbery Banke is open: Daily, 10–5, May–October. Admission fee. Telephone: 433-1106 for recorded information twenty-four hours a day; 433-1100 for office staff during business hours.

The Historic Houses of Portsmouth (in alphabetical order; the more important houses are starred)

John Paul Jones House, 43 Middle Street. Open: Daily, 10–4, mid-May to mid-October. Admission fee. One-hour guided tour. Telephone: 436-8420.

John Paul Jones stayed twice in this 1758 house. It's handsome, with a particularly fine front doorway. Inside, the Portsmouth Historical Society displays its collection of memorabilia.

*Governor John Langdon House, 143 Pleasant Street. Open: Wednesday–Sunday, 12–5, June to mid-October. Closed: Holidays. Admission fee. One-hour guided tour. Telephone: 227-3956.

Of this 1784 Georgian mansion George Washington, who stayed there (honest!), wrote in his diary: "Col. Langdon's may be esteemed the first" of all the houses in Portsmouth. Langdon was an important figure in New Hampshire history; he was a signer of the Constitution, the first president of the United States Senate, and a five-term governor. Washington was not his only prominent visitor; he also entertained Lafayette, James Monroe, and Louis Philippe of France in this splendid dwelling. This is Portsmouth at its grandest. There is an addition at the back done by the great American architectural firm of McKim, Mead, and White in 1906, and the gardens are quite nice.

*Moffatt-Ladd House, 154 Market Street. Open: Daily, 10–4, Sundays and holidays, 2–5, mid-June to Mid-October. Admission fee. One-hour guided tour. Telephone: 436-8221.

Built in 1763 by Captain John Moffatt for his son Samuel, this is one of the finest Georgian houses in the country. The interior is magnificent. The entrance hall has a splendid staircase, elaborate paneling, and French wallpaper. As for the eighteenth- and early-nineteenth-century furnishings, many

Ah, the great houses of Portsmouth—always a magnificent surprise. This one, the Moffatt-Ladd House (1763), is among the finest Georgian houses in the country.

are original to the house, as are the jewelry, silver, portraits (including a Gilbert Stuart), and even clothing. The garden at the back of the house should be seen, too.

Rundlet-May House, 364 Middle Street. Open: Wednesday–Sunday, 12–5, June to mid-October. Admission fee. One-hour guided tour. Telephone: 227-3956.

Built in 1806–1807 for the self-made merchant prince James Rundlet, this four-columned Federal mansion lords it over its neighbors on an artificial terrace eight feet above the level of the street. (You know what they say about new money.) It is entirely furnished with family pieces and accessories, and the Federal furniture was made in Portsmouth.

*Warner House, 150 Daniel Street. Open: Tuesday–Saturday, 10:00–4:30, June to mid-October. Closed: Sunday and Monday. Admission fee. Forty-minute guided tour. Telephone: 436-5909.

If you have time to see only one house, this is the one to choose. A 1716 brick Georgian, and Portsmouth's oldest brick residence, it is considered by some to be the finest example in New England of an early-eighteenth-century brick residence. Built by a Scottish sea captain, Archibald MacPheadres, of bricks he had used as ballast in one of his ships, the house has a particularly harmonious façade, with its perfectly integrated front door and superb proportions. Inside, the painted murals in the staircase are in themselves worth the visit. They were painted about 1720 and are among the oldest in the country. The oddly disparate subject matter includes portraits of two Mohawk sachems, a portrayal of the angel interrupting Abraham as he is about to sacrifice Isaac, and hawks attacking a chicken. There are excellent examples of New England and European furnishings, and a group of portraits.

*Wentworth Gardner House, 140 Mechanic Street. Open: Tuesday–Sunday, 2–4, June to mid-October. Closed: Monday. Admission fee. One-hour guided tour. Telephone: 436-4406.

Built about 1760 by Mrs. Mark Hunking Wentworth as a wedding gift for her son Thomas, this house, with its large windows and lovely central doorway topped by a carved pineapple, long the symbol of hospitality, has the most welcoming, "homey" façade of all those in Portsmouth. Perhaps that's why it has been photographed so frequently. Its setting on the Piscataqua is extremely pleasant, too, and the interior, with carving said to have taken a year to complete, is worth the visit. The Metropolitan Museum of Art once owned this house and at one point planned to move it to New York City and place it in Central Park.

Nearby Excursions

The Isles of Shoals   These nine islands, two with the wonderful names of Appledore and Smuttynose, are 10 miles from Portsmouth and well worth seeing.

The boat trip out and back—about two and a half hours—is both pleasant and a good way to get an overview of Portsmouth's history, for it is unobtrusively narrated and, of course, so much of Portsmouth's history is associated with this river and the sea.

For the first five miles you go out the Piscataqua, passing the famous Naval Yard, Fort Constitution (once Fort William and Mary), and some of the houses lining the waterfront in New Castle (see page 116).

Not long after you have been at sea, you will see the islands.

Captain John Smith is said to have discovered them, and they were originally named Smith's Islands. They were first settled by fishermen, but families soon arrived, and by the early eighteenth century they were prospering from fishing and trade.

When the Revolution began, however, their vulnerability to attack was only too obvious, and the islanders moved to the coast. Then, in 1848, Thomas B. Laighton established a summer resort hotel, to which came many of New England's leading cultural and artistic lights, including Nathaniel Hawthorne and Childe Hassam.

I mention Hassam for a particular reason. It was on Appledore that Celia Thaxter, a member of the Laighton family, had her cottage and created a garden that would become famous because of the delightful book she wrote about it, which was published in 1894, a few months before she died. It was exquisitely illustrated with watercolors created by her friend Hassam—her home by that time had become something of a salon for many famous American painters and musicians—and now a facsimile edition has been issued. If you have any interest in gardening and/or art, you will want to own it. (*An Island Garden,* by Celia Thaxter, and illustrated by Childe Hassam, Houghton Mifflin Co.) Unfortunately, Celia Thaxter's cottage was destroyed by fire in 1914 and her garden disappeared. Then, many years later, in 1978, the director of Cornell University's marine laboratory, John Kingsbury, began the superb restoration of the garden based on the plans in her book. A special excursion can be made to see it; the necessary information follows below.

This is an unusual trip. On Star Island, for example, the nineteenth-century hotel is now owned and operated by the Unitarian and Congregational churches as a religious conference center. This in itself is a nineteenth-century concept, and a visitor to the island does get a sense of stepping back in time.

For complete information on cruises to the Isles of Shoals, telephone the Isles of Shoals Steamship Co., 315 Market Street, 800-441-4621 or 431-5500. To visit Celia Thaxter's garden, reservations are required. Telephone Shoals Marine Laboratory, Cornell University, Ithaca, N.Y., 607-255-3717. Tours are on Wednesdays from mid-June to Labor Day.

New Castle   Just off the coast on Great Island, and linked to
Portsmouth by a bridge, New Castle is a delightful New
England village whose narrow streets contain a wonderful collection of eighteenth- and nineteenth-century homes. It is
pleasant to drive about there, making sure to pass by
Wentworth-by-the-Sea, the only great Victorian seaside
summer resort hotel left north of Boston. Built in 1874, with
later additions extending its façade to a length of about 1,000
feet, it has deep, long verandas that look out to the Isles of
Shoals. It is closed now, but it would be wonderful if it could be
restored to its former glory.

*Wentworth-Coolidge Mansion, Little Harbor Road, off
Route 1A. Open: Mid-June to Labor Day, daily, 10–5;
Memorial Day to late June, and Labor Day to Columbus Day,
10–5, Saturday and Sunday only. Admission fee. Telephone:
436-6607.
   Built in three stages in 1650, 1700, and 1750, this house is
a study in domestic architecture over this hundred-year period.
It is said that lilac was introduced to the country here, brought
by Governor Benning Wentworth, whose official residence this
was from 1741 to 1766. Because the house is very near the
harbor, the governor could keep an eye on the traffic entering
the port.
   I am particularly fond of this wonderfully rambling mustard-
yellow clapboard building with green shutters, full of angles
and surprises and additions that make it an endearing jumble.
Inside, it is largely unfurnished, but the rooms are lovely
enough in themselves to be worth a visit, and there are a few
pieces here that belonged to Wentworth, as well as some original wallpaper.

Exeter   One of New Hampshire's earliest settlements (1638),
Exeter is on the Squamscott River, 13 miles southeast of
Portsmouth. Unlike Portsmouth, which always had loyalist
tendencies, Exeter was at odds with the mother country as
early as 1734.
   At that time, the Crown's agents, wanting to ensure that
pines would be reserved for masts for England's navy—the

Exonians had been selling to the highest bidders—came to the town to reassert their authority. The townspeople promptly burned their ship. Then, when the Revolution started, the capital was moved from Portsmouth to Exeter, where it would remain throughout the war.

Today it is a lovely colonial town of some 12,000 souls and contains a distinguished collection of houses and public buildings, as well as **Phillips Exeter Academy** (1781), one of the country's finest prep schools, which is at the center of the town.

Take time to stroll on the Exeter campus, as well as on the town streets. The campus, primarily in the Georgian style, has some excellent contemporary buildings, including two by Louis Kahn: the library and the Elm Street Dining Center.

As for the town, be sure to see the 1855 **Town Hall,** with its magnificent octagonal cupola and dome topped by a statue of Justice. The dome looks to me like a turban, giving the whole a slightly raffish air. I also like the **First Parish Meeting House,** a Federal building completed in 1800 and one of the loveliest meeting houses in the state, the **three Federal houses** at 4 (1809), 12 (1826), and 14 (1815) Front Street, and the **Gilman Garrison House** at 12 Water Street, which was built around 1690 and is one of the oldest dwellings in the state. Originally it was a fortified house, built of massive timbers sawed at John Gilman's mill. It even had a portcullis protecting the front door, and one of the rooms on the first floor has a ceiling nearly as thick as its walls. The long wing was added around 1772, and this is more Georgian, with elaborate paneling and moldings. The Gilman House is open: mid-June to mid-October, 12–5, Wednesday–Sunday. Admission fee. Telephone: 227-3956.

WHERE TO STAY AND EAT

New Hampshire, oddly enough, does not have many inns of the quality of those in Vermont. Nor are there many outstanding restaurants; dining is good, but is rarely memorable. There are, of course, splendid exceptions, and I have included all of

them in this section, together with others that are comfortable
and conveniently located for touring the various regions. All
that are listed, I hasten to add, are more than acceptable.

Like Vermont, New Hampshire is not a large state, and it is
important to remember that an inn in one region may well
serve as your headquarters for another region.

Reservations are most easily made in the summer. The fall is
the most difficult time, and in the ski season, too, it can be hard
to get the inn of your choice. So, whenever possible, reserve
early.

Where to Stay

Area code: 603

NORTHERN NEW HAMPSHIRE—THE WHITE MOUNTAINS

Jackson

Christmas Farm Inn, P.O. Box CC, Jackson 03846

The inn is on a hill outside Jackson, a village just off Route
16, which you approach through a small red covered bridge
over the Wildcat River, rushing here toward Jackson Falls.
Jackson has been a favored spot for hotels and inns since the
nineteenth century yet has managed to maintain its village flavor; it is neither touristy nor crowded—another reason I like to
stay here.

I also like the fact that from the inn there are quiet drives
and walks, away from the hustle and bustle, that let you catch
your breath and recover from all the mammoth scenery that
bears down on you. (As I heard one exhausted lady say on the
way up Mount Washington, as we were negotiating a particularly hair-raising curve, "A view may be a lovely thing, but I
think it's awfully overrated.") There is, for instance, the "five-
mile circuit," which takes you on a scenic country trip around
the village. And it's well worth mentioning that in the winter,
cross-country skiing takes over, for the Jackson Ski Touring
Foundation maintains a 154-kilometer cross-country trail system that is ranked among the best in the world.

So that's the setting. Now to the inn, which is made up of a main building, several ancillary buildings, and—the real reason I stay here—two-bedroom cottages higher up the hill and behind the main inn. Each offers a lovely view, a fireplace in the comfortably furnished living room, a refrigerator, and a sundeck. I find the cottages ideal. The inn has a swimming pool and well-tended gardens. Double room and cottages: $$$$–$$$$$. Open: All year. Telephone: 383-4313. Credit cards.

Bretton Woods

Mount Washington Hotel, Route 302, Bretton Woods 03575

The setting for this 198-room hotel (there are additional units outside the main building), one of the last two of New Hampshire's great nineteenth-century resort hotels, is spectacular. It has all the amenities of a resort—although not quite as many as the Balsams. Unfortunately, it has seen some tough times in recent years, and its future does not seem to be as secure as one might hope. Double room: Rates vary, and packages are available. For full information telephone 278-1000. Open: Memorial Day to October. Credit cards.

Dixville Notch

The Balsams, Route 26, Dixville Notch 03576

This is the other remaining great resort hotel (234 rooms) and my preferred choice of the two. It is a hotel and resort, 12 miles from the Canadian border, and if you want to relax in comfort and style, this is the place for you. Everything is here to make you comfortable and happy and keep you occupied. In the winter there is skiing (downhill and cross-country) and skating and snowmobile trails. In the summer there's golf and tennis and swimming and horseback riding and boating. There are hay rides and lawn games and hiking trails. There is a game room and a beauty shop. There is dancing and entertainment. There are movies. In short, it is a self-contained world set in the middle of 15,000 acres. Double room: Rates vary according to the time of year, and a variety of packages are available. For a complete breakdown, telephone 800-255-0600; in

New Hampshire, 800-255-0800. Open: June to mid-October, mid-December to end of March. Credit cards.

Franconia

Sugar Hill Inn, Route 117, Franconia 03580
This inn offers attractive, comfortable rooms, and there are three cottages open only in summer, and each with two bedrooms and porches. One of its pluses is the fact that it's somewhat off the beaten track. There are two common rooms, and plenty of activities in the area. Double room: Rates vary according to the season. For complete information, telephone 800-548-4748. Open: All year except for April. Credit cards.

NEW HAMPSHIRE AND THE UPPER CONNECTICUT RIVER VALLEY

Remember: Vermont is just across the river, and if none of these selections appeal to you, please check the Vermont section of the book.

Hanover

The Hanover Inn, Box 151, Hanover 03755
The location is perfect in two ways: The inn—something of a misnomer as it has 92 rooms—overlooks the Dartmouth green; and Hanover is the most centrally located of the river towns you will wish to see. For that reason, I make it the inn of choice for the region. In addition, the rooms are comfortable and service is friendly. Double room and suites: $$$$$. Open: All year. Telephone: 800-443-7024. Credit cards.

Lyme

The Lyme Inn, Route 10, Lyme 03768
Built in 1809, the inn sits at the end of the green, which

boasts a very handsome Congregational church (1812). In fact, the whole town is attractive, one reason I recommend this inn as a pleasant, quiet place to stay. Double room: $$$. Open: All year except for two weeks in April and from the Sunday after Thanksgiving to Christmas. Telephone: 795-2222. Credit cards.

New London

New London Inn, P.O. Box 8, New London 03257
Friendly, comfortable, and moderately priced, if not the last word in inn chic, and it has a good dining room. I also like the town. Double room: $$$. Open: All year. Telephone: 526-2791. Credit cards.

Plainfield

Home Hill Inn, River Road, Plainfield 03781
A wonderful 1820s Federal building set on 25 acres. The rooms—few but attractive—and the cottage overlooking the pool are comfortable. And the dining—which is where the heart of the matter lies—is very good, indeed. Double room: $$$ Open: Tuesday–Saturday, all year except two weeks in November and two weeks in March. Telephone: 675-6165. Credit cards.

CENTRAL AND SOUTHERN NEW HAMPSHIRE

Hancock

The John Hancock Inn, Main Street, Hancock 03449
My choice for this region because of the beauty of the surrounding village, the comfortable charm of the rooms, and the pleasant owners. In addition, it is the oldest operating inn in the state. For some of your touring in this part of New Hampshire it is a little out of the way, but the travel to and from is beautiful enough to make staying here worth it.

Double room: $$$. Open: All year. Telephone: 525-3318. Credit cards.

Bedford

The Bedford Village Inn, 2 Old Bedford Rd. (Route 101), Bedford 03110-5923

The suites in this inn, very close to Manchester, all have four-posters, Jacuzzis, marble bathrooms . . . in short, it's fancier than most, and no expense has been spared in its restoration. Suites: $$$$. Open: All year. Telephone: 472-2602. Credit cards.

LAKE WINNIPESAUKEE REGION

Meredith

The Inn at Mill Falls, Route 3, Meredith 03253

The waterfall is really the star attraction of this large (54 rooms) hotel-resort, which offers boating, swimming, and fishing and has an indoor pool, sauna, shops, etc. Upscale, with "decorator designed rooms." Double room: Seasonal changes and available packages make it wise to call for full information. Open: All year. Telephone: 279-7006. Credit cards.

Wolfeboro

The Wolfeboro Inn, 44 North Main Street, Wolfeboro 03894

If you want to be at the center of things, this is the place to be. Some of the rooms have water views, and the inn has a private beach on the lake. The inn has conference facilities and more than 40 rooms. $$$$–$$$$$. Open: All year. Telephone: 569-3016. Credit cards.

PORTSMOUTH AND THE SEACOAST

As far as inns go, this area hasn't one notable place to stay. Therefore, I would make my headquarters Portsmouth—where you'll be most of the time anyway.

Portsmouth

Sheraton Portsmouth, Market Street, Portsmouth 03801
Would you believe that in all of Portsmouth the place to recommend is a 148-room Sheraton? There is nothing special about it, although there are rooms with harbor views, but it is well located for convenient walking tours of the city, and it's comfortable. $$$$. Open: All year. Telephone: 431-2300. Credit cards.

Where to Eat

Area code: 603

The inns I have recommended all have dining rooms and, with the exception of Hanover and Portsmouth, the food served is as good as that of any of the local restaurants.

NORTHERN NEW HAMPSHIRE—THE WHITE MOUNTAINS

All the places to stay in this area include the price of dinner in the rate.

Dixville Notch

The Balsams, Route 26. Open: Dinner (lunch is available in the ski lodge or the café). $$$$. Phone: 800-255-0600; in New Hampshire 800-255-0800. Credit cards.
The food is well prepared and good, no mean feat considering the number of meals served.

Franconia

Sugar Hill Inn, Route 117. Open: Dinner. $$. Phone: 823-5621. Credit cards.
Dinner here—primarily New England fare—is consistently good.

Jackson

Christmas Farm Inn, Route 168. Open: Breakfast, dinner. Credit cards. Phone: 383-4313.

The dining room is pleasant and the food is good, if not memorable. Rates here include dinner and breakfast, making it something of a bargain.

NEW HAMPSHIRE AND THE UPPER CONNECTICUT VALLEY

Hanover

Café Buon Gustaio, 72 South Main Street. Open: Dinner. $$. Phone: 643-5711. Credit cards.

If you are looking for good, plain Italian cooking in an unpretentious setting, search no farther.

The Hanover Inn, Dartmouth Green. Open: Breakfast, lunch, dinner. $$$. Phone: 643-4300. Credit cards.

The food is pretty good but sometimes can get a little too audacious for its own well-being.

Lyme

D'Artagnan, 13 Dartmouth College Highway (Route 10). Open: Sunday lunch, and dinner except for Monday and Tuesday. $$$. Phone: 795-2137. Credit cards.

Very pretty setting. The dinner, either à la carte or a four-course, prix fixe affair, is quite good.

The Lyme Inn, The Common. Open: Dinner. $$$. Phone: 795-2222. Credit cards.

Not bad at all. I like the homemade soups, in particular, and find the food very satisfying.

New London

New London Inn, Main Street. Open: Breakfast, dinner. $$$. Phone: 526-2791. Credit cards.

Sometimes the food here is very good. At other times, something is missing and it's only fair. Even so, I like to come here

because the service is warm and friendly and the food is good
often enough so that the odds are on your side.

Plainfield

Home Hill Inn, River Road. Open: Dinner, Tuesday–Saturday.
$$$. Phone: 675-6165. Credit cards.

Offering a four-course, prix fixe menu, this certainly is one of
the best restaurants in the region and well worth a visit. In ad-
dition, the dining rooms are attractive and the service impec-
cable.

CENTRAL AND SOUTHERN NEW HAMPSHIRE

Bedford Village

Bedford Village Inn, 2 Old Bedford Road. Open: Breakfast,
lunch, dinner. $$–$$$. Phone: 472-2602. Credit cards.

Lots of dining rooms here, so if possible select the one you
prefer in advance. The emphasis is on traditional New England
foods. It's good, with no surprises.

Canterbury Shaker Village

The Creamery Restaurant. See page 100.

Hancock

The John Hancock Inn, Main Street. Open: Dinner. $$–$$$.
Phone: 525-3318. Credit cards.

The food is good here, and the dining rooms are warm and
cozy. I like it well enough to say it's my favorite in the area and
to recommend that you consider eating here whether you stay
here or not.

LAKE WINNIPESAUKEE REGION

Meredith

The Inn at Mill Falls, Route 3. Open: Breakfast, lunch, din-
ner. $$$. Phone: 279-7006. Credit cards.

There are two restaurants here. Neither is memorable.

Wolfeboro

The Wolfeboro Inn, 44 North Main Street. Open: Lunch, dinner. $$–$$$. Phone: 569-3016. Credit cards.

The tavern here has an enormous menu with everything from sandwiches on up. The dining room specializes in seafood and beef.

PORTSMOUTH AND THE SEACOAST

Best in the Region: The Blue Strawbery

The seacoast region has no other notable restaurants, and you will do best if you confine yourself to Portsmouth.

Portsmouth

The Blue Strawbery, 29 Ceres Street. Open: Dinner, except Monday. Confirmed reservations only. $$$. Phone: 431-6420. Credit cards.

The prix fixe dinner consists of six to eight courses, but before you expire at the thought, let me add that each course is small, and service is comfortable and—rightly—leisurely, so you can enjoy your selection and have some breathing space before the next one arrives. The setting is very attractive, in an old warehouse on the waterfront. This should be a memorable evening.

The Oar House, 55 Ceres Street. Open: Lunch, dinner. $$–$$$. Phone: 436-4025. Credit cards.

I like sitting on the deck here, looking out on the harbor and watching the boats and people. You can also get an award-winning Bloody Mary that helps the afternoon drift by, and the seafood selections are very good.

Portsmouth Gaslight Co., 64 Market Street. Open: Lunch, dinner. $$. Phone: 430-9122. Credit cards.

Very good burgers, snacks, sandwiches, homemade soups, and so forth, in an attractive setting.

State Street Saloon, 268 State Street. Open: Lunch, dinner. $$. Phone: 431-4357. Credit cards.

Good, old-fashioned Italian cooking and seafood. Lots of pastas and sauces, plus chicken and meats, all served in more-than-generous portions at more-than-generous prices.

Finally, if you're an ice-cream freak, be sure to visit **Annabelle's** at 49 Ceres Street. Although they also serve sandwiches and soups, it's the ice cream you come here for—as did George Bush, who asked them to serve red, white, and blue ice cream at the White House one July 4.

Western and
Central Massachusetts

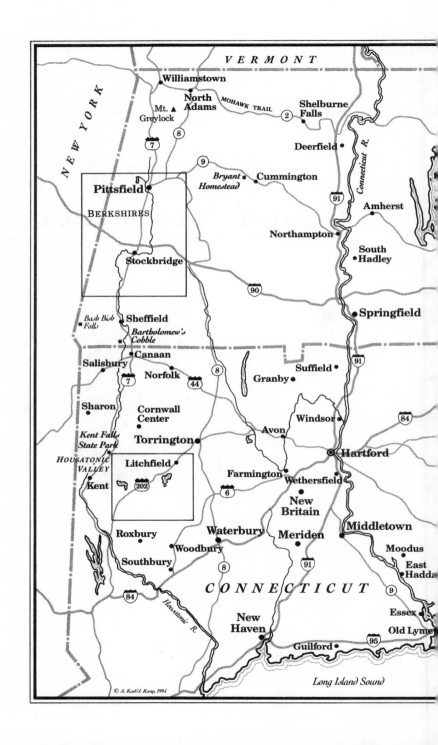

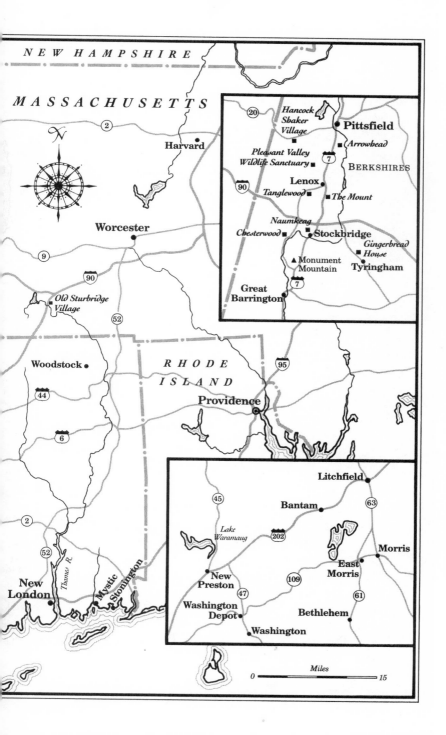

THE BERKSHIRES

Area Code: 413

Only 45 miles long and about 25 miles wide, this westernmost area of Massachusetts is one of that state's most beautiful and popular regions. Through its gentle valley flows the Housatonic River, which rises near Pittsfield and eventually passes into Long Island Sound at Stratford, Connecticut. To the west is the Taconic Range, which runs along the New York–Massachusetts border. To the east, the natural border is the Hoosac Range, called the Berkshire barrier by the early settlers because it slowed access to the region from the Connecticut Valley.

Until the mid-nineteenth century, this was a quiet area, with typical New England mill towns and farms and villages dotting the landscape. Then the writers began to come—William Cullen Bryant was the first, in 1820, but by 1850 Oliver Wendell Holmes was here, as was Herman Melville, and Nathaniel Hawthorne had also established residence. They preceded the monied wave that would "discover" the Berkshires after the Civil War, just as they would discover Newport and the Hudson Valley, and build "cottages" that were the equivalent of palaces—about seventy-five of them in this region, each grander than the last, an exercise in excess if there ever was one.

The artists and millionaires have both left legacies, but that of the artists is the stronger, for the arts are omnipresent in the Berkshires today—dance, opera, chamber music, theater, the symphony, choruses . . . the list is endless. As for the great houses, many have been lost, but enough remain and are open to the public to provide provocative glimpses of what life was like, and a few have been turned into resorts and hotels, so we can even have a taste of the luxury once so common in this area.

Today the Berkshire region is as lovely as ever; although it is overdeveloped and tacky in patches, you can soon get away from the ugliness and into an atmosphere as serenely beautiful as any in New England. You can find pretty much anything here you might desire—excellent food, handsome and varied accommodations, almost every kind of sporting activity, cultural events—in every season of the year. Or you may just want to settle down with a good book and relax in these lovely surroundings.

Special Interest Services

For complete information, including touring maps, ski information, and a calendar of events, telephone the Berkshire Visitors' Bureau at 800-237-5747.

The Great Barrington Area

Did you know that Great Barrington was one of the first cities in the world to have its streets and homes electrified? Well, that happened, on March 20, 1886, because the inventor William Stanley, who first demonstrated the use of alternating current, lived here. And that's not all. W. E. B. Du Bois, the great black educator and civil rights pioneer, was born here in 1868, and during the Revolutionary War, the sixty tons of cannon and mortars captured by Ethan Allen at Fort Ticonderoga passed through here on their way to help George Washington expel the British from Boston.

Today this little town of slightly more than 7,500 people is the commercial center for the many weekend homes surrounding it, as well as an arts center in and of itself, and in the summer the sidewalks and shops are filled with visitors.

Great Barrington also is home to the **Albert Schweitzer Center,** which is located on Hurlburt Road. The Center's library and museum house writings by and about Schweitzer as well as memorabilia concerning this great humanitarian. There also is a wildlife sanctuary with trails and a children's garden. Unfortunately, the center will be closed for reorganization from April 1994 until further notice. Please be sure to phone ahead before making a visit. Telephone: 528-3124.

In addition, a great deal of musical activity takes place here, including Aston Magna, a group specializing in seventeenth- and eighteenth-century chamber music, which plays each July and August in St. James Church (528-3595); the Berkshire Bach Society, specializing in Bach cantatas—it, too, performs at St. James (528-9277); and the Berkshire Choral Festival in nearby Sheffield (229-3522).

The Colonel John Ashley House and Bartholomew's Cobble One of the most delightful days I have spent in the Berkshires centered on a visit to these two sites, so you know I will be prejudiced.

First go to the John Ashley house, which is about 8 miles south of Great Barrington via Routes 7 and 7A; you will take the latter to Ashley Falls. Then take Rannapo Road to Cooper Hill Road.

On the way to the house, you will pass through the town of **Sheffield.** (You may want to get out on Main Street to take a closer look at the First Congregational Church, known as Old Parish, which was built in 1760.) If you have any interest at all

Stone, trees, a view across fields to mountains . . . I feel I should settle down, put a straw in my mouth, and chew the fat with the first person to come along.

in antiques, you will want to spend at least an hour here, for it is an antique center and there are many fine shops, perfect for browsing.

The Ashley house was built in 1735 and is the oldest house in Berkshire County. It's interesting both for its history and because the interior is, particularly for the time, very handsome and beautifully furnished.

First the history. John Ashley built this house for his Dutch bride, who came from the town of Claverack, N.Y. He was a Yale graduate, and as a successful businessman, lawyer, and entrepreneur, he quickly became the leading citizen of Sheffield, not only because of his business success but also because of his deep interest in (and talent for) the affairs of the church, the local militia, and politics. He was, for example, a major contributor to the building of the Congregational church mentioned above, and he became a colonel during the French and Indian War. By 1760 he was a very rich man, but it was an event in January 1773 that has given him a footnote in American history. During that month an eleven-man committee under his leadership gathered in the second-floor study at his house and produced the Sheffield Declaration, often referred to as the forerunner of the Declaration of Independence because it expressed such sentiments as "that mankind in a State of Nature are equal, free, and independent of each other, and have a right to the undisturbed Enjoyment of there Lives, there Liberty and Property," or "that the great end of political society is to secure in a more effectual way those Rights and priviledges wherewith God and Nature have made us free." The full text of the Sheffield Declaration would eventually circulate throughout the colonies.

Colonel Ashley died in 1802 at ninety-two years of age, and the house went out of the family, passing through various vicissitudes until, in 1924, it was bought by Harry Hillyer Brigham, a great-great-grandson of Ashley, who moved it from its original location to the present site, 1/4 mile away. It was he and his wife, Mary, a professional architect, who did the restoration that you see today and created the collection of first-rate furnishings.

All the rooms are worth seeing, but far and away the most beautiful—and by itself a reason to visit the house—is the study where the Sheffield Declaration was composed; its walls are completely covered with brilliantly carved paneling, and a carved cupboard is inset near the fireplace. Almost as beautiful is the master bedroom, with white-and-yellow pine paneling. But, as I've noted, all the rooms are interesting, and the furnishings are perfectly in tune with the period and quality of the house.

The Colonel John Ashley House is open: Weekends, Memorial Day through June and Labor Day to Columbus Day; Wednesday–Sunday, July and August, 1–5. Admission fee. Telephone for exact times: 229-2600.

When you leave the house, take one of the most delightful walks in the Berkshires, following the signs for Hulburt's Hill, which will lead you through a section of Bartholomew's Cobble (277 1/2 acres). The Cobble is a nature preserve operated by The Trustees of Reservations, a Massachusetts group that preserves and maintains properties—currently more than seventy, including the Mission House and Naumkeag in Stockbridge and the Bryant Homestead—all over the state. They own both the Cobble and the Ashley house.

This walk is not a long one, but you will want to stop several times to enjoy your surroundings. It takes you first through the cow pasture—don't be startled to see a cow loom up in front of you—and then through woods and meadows filled with ferns and flowers (over 740 species of plants, including 45 of ferns alone) and birds (240 recorded species), and always upward, until you climb the last ascent to the top of the hill, where you will enjoy what is my favorite view of the Housatonic River Valley and the Berkshires.

The reason I favor this vantage point above all others is that the height is not so extreme as to make everything lilliputian but instead allows you to see far and wide with a more human perspective. It is like viewing a lovely nineteenth-century American landscape painting, in which you can pick out details that must be many miles away. I was last there in early fall, just as the coloring was beginning to deepen and spread across the landscape; it was an extraordinarily bright, clear day, with light carving the scenery like an etcher's tool—the kind of day that seems to occur only in New England, and then only in October.

From there, I like to go to the formal entrance to the Cobble and take the 1/2-mile or so Ledges Trail. Here you can get a booklet that tells you of the Cobble's natural history and is an invaluable aid. This walk will take you along the Housatonic River and through a captivating landscape that will leave you refreshed and rested.

Bartholomew's Cobble is open: April 15–October 15, 9–sunset. Admission fee.

Bash Bish Falls   Another of my favorite walks. This spot is about 16 miles southwest of Great Barrington and the route (23/41) will take you through one of the Berkshire villages I like best, **South Egremont,** where you may wish to get out of your car to visit some of the shops. When you leave South Egremont, take Route 23 to Route 41. It will be on your left and not long after you leave the village. Then turn right on Mount Washington Road. From there, just follow the signs, and eventually, after a beautiful drive that will take you deep into Mount Washington State Park, you will come to two parking spots for the trail to the falls; park in the second one, about a mile beyond the first—the walk is longer from there, but it is easier and has prettier scenery. (Because the falls are almost at the New York–Massachusetts border, this parking lot is actually in New York State.)

Long before I actually saw the falls, or even knew exactly where they were, I had known them because they were the subject of several paintings by John F. Kensett (1816–1872), a prominent Hudson River School painter. In the nineteenth century, the falls were the focus of many a romantic pilgrimage—"one of the wildest and most beautiful cascades in the country," one writer pronounced—and their romantic appeal was enhanced by a legend of an Indian maiden, Bash Bish, who was driven insane and, falling under the spell of the witch of the cascade, leapt to her death. Her lover followed her. Another legend has it that her father, disapproving of her lover, had her tied to a canoe and thrown over the falls. If you are very quiet you can hear the falling water whisper "Bash Bish, Bash Bish."

Today the scenery surrounding the 275-foot-high gorge is the same as that which enchanted Kensett. This trail takes you along the stream, climbing slowly through the woods, until you come out rather dramatically at the falls, which cascade down the gorge. It is a memorable sight.

Monument Mountain This peak achieved some of its fame as the object of a climb by Herman Melville, Nathaniel Hawthorne, Oliver Wendell Holmes, and others in 1851. It was the first occasion on which Melville and Hawthorne met, and, caught in a thunderstorm on the way up, they and the other climbers polished off several bottles of champagne while one of the party read William Cullen Bryant's poem "The Story of the Indian Girl," for here too, as at Bash Bish Falls, an Indian maiden is said to have leapt from the escarpment, this time because her lover had been killed in battle. (For some reason, suicide by jumping from high spots seems to have been a favored way to go for the Indians of the area. Two young chiefs supposedly jumped from Mount Tom in Litchfield, Conn., another Indian leapt from the top of Nonewaug Falls, and so on. Curious.)

In any case, you, too, can make the ascent to the top of Monument Mountain. Simply take Route 7 about 4 1/2 miles north of Great Barrington, where you will see a parking area. There are two trails. I take the easier one, the Indian Monument Trail, which takes about an hour. At the top you will be on Squaw Peak, named for the maiden who leapt from here; the cairn at the base of the mountain supposedly marks her grave. The view of the Berkshires from here is worth the climb, but I still prefer the view from Hulburt's Hill at Bartholomew's Cobble.

The Lenox Area

In 1894, *Scribner's Magazine* pointed out that a self-respecting member of society could no more neglect a visit to Lenox during some part of the season than he could omit observing Lent or speaking French at table. Earlier, around 1850, when the actress Fanny Kemble wished to give a benefit reading for the village poor, she was told, "But we have no poor." Lenox, in short, was the ne plus ultra of Berkshire resorts, surrounded by roughly 100 magnificent estates. Today it still has an air that sets it apart from the rest of the Berkshire towns and villages.

The town was incorporated in 1767 and named after the Duke of Richmond, Charles Lennox. In 1787 it became the county seat, which it remained until 1868 (when Pittsfield was named county seat), and it is to this period that we owe the splendid public buildings on Main Street—the Greek Revival Berkshire County Courthouse, now the **Lenox Library** (1815); the Federal-style **Lenox Academy** (1803); and the magnificent **Church on the Hill** (1805). In addition, dominating the center of the town is the old **Curtis Hotel,** now an apartment complex with shops on the first floor. Allow yourself time to walk and drive in this beautiful town, which is less crazed with tourists than Stockbridge, 6 miles away.

Tanglewood   The summer home of the Boston Symphony Orchestra and site of the most famous music festival in this country, this estate was formed by William Aspinwall Tappan, who bought the property in 1849. His granddaughter, Mrs. Andrea Hepburn, gave the 210-acre estate on the Lenox-Stockbridge border to the orchestra in 1937. In 1938 the 6,000-seat shed, designed by Eliel Saarinen, was opened, and today there is also a chamber music hall and a theater-concert hall, as well as the main house, which is now the administrative building. The orchestra performs here for eight weeks, and 300,000 people attend the concerts each summer.

In season, anyone visiting the Berkshires should attend at least one concert. You can either sit inside the shed or bring a picnic and sit on the lawn. Get there early in order to enjoy the grounds and lovely views over the Stockbridge Bowl to Monument Mountain. And if you can't go to a concert, you can at least visit the grounds.

Also on the estate is the **Little Red Cottage,** a replica of the house Nathaniel Hawthorne rented from the Tappans in 1850. He said it was "as red as the Scarlet Letter." He stayed there only eighteen months, but during that period he wrote *The House of the Seven Gables,* among other things. Some sources credit Hawthorne with naming the estate Tanglewood because there was a glen filled with brush and vines between his house and the bowl. The cottage is open to the public during the season—it contains some Hawthorne memorabilia and period furnishings—and is used for music classes.

The Mount This was Edith Wharton's home from 1902 to 1911. It was her own creation, although she hired the architect Francis V. L. Hoppin to carry out her ideas. (She was well equipped to design a house. In 1897, she published, with the architect Ogden Codman, Jr., a book called *The Decoration of Houses,* which swept away the Victorian precepts of the Mauve Decade and introduced concepts that are used in interior decoration to this day. It has taken its place as a classic.)

Here is how Mrs. Wharton describes her house and her life there in her autobiography, *A Backward Glance.* "On a slope overlooking the dark waters and densely wooded shores of Laurel Lake we built a spacious and dignified house, to which we gave the name of my great-grandfather's place, the Mount. There was a big kitchen garden with a grape pergola, a little farm, and a flower-garden outspread below the wide terrace overlooking the lake. There for over ten years I lived and gardened and wrote contentedly, and should doubtless have ended my days there had not a grave change in my husband's health

The Mount, Edith Wharton's home from 1901 to 1911. Many years later she would write: ". . . its blessed influence still lives in me."

made the burden of the property too heavy. But meanwhile the Mount was to give me country cares and joys, long happy rides and drives through the wooded lanes of that loveliest of regions, the companionship of a few dear friends, and the freedom from trivial obligations which was necessary if I was to go on with my writing. The Mount was my first real home, and though it is nearly twenty years since I last saw it (for I was too happy there ever to want to revisit it as a stranger), its blessed influence still lives in me."

Today, after many vicissitudes, including a period as a girls' school, the Mount is being restored and revitalized both as the home of **Shakespeare and Company at the Mount**—a first-rate theatrical group that gives its productions on the grounds and also performs plays based on Mrs. Wharton's life and writings—and by Edith Wharton Restoration Inc., the organization responsible for the house. The grounds, by the way, were designed by Edith Wharton with her niece, the great American garden designer Beatrix Jones Farrand. The restoration of both gardens and house is slow, but the tour is excellent and informative, and there is a well-provisioned book-and-gift shop where you can stock up on Edith Wharton novels. I think this is as imaginative a use of a historic house as any I know.

The Mount is located at the southern junction of Routes 7 and 7A. Open: Tuesday–Sunday, late May–Labor Day, 10–5. Thursday–Sunday, Labor Day–October, 10–5. Admission fee. The Mount phone: 637–1899; Shakespeare and Co: 637-3353.

Pleasant Valley Wildlife Sanctuary   This refuge, only 3 miles from Lenox (off Route 7 on West Dugway Road, which is opposite the All Seasons Inn), has splendid trails through woods and fields that will give you some idea of what the region was like before the white man came along. There is a total of 700 acres, and one of the highlights for me is that it is home to a beaver colony. If you're there at dusk, you can watch them at work.

The Sanctuary is open: Tuesday–Sunday, dawn to dusk. Admission fee. Telephone: 637-0320.

Berkshire Scenic Railway Museum   This is located in the old Lenox Station, at the foot of Housatonic Street. The museum features railroad memorabilia, videos, and a model railroad. The real reason to visit, though, is to take a ride in a vintage 1920 coach that goes along the Housatonic River. Most of the work of running the train and museum is being done by volunteers, and there is a feeling of camaraderie that makes it all great fun.

The museum is open: Weekends and holidays, Memorial Day through October, 10–4. Free admission to the museum; fee for the train ride. Telephone: 637-2210.

The Pittsfield Area

Settled in 1743, Pittsfield, a small city of about 48,500 people, reached its apogee as a manufacturing center in the nineteenth century. Today it is the county seat—the **Berkshire County Courthouse** (1872) on Park Square is a handsome Renaissance Revival building; next to it is the Gothic Revival **Berkshire Athenaeum** (1876)—and the home of a major insurance company, several light-industry operations, and a division of General Electric.

Hancock Shaker Village   One of my favorite sites, not only in the Berkshires but also in New England.

The Shakers, who received their name from their ecstatic worship, came to this country from England in 1774 under the leadership of Mother Ann Lee (1736–1784). They—Mother Ann and eight disciples—established their first community on some land near Albany, N.Y., initially known by its Indian name of Niskayuna, and now known as Colonie.

Mother Ann converted many followers, but she died after only ten years in the country. Fortunately, she was succeeded by several talented leaders who spread the faith not only throughout New England but as far away as Ohio, Indiana, and Kentucky.

They called themselves the United Society of Believers in Christ's Second Appearing, and by 1821 they had codified their beliefs and way of life into what they called the Millennial Laws. (They were believers in the second appearance of Christ because of Mother Ann's single most important vision, which occurred while she was in an English jail, that Jesus came to her and became one with her.)

The Millennial Laws established how the Shaker communities would be run. Heading each Family (organized groups of believers designed "to accommodate and provide for the different circumstances of individuals in temporal things and . . . for the advancement of spiritual travel in the work of rejuvenation, and the universal good of all the members, composing such society") were elders and eldresses, whose primary responsibility was the spiritual welfare of their Family. Under them were deacons and deaconesses, who were in charge of the family's material welfare. (One of the primary distinguishing characteristics of the Shakers was the complete equality of the sexes. Another was that men and women were to live separately, which eliminated sexual activity. The community children—other than those of converts—were placed there by non-Shaker parents or came as orphans. All rights to the children were relinquished by their parents, and they lived under caretaker supervision until maturity, when they had the right to leave or stay.) Finally came the trustees, who performed business transactions with the outside world and with Shakers in other colonies.

The Millennial Laws governed every conceivable aspect of Shaker life. In education, for example, the laws decreed that

Andrew Carnegie endowed more than two thousand five hundred libraries in this country, many of which—like the one above—are still operating and are among the most handsome buildings in their towns.

"girls' school should be kept in the summer and boys' school in the winter, and they should never be schooled together." Like so much of what they undertook, their educational system was so good that non-Shaker parents often sent their children to the Shaker schools. As for personal property, "No private interest or property is, or can be allowed of, in families that have come into the covenant relation of a full dedication." Even appropriate clothing was described—no unnecessary pockets—as was the ordering of each day.

The quality and beauty of what they produced in music, furniture, architecture, art, farm product, medicinal herbs, technology and inventions (the flat broom; the circular saw, credited to a sister; the clothespin) have kept their fame in front of us to this day. And when you know that throughout their history their total, accumulated membership probably never exceeded 17,000, their accomplishments become staggering.

The twenty buildings at Hancock Shaker Village make it the most complete example of a Shaker community left. Founded in 1790, it continued in Shaker hands until 1960, when it became a museum village. Today, in no little part thanks to brilliant administration that has seen to everything from excellent signage to a superbly trained and friendly staff, this is one of the most pleasant and interesting sites described in this book, and you will want to spend several hours here.

After you leave the **Visitors' Center** (where you will find an excellent gift shop offering those famous Shaker herbs as well as video and music tapes about the Shakers, examples of their crafts, and so forth) you will pass through the **herb garden.** It is one of my favorite places in the village, this large, beautifully tended, absolutely fascinating representation of what the Shakers grew for their own use and for sale to the outside world. Once I was lucky enough to be able to sit and talk to one of the gardeners about medicinal uses for herbs, which ones were invasive in the garden, drying techniques . . . it was like visiting with an old friend.

But all the staff are like that—warm, extremely knowledgeable and intelligent, and with an exact sense of what you would like to hear and how to give it to you in the most interesting way possible. The Shakers would be pleased, they who were so filled with gentleness and love, to see their ideals carried forward so well.

You will already have noticed the architecture, and particularly the huge **round stone barn** (1826) that dominates the village and is one of the great masterpieces of vernacular American architecture. This building alone is worth the trip. First of all, the masonry work is superb, and the overall design—window placement, the cupola, the proportions—gives the barn a serenity and dignity that make it unique. Inside, the functional design is so well executed and so balanced as to become a major factor in the viewer's sense of satisfaction and enjoyment.

The barn has three levels. On the first level were the manure pits. On the middle level, radiating out from the central haymow, were stabled the 54 cows the building could contain. On the third level, wagons could enter from a ramp and empty their hay into the mow. It is so ingeniously designed that one person, standing at the center, could easily feed the entire herd. On the third level there is exhibition space where you can learn more about Shaker farming.

There are shops where you can watch a cabinetmaker at work, a basket maker or a weaver. Again, each craftsman is informative and natural, never condescending or dull. My other favorite building is the **brick dwelling,** whose simple yet elegant architectural forms and symmetry, in the wide hallway, in particular, remind me of certain Italian Renaissance spaces, for both exemplify the aesthetic value of proportion and craftsmanship. Exploring this building is fascinating, for here you will see how the brothers and sisters lived, in their functional rooms with pegs to hang the chairs on and that exquisite sense of design in furniture that makes their work so valued today.

Other buildings are fascinating in their own right, and you will want at least to stop in at all of them and hear the explanations of how they were used—in the laundry and machine shop, for instance, you will see an ingenious arrangement involving a water-powered turbine—but you must be sure to save time to see the **cemetery** across the street and the nearby **schoolhouse.** The tombstones are gone now, but the area is fenced and has a monument at the center; beyond, you look up to their sacred mountain, where they once held ceremonies on very special occasions. It's a wonderful opportunity to reflect on what you have seen and learned about these special people whose benign and loving presence can still be felt in everything, from the buildings to the plants and animals to the landscape itself. Visiting here is a wonderful experience.

Hancock Shaker Village, on Route 20 west of Pittsfield, is open: Daily, May through October, 9:30–5:00. April and November: 10–3. Admission fee. Telephone: 443-0188.

Arrowhead   This was, for the thirteen years between 1850 and 1863, the home of Herman Melville (1819–1891). It was here that he finished *Moby Dick* and wrote two other masterpieces, *Pierre* and *The Confidence Man,* and from here he would return to New York City to live out the rest of his days as a customs inspector.

The house was built in 1780. It is far enough removed from the city to give you some sense of what it must have been like in Melville's day—particularly when you are in Melville's study on the second floor and look north to Mount Greylock. The study, of course, holds the greatest interest to anyone who loves Melville, for it was his workplace, and the women of the house used to leave his meals on a tray outside the door when he was working. There are some Melville mementos here, but true Melville aficionados will want to visit the new Berkshire Athenaeum at 1 Wendell Avenue in Pittsfield, where the Herman Melville Room has some fascinating memorabilia, including the desk on which he wrote *Billy Budd,* first editions of his work, and autograph letters.

The remainder of the house is attractively furnished; the most interesting room is the old kitchen with its great stone hearth.

You should be aware that this is the home of the Berkshire County Historical Society, and in the nearby barn you can see an interesting film on Berkshire history.

Arrowhead, just south of Pittsfield and off Route 7 on Holmes Road, is open: Memorial Day weekend to Labor Day, Monday–Saturday, 10:00–4:30; Sunday, 11:00–3:30. Labor

Day through October, closed Tuesday, Wednesday. Admission
fee. Telephone: 442-1793.

Berkshire Museum   I happen to be a great fan of the regional museums, founded many years ago by some local phil-
anthropist or other, that dot the old towns of New England. It's
not that there are great treasures waiting to be uncovered—
that's not often the case, although there are pleasant surprises—it's that they seem to embody the New England spirit
of respect for the arts and a desire to share their beauty with
others.

This very pleasant museum is just off Park Square at 39
South Street, which is also Route 7. It is dedicated to the arts
and the sciences, and was founded in 1903 by Zenas Crane,
owner of the Crane Paper Company, which makes the rag
paper on which our currency is printed. (There is also a **Crane
Museum,** lodged in a restored paper mill, and dedicated to the
craft of papermaking, in nearby Dalton. It is open: June to mid-
October, Monday–Friday. Admission: Free. Telephone: 684-
2600.)

The Berkshire Museum's collections include Chinese porcelain, abstract art, minerals and shells, early American silver,
and Hudson River paintings—and by no means does that fully
describe the contents. It's a delightful hodgepodge, perfect for
whiling away a rainy day and learning comforting odds and
ends about such esoterica as owls and birds common in the
Berkshires or looking at the clothing and a sledge that accompanied Peary to the North Pole or even examining live fish and
animals in exhibits designed to resemble their normal habitats.

I particularly like the collection of American paintings, ranging from the eighteenth century to today, with one very handsome gallery dedicated to the Hudson River School. It's almost
impossible not to find something to enjoy.

The Berkshire Museum is open: Year-round, Tuesday–Saturday,
10–5; Sunday, 1–5. Monday, 10–5 in July and August. Admission
by donation. Telephone: 443-7171.

Bryant Homestead   This isn't really in the Berkshires—it's
in the Connecticut River Valley and can be conveniently

There's something joyous about the Bryant Homestead and its beautiful setting, something that sends you away satisfied.

reached from Northampton (see page 173)—but it's also easy to get to from Pittsfield, and the drive is very pretty. (Go east on Route 9 to where it intersects with Route 112 in Cummington. Take Route 112 south for a mile and a half, where there is a five-way intersection—it's not as bad as it sounds—and take Bryant Road to the entrance.)

This was the home of William Cullen Bryant (1794–1878), one of the major literary figures of the nineteenth century but almost forgotten today. You do not have to be a fan of Bryant, however, to enjoy this beautiful spot overlooking the Westfield River Valley, with views off into the Hampshire Hills, and the surrounding area, which has a rural quality that is hard to find in most of Massachusetts.

The house was built in 1785 and much altered by Bryant, who made it his summer home. I find the exterior of the building most attractive; the interior is interesting, even eccentric, and filled with memorabilia of Bryant. It provides a particularly interesting opportunity to see how a major intellectual figure of great influence and power lived.

The Bryant Homestead is open: Last weekend in June to Labor Day, Friday, Saturday, Sunday, holidays, 1–5; Labor Day to Columbus Day, Saturday, Sunday, holidays, 1–5. Admission fee. Telephone: 634-2244.

The Stockbridge Area

Stockbridge   This is one of the prettiest—and most visited—towns in the Berkshires. The village is set on a plain through which the Housatonic River, a comfortable, lazy river, meanders. Because Stockbridge has attracted people of wealth since the nineteenth century, the village is particularly well kept and the homes and gardens are models of their sort. This is one of the primary reasons so many people come here.

Stockbridge also has a more interesting history than most villages. In 1734, it decided to organize a mission to the Housatonic Indians, whose tribal name was the Mahicans. (Among those deciding was Jonathan Edwards, the greatest mind of his time, and an eventual head of the mission.) Funds for that purpose were provided by the British Society for the Propagation of the Gospel in Foreign Parts, and the missionary selected was John Sergeant (1710–1749), a recent Yale graduate, who would eventually build the Mission House (see page 152).

Sergeant was totally dedicated to his Indian parishioners and much loved by them. In 1739, the town of Stockbridge (named after a town in Hampshire, England) was incorporated, and the Indians began officially calling themselves Stockbridge Indians, relinquishing their old designation, Mahicans.

By 1749, more than fifty Indian families lived in the village and were on the way to being truly integrated into the white man's culture and society. But Sergeant, who, despite a paralyzed left arm, had managed thus far to work his farm, teach, preach, raise money, and do a hundred other things necessary to keep his community going, was exhausted. In July of that year he died.

With Sergeant's death the Indians themselves were doomed, for they were left to face the rapacious English alone. At the end of the Revolution—during which, by the way, they had loyally served the American cause—the Indians were forced to begin their migration westward, first to New York State and then to Wisconsin, where their descendants live today.

What to See and Do

A Brief Walking Tour   A good deal of Stockbridge is encompassed by Main Street, and a walk along here will both orient you and give you an introduction to the highlights of the village. Start from the **Red Lion Inn** at the heart of Stockbridge. The original inn was built in 1773 and was an important stop on the stagecoach route between Boston and Albany. The building you see today, however, was built at the end of the nineteenth century after a fire destroyed the original. The famous veranda, with its comfortable chairs and rockers, is ideal for watching the passing parade. From the end, overlooking the small plot of the junction of Main and South streets, you can see the Cat and Dog Fountain, with the two animals spitting at each other.

Across from the inn is **St. Paul's Episcopal Church,** designed by Charles F. McKim of McKim, Mead, and White. McKim has taken elements of the Gothic and the Romanesque and elegantly combined them to create this small yet imposing building. The statue *The Spirit of Life* is by Daniel Chester French (see page 155); the chancel window is by John LaFarge, a window in the nave by Tiffany.

As you leave the church, go to your right. Across the way, at 14 Main Street, you will see the **Merwin House,** a handsome brick Federal building from about 1825. This was the summer home of William and Elizabeth Doane, who named it Tranquility. It is now operated by the Society for the Preservation of New England, and the eclectic collection of antiques and family memorabilia is open to the public from June 1 to October 15, Tuesday, Thursday, Saturday, and Sunday, with tours at 12, 1, 2, 3, and 4. Admission fee. Telephone: 298-4703.

Continue your walk, enjoying the handsome dwellings, including the **Mission House** (see page 152), and eventually coming to the **Children's Chimes Bell Tower** (1878), built as a memorial to his grandchildren by David Dudley Field. It marks the spot where John Sergeant preached to the Indians, and there are carillon concerts here each day from June through August. There is also an Indian Burial Ground, with a monument to the Indians and a splendid view from the rise. The red-brick **Congregational Church** (1824) has plaques describing the ministries of some of its pastors, including Jonathan Edwards. If you decide to explore the village cemetery, you will find the graves of John Sergeant and Joseph Choate (see page 154), who remarked, on purchasing a plot, that he had decided to become a permanent resident of Stockbridge.

At the other end of town, at the intersection of Main Street and Yale Hill, is the **Berkshire Theater Festival** building, home to one of the better regional theaters in New England. This handsome building (1887) has an interesting story. It was designed by Stanford White for use as a casino and a tennis club, as well as for art shows and local theatricals, and was located on Main Street where the Mission House now stands. Eventually it fell into disuse and was purchased by Mabel Choate, who, in turn, sold it to the Three Arts Society, who moved it to its present location.

The Mission House   Originally placed on Eden Hill, outside the present town, the house was moved to its present site at the corner of Main and Sergeant streets in 1928 by Mabel Choate, who inherited Naumkeag. She had her landscape architect, Fletcher Steele, create the original version of the exquisite eighteenth-century garden that is there, and he supervised much of the work on the restoration. Miss Choate, however, is responsible for all the furnishings.

In 1739, John Sergeant married Abigail Williams, daughter of Ephraim Williams, a settler who had moved to Stockbridge along with three other families in 1737 at the request of the governor of Massachusetts, Jonathan Belcher. The governor wanted them to represent to the Indians the English way of life. Williams did just that, but not in the way the governor expected—he promptly built a house on a hill overlooking the Indian settlement, fortified it, and made it abundantly clear that he would stay as far away from the natives as he possibly could.

Abigail, as sensitive and caring as her father, immediately made it clear to her new husband that she also wanted a fine house on a hill away from the Indians, and John obliged, probably getting his Indian friends to help, and using Connecticut craftsmen as well. The magnificent carved Connecticut doorway that so distinguishes the house today was brought here by a team of oxen from Westfield, Conn. (Examine the panels. They depict Saint Andrew's Cross, the Ten Commandments, and an open Bible.) Poor John. The house put him in such debt that when he died in 1749 he still owed £700.

The house remained in the Sergeant family until 1867, and then remained vacant until 1927, when Mabel Choate arrived on the scene, bought it, moved it to its present site, restored it, and opened it as a museum in 1930.

Today the house is particularly interesting for its collection of primarily seventeenth- and eighteenth-century decorative arts (including five pieces from the original house and ranging from pewter to tiles to textiles, mezzotints, and the original conch shell used from 1734 on to call worshippers to the mission church), the rooms themselves, the garden, and a small collection of Indian artifacts in a building near the house.

The parlor is a good example of what you can expect to see. The pine paneling, exquisitely carved, has been stained to resemble walnut. A handsome cupboard to the right of the fireplace contains fine examples of English and Dutch earthenware of the seventeenth and eighteenth centuries. Three superb chairs represent Connecticut in the early eighteenth century, Massachusetts in the early seventeenth century, and New York City in the late eighteenth century. Other furnishings include a Delft plaque (c. 1705), eighteenth-century candlestands, and a New England highboy (c. 1720).

In short, this is not meant to be an accurate re-creation of how the Sergeants lived, but it is a museum of the period and region and, as such, is fascinating. As for the garden, it is superbly planted and maintained and is worth an investigative stroll.

Mission House is open: Tuesday–Sunday and on Monday holidays, from Memorial Day weekend through Columbus Day, 11–4. Closed Tuesdays following holidays. Admission fee. Telephone: 298-3239.

Naumkeag A 26-room shingled "cottage" on the west side of Prospect Hill, 3/4 mile from the center of Stockbridge,

Naumkeag (it means "place of rest" in Mahican) was designed by Stanford White in 1885. It was the summer home of Joseph Hodges Choate (1832–1917), a well-known attorney and an ambassador to the Court of St. James appointed by President McKinley. His brother, William, founded the Choate School in Connecticut in 1896.

Mr. Choate's charm, manners, and humor were legendary. A story that is my particular favorite concerns his reply to the question of who he would most like to be if he could have his choice. "I should like," he replied, "to be Mrs. Choate's second husband." On another occasion, when viewing a nude sculpture by Frederick MacMonnies, *Young Faun with Heron,* which was to adorn his home, he said, "Fig leaf or no, it has an honorable mention." And when asked to contribute to a fence to surround a cemetery in Stockbridge he declined, explaining, "No one inside can get out, and no one outside wants to get in."

My favorite part of the estate is the grounds; the house itself is its least interesting facet. It is true that there is a significant collection of porcelain, particularly Chinese Lowestoft, and

An entrance to the Chinese Garden at Naumkeag. No one interested in landscape architecture should miss visiting the superb and varied gardens here.

there are some good antiques, including some excellent early American pieces, a bust of Ruluff Choate by Augustus Saint-Gaudens, two drawings of Mabel and Joseph Choate by John Singer Sargent . . . but all in all, what is here is just the sort of thing you would expect to find, and the rooms themselves are not Stanford White at his best. But the grounds—that is a different story, for the gardens can be ranked with the best in New England.

What you see today is largely the result of a collaboration between Joseph's daughter Mabel and the American landscape architect Fletcher Steele. There are twelve divisions—the Oak Terrace, the Perugino View, the Birch Walk, the Rose Garden, the Peony Terraces, the Chinese and Evergreen and Afternoon gardens, and so on. Each is superb, but I must tell you of my favorites.

The first is the **Birch Walk.** An extraordinary staircase with Art Nouveau stair rails flows outward on the steep slope, centering on a channel of water that is interrupted by four basins. Walking down this staircase, and then looking back on it from the bottom of the slope, is an experience that anyone interested in landscaping or gardening will never forget.

Next I must mention the **Afternoon Garden,** where oak pilings, dredged from Boston harbor and carved and painted to resemble Venetian posts, have been placed to frame the views of the Berkshire Hills. And the brick-walled **Chinese Garden,** with its Buddhas, carved dogs, and other figures, its ginkgo trees and water flowing through marble channels, its temple and Moon Gate . . . The grounds, in brief, are captivating and original, so interesting, in fact, that you should make every effort to see them.

Naumkeag is open: Daily, except Mondays, late May to Labor Day, 10:00–4:15. Labor Day to Columbus Day, weekends and holidays. Admission fee. Telephone: 298-3239.

Chesterwood   This was the summer home of the American sculptor Daniel Chester French (1850–1931), whose most famous works are the *Abraham Lincoln* for the Lincoln Memorial in Washington and *The Minute Man* in Concord, Mass. After Augustus Saint-Gaudens (see page 86), he was the most important American sculptor of the nineteenth century.

In fact, he spent some time in Saint-Gaudens's beloved Cornish, but when it came time to buy a summer home, he and his wife, Mary, fell in love with the Berkshire region, and in particular the Stockbridge area. Said Mary on her first visit to Stockbridge in 1895: "I don't know what you're going to do, but I am going to live here."

In the summer of 1896, a friend showed them the farm and land that French would buy and transform into Chesterwood, named after his grandfather's house in Chester, N.H. What decided him to buy the property was the magnificent view to Monument Mountain, and to raise the necessary funds he asked for and received an advance on a commission he had accepted for an equestrian statue of General Grant. He would live here for six months of each year until his death and said it was "as beautiful as Fairyland. . . . I go about in an ecstasy of delight over the loveliness of things."

To transform the property, French hired his friend the architect Henry Bacon—it was he who would design the Lincoln Memorial—to build his studio (1898) and then the Colonial Revival house (1901).

The Studio: This is my favorite of the two buildings. There is an especially appealing reception room, with art catalogues and books, a grandfather clock, a fireplace, carved chests, and an Egyptian-style daybed. The studio itself has a 23-foot ceiling with a skylight, a 30-by-29-foot floor area, and banks of windows on the north and east walls. But its most immediately noticeable feature is the railroad track that disappears through huge (22-foot) doors. French could place a sculpture on a flatbed railroad car and have it rolled out into the light, where he could examine it in the conditions under which it would be seen and then make any adjustments he might feel necessary.

His daughter, Margaret French Cresson, lived here until she died in 1969, when the estate was bequeathed to the National Trust for Historic Preservation. She maintained the studio as French left it, and his tools and supplies are all in order. (She also added to what already was there, and the estate now contains over 500 casts and models of his work, making it the largest collection in existence for the study of an American sculptor.)

The House: I first came to Chesterwood when Margaret Cresson was still alive, and I remember seeing her enter the house, first giving a welcoming wave to my little group. I thought then how much I would like to see the interior of the house, and of course I now have. It's pleasant, rather cozy, in fact, but if your time is at all limited, save it for the studio, the garden, and the trails.

The Garden and Trails: I can think of nothing more pleasurable than spending time wandering about in the formal yet simple garden, with its handsome fountain designed by Bacon, that adjoins the studio and complements it so beautifully, tying it in to the surrounding landscape with casual elegance. The nature trails that lead you off into the woods have wonderfully placed statuary and planned vistas that create a sense of intimacy between man and nature that can only be described as remarkable. I believe that Chesterwood is one of French's greatest creations, in its own way as powerful and moving as anything he sculpted. Today, each summer, there is an outdoor sculpture exhibition. It's a wonderful idea, and in the exhibitions I have seen, some of the sculpture has been quite good. But much of it is second-rate and extremely jarring in an environment so carefully designed as one man's artistic vision.

The Barn Sculpture Gallery: Special exhibitions are held here of models and casts of French's work, as well as the work of his daughter. This is the only building left of those that were on the property when French bought it.

There is a gift shop with an excellent selection of books and other attractive things to buy.

Chesterwood is open: Daily, May 1–October 31, 10–5. Admission fee. Telephone: 298-3579.

The Berkshire Botanical Garden   About 2 miles outside Stockbridge, at the junction of Routes 102 and 183, this 15-acre botanical garden, founded in 1934, is extremely well done and will be of interest not only to gardeners but also to all those who enjoy flowers. You enter the Visitors' Center and gift shop—a very nice one, by the way—where you will pay your admission and receive a map to the gardens.

A real Connecticut door—exuberant, brilliantly carved, excessive in almost every detail—and who wouldn't kill to have one? See one of these and you have to be in the Connecticut River Valley.

Depending on your interests and the time of year, you will find that a visit of anywhere from one to two hours is necessary. To give you an idea of what is available: There is a section devoted to primroses and another to daylilies . . . there is a pond garden and a spectacular terraced herb garden . . . there is a daffodil meadow, a rose garden, and exquisite perennial borders . . . there are vegetable gardens, greenhouses, and a section devoted to conifers. In addition, the Botanical Garden offers special events and lectures and has an excellent reference library.

The Berkshire Botanical Garden is open: Daily, 9–sunset. Admission fee. Telephone: 298-3926.

The Norman Rockwell Museum Norman Rockwell (1894–1978) lived in Stockbridge for the last twenty-five years of his life. From 1969 to 1993, this museum was located on Main Street in Stockbridge in a building known as the Old Corner House, where an estimated two million people passed through the exhibitions, making it one of the major tourist attractions in the Berkshires.

That space was inadequate to the needs of the museum—only 50 paintings at a time could be shown from the collection of 500 works, the largest holdings in the world of Rockwell's art—and the museum therefore decided it would have to find more suitable quarters.

In 1983 it acquired Linwood, a magnificent 36-acre site with views to the Housatonic and the surrounding hills, just 2 miles from Stockbridge, and successfully embarked on a fund-raising campaign to build the new $4.4 million museum. Designed by Robert A. M. Stern Architects, the building contains 27,000 square feet of exhibition space to display 150 of Rockwell's paintings, as well as classrooms, a library, studios, storage space, and an auditorium. This handsome building is evocative of a New England town hall. Rockwell's studio is also on the grounds, and the Victorian house (1859), separated from the museum by a 25-foot hemlock hedge, and the carriage house have been remodeled for administration and staff offices.

The Norman Rockwell Museum, 9 Glendale Road (Route 183), is open: May–October, daily, 10–5. November–April, weekdays, 11–4, weekends, 10–5. Closed: Last two weeks of January. Admission fee. Telephone: 298-4100. The studio is open: May through October.

Tyringham Valley

Down on the meadow and up on the height
The breezes are blowing the willows white.
In the elms and maples the robins call,
And the great black crow sails over all
In Tyringham, Tyringham Valley.

—From "A Rhyme of Tyringham" by Richard Watson Gilder

Tyringham is as sweet and peaceful as ever. One house has burned down and one has been built and three have been painted and Miss Beulah has put in two dormer windows—with these slight exceptions the town knows no change ... I eat

alone and sit alone at night and climb the cobble alone, but—
so far at least—I haven't got lonely.

—Jean Webster to her husband

These excerpts, drawn from *Views of the Valley: Tyringham*
1739–1989 (The Hop Brook Community Club), well define the
"feel" of this area, perhaps my favorite in the Berkshires because it is still unspoiled and uncommercial.

If you don't have time to climb the Cobble, with its lovely
trails and views (telephone 458-3144 for directions), or wander
through the valley on any of the back roads, there is a pleasant
short drive that will at least introduce you to the gentle beauty
of this forgotten area, and you also can visit an extremely attractive dwelling, the Bidwell House (see below).

Take Route 23 from Great Barrington to Monterey. At
Monterey, take a left on Tyringham Road, which will eventually become Monterey Road. It is here that you should turn left
onto Art School Road to see the **Bidwell House,** set on 190
acres of land.

Adonijah Bidwell, a graduate of Yale and the first minister
in Monterey, was the builder of this fine 1750 clapboard house,
with its large and well-proportioned rooms. When he died in
1784, he left a complete inventory of his household furnishings, which turned out to be extremely fortunate as it survived
through the centuries and enabled the last owners of the house
to re-create, to a large extent, the look the house must have had
in the later eighteenth and nineteenth centuries, and to include some furnishings known to have belonged to the Bidwell
family.

This restoration is different from many others because the
owners lived here among the furnishings, so the house has a
pleasantly "used" feeling, making it particularly welcoming, as
if you were there for a country weekend. In addition, because
one of the owners was particularly interested in textiles, there
is an unusually fine collection of period bed coverings, and
there also are interesting collections of redware, delft, and iron
domestic tools.

The Bidwell House is open: Memorial Day weekend to mid-
October, Tuesday through Sunday and holidays, 11–4.
Admission fee. Telephone: 528-6888.

Turn left when you leave and go to the end of the road. Turn left again, and soon you will enter the town of **Tyringham,** which is worth a stroll and exploratory drive not so much because of any one building or house but because the overall ensemble is so pleasant and unpretentious.

Continuing on, you will see the—to put it mildly—unusual **Gingerbread House.** This was built by the sculptor Sir Henry Hudson Kitson (he sculpted *The Minuteman* at Lexington) in the early 1930s. You can't miss it. In fact, it's worth quoting from a postcard description to give you an idea of what is going on here:

Construction—The roof is fashioned of conventional materials to simulate thatching, specially cut and shaped to achieve the rolling effect, actually a gigantic sculpture constructed on a massive armature of heavy chestnut beams. Total weight is estimated at 80 tons. The footings are concrete, to support the tremendous weight. The shingles were applied over a period of two years by English workers imported for the purpose, it is said. The tremendous rocks [which you see outside the house from the road] were brought in by horse and stone boat, and the fronting pillars were erected (as was the rest of the building) under the direct supervision of Sir Henry, who was said to be a most difficult and temperamental man to work for. . . .

Motif—The roof was designed to represent the rolling hills of the Berkshires in the Autumn. The fronting rock pillars and the grottoes between them are fashioned after similar edifices in Europe, and the gardens in the rear were primarily wild, and intended to attract wildlife, particularly birds. At one time the pond was full of goldfish, and it is said that Sir Henry used to call them and feed them oatmeal.

Today the building is home to the Tyringham Art Galleries and is open to the public.

Next you will come to Route 102, which you can take to Lee, the town that supplied the marble for the Capitol in Washington, D.C. Lee is the commercial center nearest to the **Jacob's Pillow Dance Festival,** which is eight miles east, off Route 20 on George Carter Road in Becket. This, the oldest and

most prestigious dance festival in this country, was created by
Ted Shawn; he and his wife, Ruth St. Denis, are considered to
be the first true American dancers. For information on the
summer season, telephone 243-0745 or write: Jacob's Pillow,
P.O. Box 287, Lee 01238.

The Williamstown Area

Williamstown is almost too pretty. I wouldn't mind seeing
just one ramshackle ranch house with a pink flamingo on the
lawn amid all this pristine white New England clapboard re-
spectability. But it never will be.

The town was established in 1753 as West Hoosuck by soldiers from Fort Massachusetts. One of the these soldiers was
Colonel Ephraim Williams, who wrote into his will a bequest to
found a free school provided the town was named after him. He
was killed in 1755, in the French and Indian War, and both
town and college took his name.

Sterling and Francine Clark Art Institute   This superb
museum is one of the best small museums in this country.
Make every effort to see it. It will be a highlight of your trip.

Robert Sterling Clark (1877–1956) began collecting seri-
ously in 1912. Over the next forty years and more, he and his
wife, Francine, (1876–1960) created an extraordinarily personal and diverse collection that includes great masterpieces
by Piero della Francesca, Botticelli and his studio, Goya and
Rubens, Fragonard and Gainsborough, Degas and Homer,
Tiepolo and Corot, among others. There are more than thirty
paintings by Renoir, eight by Corot, and eight by Monet. But if
one were to characterize the collection as simply as possible,
one could say it is oriented primarily toward French paintings
of the second half of the nineteenth century.

Needless to say, every museum in this country would have
killed to get the collection, but it came to Williamstown primarily because the Clarks felt it would be safe here from the
possibility of atomic attack (remember, the cold war was at its
height in the 1950s), because of the beauty of the site, and because they had connections at the college. Since the death of

Mr. and Mrs. Clark, the collection has continued to expand through gifts and purchases.

It it necessary to mention only a few works from different periods to give you a flavor of the whole.

From the Renaissance, my favorite picture is della Francesca's *Virgin and Child Enthroned with Four Angels.* This late work is a masterpiece, and particularly brilliant in its study of proportions and the relationship of figures to one another and to the architecture. It is the finest work of this master in the country.

The seventeenth and eighteenth centuries are well represented. Among the best canvases certainly would be included J. M. W. Turner's *Rockets and Blue Lights (Close at Hand) to Warn Steamboats of Shoal Water,* Francisco Goya's *Asensio Julia* and Claude Lorrain's *Landscape with the Voyage of Jacob.*

As for the nineteenth century, certainly the collection of French paintings, and particularly those by Renoir, is exceptional, and they also are the best known. Therefore, I would like to call your attention to the often overlooked American canvases. Winslow Homer, for example, is represented by ten superb canvases, including a particular favorite of mine, *Sleigh Ride.* There are a dozen paintings by John Singer Sargent, as well as excellent examples of the work of Frederic Remington, John Frederick Kensett, and Mary Cassatt, among others, and such pleasant surprises as a particularly satisfying picture by the little-known painter Clarence Johnson (*At the Hill's Top—Lumberville*).

Finally, it is a pleasure to be able to say that the paintings that have been added to the Clarks' collection are of the same high quality. For example, there is a brilliant Jean-Honoré Fragonard portrait (*The Warrior*) that would be the envy of any museum; a Gustave Caillebotte that not only is lovely but also helps to fill a hole in the collection; one of the American folk artist Ammi Phillips's greatest portraits, *Portrait of Harriet Campbell;* a group of paintings from the Lehman collection, including several by Jan Gossaert (Mabuse); Paul Gauguin's *Young Christian Girl.*

The Clark also has first-rate collections of porcelain and furniture. The collection of American and European silver is among the finest in the world and includes several dozen(!) pieces by that greatest of English silversmiths, Paul de Lamerie.

The Sterling and Francine Clark Art Institute is open: Tuesday–Sunday, 10–5. Free admission. Telephone: 458-9545. Follow the signs in Williamstown.

Williams College   The campus is certainly among the most beautiful in New England, and you should leave yourself ample time to stroll among the buildings, which cover every style from the colonial period up to today. **The Chapin Library** has a rare-book collection that places it among the best in the country. The **Williams College Museum of Art,** with an interior space brilliantly designed by Charles Moore yet retaining a particularly beautiful neoclassical rotunda from 1846, contains 11,000 works of art from all periods but emphasizes contemporary and modern art. There is also a major collection of paintings by the American Charles Prendergast, as well as some by his brother, Maurice, and important American works from the late eighteenth century to the present. Their changing exhibitions are good enough to receive widespread coverage and add immeasurably to a visit. The museum is open: Tuesday–Saturday, 10–5; Sunday, 1–5. Free admission. Telephone: 597-2429.

A DRIVE: THE MOHAWK TRAIL

The Mohawk Trail, about 65 miles along Route 2, is only partially in the Berkshires, for it runs from Williamstown in the west to Greenfield in the Connecticut River Valley. It is named for the Mohawk Indians because they used it during the French and Indian War as a passage from the Hudson River Valley in New York State to the Connecticut River Valley. The drive is extremely scenic, varied, and really quite special, and it takes you to interesting places. It can therefore be highly recommended as a pleasant and interesting way to spend a day.

From Williamstown you will drive east, making your first destination the summit of **Mount Greylock,** named for an Indian chief and, at 3,491 feet, the highest point in Massachusetts. Access to the summit is easy by car, and the

The house by the side of the road. A massive central chimney, weathered clapboard . . . only the door has been "designed." And yet the whole has a dignity and quiet beauty that are soberly moving.

road is pretty enough to be of interest in itself. At the summit there is a tower that was erected as a war memorial, and as you can imagine, the view is spectacular and includes the Berkshire Valley and the Taconics. It makes an excellent introduction to the countryside you will be visiting.

North Adams is hard by, and a stop here can be very interesting. First of all, this is the proposed site for one of the most interesting museum projects conceived in this century, known by its acronym, MassMoCA (Massachusetts Museum of Contemporary Art). Let me back up a little.

At one time, North Adams was the home of Sprague Electric division, which occupied huge nineteenth-century buildings, quite beautiful in their own right. Then Sprague Electric left, and no one was interested in the structures. And then someone had a brilliant idea: Why not rehabilitate them and dedicate them to modern art, making the facility one of the great museums for modern art in the world? After all, many contemporary art pieces are enormous, far too large for the average museum to hold more than one or two. These buildings, with their acres of walls, would not only be the ideal site but also could be made ready at a fraction of the cost of building a new facility. The idea was that both the state of Massachusetts and private sources would contribute to the creation of this museum, which would be a great tourist attraction. Then the recession hit, Massachusetts went into a decline, and the project, although not dead, has not received the attention it once did. I personally hope it happens, at least in part, for it's a visionary plan that could do much to help this depressed mill town, and you should try to save enough time to drive by the buildings and make up your own mind.

Western Gateway Heritage State Park is a restored railyard, with six buildings set around a cobbled courtyard whose most interesting feature is its display about the 4.7-mile Hoosac Tunnel. This was a railroad tunnel built between 1851 and 1875 to facilitate rail traffic between Massachusetts and the West. It was a brilliant and innovative engineering feat in its time but, tragically, the cause of the death of almost two hundred workmen. Certainly one of the reasons for this appalling mortality rate on what would then be the longest tunnel in this country was that nitroglycerin was first used here as a blasting agent.

In any case, the exhibitions here—films, slides, and excellent signage—illuminate a little-known but fascinating footnote to our history, and when you are done, there are some attractive shops to visit including one highlighting regional crafts.

Western Gateway Heritage State Park is open: All year. Admission: Free. Telephone: 663-6312.

From here, between North Adams and Florida, you will pass through the most dramatic scenery of the drive, with expansive views opening up of the Hoosac and Berkshire valleys and the Taconic Mountains. Whitcomb Summit, Hairpin Turn, Western Summit . . . all offer spectacular views.

Next visit **Shelburne Falls,** off Route 2, a pleasant village alongside the falls of the Deerfield River. The old trolley bridge that crosses the river has been transformed into the **Bridge of Flowers,** a 400-foot-long garden, with flower beds on either side of the footpath. It's an ingenious reuse of an outmoded facility. This is a favorite spot for glassblowers, among other artists, and you can visit the **North River Glass Studio** and watch artists create their pieces.

From here you will descend into *Greenfield*, from which you can visit Deerfield or wend your way home.

THE CONNECTICUT RIVER VALLEY

Distances between the towns and villages in this region are very short—the Connecticut River Valley in Massachusetts is only about 45 miles long, and all the sites mentioned, with the exception of Sturbridge and Worcester, lie within that range. You can easily stay in any town and comfortably visit all of the others. I have listed the sites from north to south.

Deerfield

The town was incorporated in 1673 and was twice devastated in Indian wars. The first time was in 1675, during King Philip's War, in what has become known as the Bloody Brook Massacre, when 64 people lost their lives. Those left fled south, and Deerfield reverted almost to a wilderness tract.

Slowly the community reestablished itself, and by 1700 it was a substantial little village. Then, in February 1704, during Queen Anne's War, the Canadian French and Indians struck, killing 49 people and taking 111 captives north to Canada, an agonizing and brutal march of some 300 miles. Many died before they reached Canada, and it was said that women with newborn babies who fell behind were left to die. Those who survived in Deerfield, were committed to keeping the community alive, and by 1706 the town had become a prosperous agricultural center.

Today Deerfield is famous for two reasons. The first is that it is the home of Deerfield Academy, founded in 1797. The school achieved national fame during the sixty-six-year headmastership of Frank Boyden, who took over the reins of a nearly defunct country school in 1902. By his retirement in 1968, Deerfield Academy had become one of the country's premier educational institutions.

The second is **Historic Deerfield,** whose 14 museum houses open to the public line a mile-long thoroughfare with Georgian and Federal houses that make it one of the most historically important and lovely streets in this country. Usually referred to simply as The Street, it has forty-six buildings that antedate 1850, including two churches, and was laid out as part of the original plan of the village, which contained forty-three home lots. Fortunately for us, very little has changed in the past three hundred years in the relationship of town and The Street to the adjacent two thousand acres of surrounding open farmland.

Historic Deerfield was founded in 1952 by Henry and Helen Flynt, who bought most of these old houses and other buildings, did the original restoration, and filled them with splendid examples of the decorative arts. Today, thanks to the Flynts and others, the Deerfield collections of colonial and Federal silver, textiles, and clothing have an international reputation, while the collections of ceramics and furniture, particularly objects made and used in the Connecticut River Valley, are of the highest quality.

The Flynts first began going to Deerfield in 1936, when their son was attending the academy. By 1939 Henry Flynt was exploring the possibility of preserving and restoring the entire length of The Street. In 1942 they bought their first house, and in 1945 the Deerfield Inn was purchased; eventually they would move two colonial houses to the village from other locations.

There is no need to describe every building in detail, but a few of my favorites will give you an idea of what you can expect. In fact, there is so much to see and do here that you should plan on staying overnight, easy enough as the Deerfield Inn is right on The Street.

Asa Stebbins House (1799): This simple Federal structure was the first brick house in Deerfield. It is my personal favorite, perhaps because there's something about it that always makes me feel happy and welcome as I pass through the door. Or perhaps it's because it offers the visitor the warmth that comes from restrained elegance in proportion, the carving of the moldings, the lovely curved stairway, and the plasterwork trim. And then the dining room is one of the most charming rooms imaginable, with walls painted in a delightful freehand design by an itinerant artist named Jared Jessup about 1813

Historic Deerfield is noted for its spectacular houses and decorative-arts collections. But I also like the wonderful old-fashioned village gardens.

or 1814. In the hall is a magnificent French scenic wallpaper (*Les Voyages de Capitaine Cook,* made between 1804 and 1806), on a wall by the staircase and on the stair landing. The furnishings, porcelains, mirrors and paintings are perfection throughout the house. There are two portraits by Erastus Salisbury Field here (see page 177). Field lived in the area, and Historic Deerfield owns a total of seven of his portraits. In addition, paintings by Ralph Earl appear in this collection, including one lovely portrait in the Sheldon-Hawks House, described below.

Upstairs, two of the bedrooms have French wallpapers, one a lavish trompe l'oeil of drapery, the other, architectural motifs and drapery. Both, like the wallpaper on the staircase, are from a house in Maine that was demolished during highway construction. And again, both rooms are perfectly furnished.

The Hinsdale and Anna Williams House (1838): The most recent restoration, this was completed in the early summer of 1993, after eleven years of work. It was built in the mid-eighteenth century, then altered in 1818 to become a basically Georgian house. But the interior has been radically changed;

what you see is the creation of E. H. Williams, begun in 1817, when he was living there. Williams was one of the richest men in the area, and what he did to this house reflected both his wealth and the new Federal fashion.

The first thing you notice over the Federal door that Williams had installed is the exquisitely delicate gilded pewter fanlight, as lovely as any I've seen. Go through the door, into the north parlor, and you're in a Federal room, beautifully proportioned and detailed, whose highlight is the French wallpaper of *Venetian Scenes* from the original Williams renovation of 1817. (The other wallpapers in the house are reproductions based on scraps found during the renovations, and they, too, are very handsome.) All the rooms are delightful, but of particular interest here is the story of how the restoration was accomplished and what was discovered during the process. It was not an easy project, for Williams reused material from the original house in rooms that would not be seen by his guests, and changed much of the interior, and the last owner of the house also made extensive changes.

Because there was a very complete inventory of what was in the house during the period Williams lived there, Historic Deerfield has been able to accurately furnish the rooms as they were then; there is even a watercolor of Mount Vernon by Williams's daughter.

Sheldon-Hawks House (c. 1743): The same family lived here from the mid-eighteenth century to the mid-twentieth, and the façade of this house is the least changed of any in Deerfield. Overall it has that Georgian dignity and restraint that makes it seem larger and more imposing than it actually is. It also has its original Connecticut Valley doorway with triangular pediment, one of only two in Deerfield.

Inside, the furniture consists primarily of examples from the Connecticut River Valley—the strongest segment of Deerfield's furniture collection—and the porcelains, particularly the blue-and-white pieces, and ceramics are very good. Upstairs, the paneling, a warm brown-honey color, is outstanding. The kitchen is furnished to look like what it was, the kitchen of a farming family, and it has its original hearthstone.

All the houses have a great deal to offer, and you should try to see as many as you can. In addition, you will want to stroll on the Deerfield Academy campus and, in particular, see the magnificent John Williams Herise's Connecticut River Valley door along Albany Road, as well as the **Helen Geier Flynt Textile Museum,** located in a converted 1872 barn (please note the knife weather vane), with its extensive and very good collection of sixteenth- to nineteenth-century clothing, needlework, and coverlets. My only complaint is that I wish they would change the rather dopey-looking mannequins.

The Textile Museum is right behind the **Henry Needham Flynt Silver and Metalware Collection** of seventeenth- to nineteenth-century American and English silver and pewter (and some beautiful tea tables, I might add). It contains pieces from all major forms made in America during the periods represented and is an extremely fine collection that is a must for anyone with any interest at all in antique silver.

Historic Deerfield also exhibits the **Frank L. Boyden Carriage Collection,** which Boyden's family gave to Historic Deerfield and which is housed in a barn behind the Williams House.

The brick **First Church of Deerfield** (1824), also on The Street, has its original pulpit, pews, and galleries and is worth visiting. The post office (1953) was designed, at the request of the Flynts, after the 1696 meeting house. The J. G. Pratt Store has an outstanding collection of books.

Finally, the **Indian House Memorial** is a reconstruction of a c. 1698 house that survived the Indian attack in 1704 but was destroyed in 1848. The original door, with tomahawk scars still visible, is in **Memorial Hall Museum,** a regional collection of historical memorabilia housed in a building designed by Asher Benjamin and built in 1798 to be the first home of Deerfield Academy. It has since been considerably altered. Both museums are separate from Historic Deerfield and are open on a seasonal basis.

Historic Deerfield's fourteen museum houses are open: Daily, 9:30–4:30. The houses are shown by guided tour, and each tour lasts one-half hour. Admission fee includes guided walks of The Street and admission to all special events. Telephone: 774-5581.

Amherst

The town was first settled in 1703 and was named after the English lord and general Jeffrey Amherst, who had fought in the French and Indian War. Amherst has a lovely situation, surrounded by hills, and the campus and buildings of **Amherst College,** which was founded in 1821 to prepare young men for the ministry, adds a great deal to the overall charm.

A slight digression is in order on the colleges in the Massachusetts section of the Connecticut River Valley. Approximately 60,000 students are enrolled in the five colleges or universities found here, and they have formed a consortium to share facilities and even faculty. The five are Amherst; Hampshire College (Amherst), created in 1971 by the other consortium members; Mount Holyoke (South Hadley), the first women's college in the country; Smith College (Northampton); and the University of Massachusetts (Amherst), where 25,000 students attend classes.

The original Amherst College buildings date from the 1820s and form a harmonious backdrop; it is the whole, in fact, that makes the town interesting, and you should take the time to drive around it first, to orient yourself, and then walk along Main Street and the Green.

Emily Dickinson House: Emily Dickinson (1830–1886) is Amherst's most famous resident, although the poets Robert Frost and Eugene Field also lived here, as did Noah Webster. The **Robert Frost Library** of the college owns about one half of the Dickinson poems in manuscript and has a Frost collection as well. For information, telephone 542-2000. (Frost lived west of the center of town in a house that is still privately owned.)

Miss Dickinson's Federal brick house was built by her grandfather, Samuel Fowler Dickinson, in 1813, and is at 280 Main Street. When her father died, in 1874, the reclusive Emily left the grounds exactly once, when her nephew died, before her own death twelve years later. Only ten of her poems were published in her lifetime—the remainder were found by her sister after her death—and a complete edition did not appear until 1955. The bulk of her personal effects and furnishings are now at Harvard, but her writing room has been re-created here. It's recommended that you call ahead before visiting the house; hours are limited. Telephone: 542-8161.

Other sites to consider include, on the Amherst campus, the **Pratt Museum of Natural History,** which holds the world's largest mastodon skeleton, as well as Indian artifacts, minerals, and fossils (Open: During the academic year. Telephone: 542-2165. Free admission), and the **Mead Art Museum,** a small but interesting collection (Open: September–July, daily; August, by appointment. Telephone: 542-2000. Free admission). The **Jones Library,** at 43 Amity Street, has collections of works by the Amherst authors, including a display of Dickinson and Frost manuscripts. (Open: Monday–Friday, 11–1 and 2–5. Telephone: 256-4090. Free admission), and the **Strong House Museum,** at 67 Amity Street, in a 1744 house, displays clothing, furniture, and household items and has an eighteenth-century garden (Open: Daily. Telephone: 256-0678. Free admission).

What you will not wish to visit is the University of Massachusetts campus. Founded as a land-grant agricultural college in 1863, it has evolved into a huge institution with a collection of modern buildings as ugly as any in the country. Particularly shocking is that so many major twentieth-century architects (Roche and Dinkeloo, Marcel Breuer, Edward Durrell Stone, and Hugh Stubbins) have done such terrible work here. The students must find it depressing and enervating.

Northampton

Two things I'll bet you didn't know until now: In 1852, Jenny Lind spent her honeymoon here ("This," she pronounced, "is the paradise of America!"), and Calvin Coolidge was once the town's mayor. Other than that, Northampton, which was settled in 1654, had its most interesting moment in history during the ministry of Jonathan Edwards, who preached here for twenty-three years, until 1750, when he was dismissed. It was here that the Great Awakening began, in 1740, when Edwards for a short time revivified Calvin's teachings of hellfire and damnation and spread the word throughout the valley. It all got rather hectic. "Infants," he preached, "if they are out of Christ are in God's sight young vipers, and infinitely more hateful than vipers." Obviously he felt his own twelve children were not "out of Christ." For a time he was very effective in attracting followers—"The noise of the dry bones waxed louder and louder," he said—but finally he was done in by a theological dispute.

Today Northampton is the home of **Smith College,** founded by Sophia Smith, which opened in 1875, the largest (2,700 women) private liberal arts college for women in this country and one of the best. The campus is well worth a stroll, particularly on Elm Street, which came to glory during the Victorian era, and at Paradise Pond—named by Jenny Lind, of course—and save time to visit the **Museum of Art,** on Elm Street, which has the best collection (Picasso, Degas, Corot, and others) of the consortium. (Open: Mid-September to May, Tuesday–Sunday, 10–5; June, by appointment; July and August, Tuesday– Saturday. Free admission. Telephone: 584-2700.)

Other sites to visit include the nearby Bryant Homestead in Cummington (see page 148) and three house museums of the

A particularly handsome 19th-century New England factory, many of which still dot the landscape. This one was built by an ancestor of mine. He also founded the first abolitionist newspaper in western Massachusetts and built Catholic and Protestant churches for his workers, as well as housing that was a model for the time.

Northampton Historical Society: Damon House (1813), Shepherd House (c. 1798), and Parsons House (c. 1712). All have changing exhibitions on aspects of local history and there are some period rooms. (Open: March–December, Tuesday–Sunday. Free admission. Telephone: 584-6011.) And if you are interested in the life of Calvin Coolidge, you should visit the Forbes Library at 20 West Street to see the Calvin Coolidge Memorial Room, which houses some of his papers and correspondence and other Coolidge memorabilia, including an Indian headdress and beadwork. (Open: Monday–Friday, but the schedule may vary, so call ahead. Free admission. Telephone: 584-6037.)

South Hadley

Yet another college town, this time the home of **Mount Holyoke.** South Hadley was settled in 1659 and incorporated in 1775. The first navigable canal in the United States operated here, one of many that would eventually allow navigation to go up the Connecticut into Vermont. Sections of the canal are now being restored, but today the main reason to visit South Hadley is the Mount Holyoke campus, which I find to be the most interesting and beautiful of the campuses of the five consortium members.

Mount Holyoke was founded in 1836 by Mary Lyon and is the nation's oldest college for women. As such, it warrants a little history.

Mary Lyon (1797–1849), the daughter of a farmer, was a brilliant student. The story is told that one teacher, to keep her busy because she seemed to learn everything instantly, gave her a Latin grammar on Friday and asked her to learn the first lesson by Monday. On Monday she recited every lesson in the book. The good news, though, is that she also was noted for a sense of humor and everyone liked her.

It was only natural that this highly talented woman would become a teacher, and wherever she went, students flocked to her and other teachers came to study her methods.

Eventually she began to dream of founding her own school, and when she was thirty-six, in 1833, she gathered together a group of men to help her with her idea for a publicly endowed school for young women that would prepare them to be well-trained teachers. Slowly her idea gained ground, and, as one of the men who supported her wrote, he and the others were asked to inspect "a few small seeds which Miss Lyon was wishing to put into the ground *somewhere* and *sometime,* allowing us to have something to say as to the place and time and so forth, yet not wholly surrendering anything entirely up to any, and still allowing us the innocent fancy of thinking ourselves for the time being co-workers with her."

Finally, on February 11, 1836, a charter was granted for the Mount Holyoke Female Seminary, and in 1837 the first students arrived. Many years later, one of Mount Holyoke's trustees described the original feeling about Miss Lyon's project: "The objections to this idea of equalizing the educational advantages of the two sexes were many and various, and not always consonant with the courtesy due to the gentler sex. It was an innovation uncalled for, unheard of until now since the foundation of the world, and unthought of now except by a few strong-minded women and radical men, who would level all distinctions and overturn the foundations of the family, of society, of the church, and of the state. It was unnatural, unphilosophical, unscriptural, unpracticable, unfeminine and anti-Christian."

Obviously, Mary Lyon paid absolutely no attention to her critics. She died twelve years later, and it isn't too much to say that she was the founding mother of higher education for women in this country.

Today, Mount Holyoke's campus is distinguished by the quality of its buildings and the splendid old trees and plantings. Don't hesitate to wander, not only on the grounds but also in some of the more intriguing buildings, such as the library addition designed by Graham Gund. There's an arboretum— **Talcott Arboretum**—that includes perennial, Japanese, and wildflower gardens, as well as a half dozen or more greenhouses filled with exotic plants. (Open: During the academic year, daily. Free admission. Telephone: 538-2116.) There also is an **Art Museum** that has a small but select collection. (Open: Daily. Free Admission. Telephone: 538-2245.) The Joseph Allen Skinner Museum, located on Route 116 and housed in a former Congregational church (1846), has an eclectic collection that includes stuffed birds, early American furnishings, medieval armor, and Indian artifacts. (Open: May–October, Wednesday and Sunday. Free admission. Telephone: 538-2085.)

Springfield

This city of almost 157,000 people is the largest city of the Massachusetts cities that lie on the Connecticut River and the third largest in the state. The federal government established an armory here in 1794—it was responsible for the first American musket in 1795 and also supplied the weapons used by the North in the Civil War—and that gave the city its first impetus toward becoming a major manufacturing center in the nineteenth century. With the money came, as always in New England, the establishment of cultural centers, and today Springfield is worth a visit for those, as well as for the quality of many of its handsome buildings. Two of the earliest works of the great American architect H. H. Richardson (1838–1886) are here—the North Congregational Church and the Hampden County Courthouse. (Unfortunately, other buildings of his in Springfield have not survived.) You can also see Augustus Saint-Gaudens's *The Puritan* (1886), one of his most famous sculptures. Last but certainly not least, in 1891 basketball was first played here, and the Basketball Hall of Fame (see page 180) is located here. In short, Springfield is a cultivated and interesting city that will repay the attention you give it, and you can easily spend a day here.

Springfield Library & Museums   Located at the Quadrangle, and founded in 1857, this is the site of four important museums and a major public library. The four museums are open: Thursday–Sunday. There is one admission fee for all four. Telephone numbers follow the notes about the institutions.

Of all the museums, my favorite is the Art Deco **Springfield Museum of Fine Arts** (1933), which contains twenty galleries and exhibits such old masters as Chardin and Monet as well as newer ones such as Frankenthaler and O'Keeffe.

These, of course, are the primary attractions, but I find this museum particularly distinguished by its collection of the paintings of Erastus Salisbury Field (1805–1900), one of the greatest folk artists this country has produced. Here you will find his most important—and bizarre—masterpiece, *Historical Monument of the American Republic,* described below.

Field was born just north of Amherst. When he was nineteen, he went to New York to study for a very brief period with Samuel F. B. Morse, the only real training he would ever have. Obviously this was too short a period to develop Field's understanding of anatomy, and this would never be his strong point, as is immediately apparent to anyone who sees his paintings.

From 1825 to 1840, he received steady employment as an itinerant portrait painter, charging $4.00 for a large portrait of an adult, $1.50 for smaller ones of children. What makes these early portraits so good is his ability to lay bare not only the psychology of the subject but also the aspect of the human condition he sees in them. In his portrait of his grandmother, Elizabeth Billings (1825), for example, which also hangs in this museum, he gives us both a particular woman whose life has formed her features and a compelling study of old age.

The 1840s found him back in New York, where the daguerreotype was all but killing the demand for his work as a portrait artist. Now he turned to subject paintings. From this would come the *Historical Monument,* a huge canvas (9'3" by 13'1") that depicts nothing less than the history of the United States.

His purpose was to display the painting around the country, charging the public a fee to come and see it. The idea was not original with Field. Artists had done this for many years, and if the public liked the painting, the profits could be very rewarding. (Perhaps the most famous example extant today is John Vanderlyn's extraordinary tour de force, a panoramic view of the gardens of Versailles, now installed at the Metropolitan Museum in New York, where you stand on a platform in the middle of the gallery and turn 360 degrees as you "tour" the gardens.)

In Field's canvas the monument is a huge, low structure surmounted by ten towers, which are connected at the top by bridges on which you see steam engines. The purpose is to tell the history of the country from the founding of the Republic to the post–Civil War period. The whole is placed in a park in which you see visitors strolling about and, off to the right, soldiers marching by. So complex is the symbolism that Field wrote a "Descriptive Catalogue of the Historical Monument of the American Republic," which was published in 1876.

To give you some idea of what is involved, let me quote one descriptive passage from a brochure on Field published by the museum, with text by Kay Nichols: "The main theme of the painting is the conflict between the northern and southern states that culminated in the Civil War. The first and eighth towers represent the war and its aftermath. The towers on the left represent the southern states and the towers on the right show events from the history of the northern states. A cluster of columns rising from the base of the second tower is topped by a figure of Satan, indicating Field's attitude toward slavery. At the right on the base of the third tower a cluster of columns is surmounted by angels. Apparently, Field saw the events as a battle between good and evil, with God on the side of the northern states. The long inscription about the bible as a source of truth and righteousness appears on the base of the columns representing the north. The work reflects the artist's belief that the optimism of the early days of the Republic, despite the disillusionment of the Civil War, could be renewed if faith in religion was restored." And that is only a beginning! It's absolutely fascinating, a surreal vision long before surrealism existed. One final note: Apparently, Field hoped eventually to build the monument. If he had, the towers would have risen 500 feet in the air. (Telephone: 732-6092.)

The **George Walter Vincent Smith Art Museum** (c. 1895), located in a very pretty Italian Renaissance building with Tiffany glass windows, has a distinct personality thanks to Mr. Smith's rather eclectic collections of nineteenth-century American paintings and sculpture, Japanese arms and armor, and Oriental jades, porcelains, bronzes, and cloisonné. I find it fascinating in both its diversity and originality. Mr. Smith, I gather, was something of an eccentric, but his highly informed taste makes this museum both rewarding and intellectually stimulating. (Telephone: 733-4214.)

The third museum at the Quadrangle, a Colonial Revival building with, as you might expect, a copy of a Connecticut Valley door, is the **Connecticut Valley Historical Museum** (1927). Inside are period rooms, paintings, Connecticut Valley furniture, pewter, and silver, and a genealogy and history library, all relating to the Connecticut River Valley. (Telephone: 732-3080.) And the fourth museum is the **Springfield Science Museum** (c. 1899), which has African, Native American, dinosaur, and habitat halls, and special exhibitions, as well as a planetarium. (Telephone: 733-1194.) As for the **City Library,** it was funded by Andrew Carnegie and finished in 1912. The architect, by the way, was Edward L. Tilton, who also designed the Currier Gallery of Art in Manchester, N.H. (see page 101).

From here you should visit the nearby **Mattoon Street Historic District,** a rare example of an intact block of nineteenth-century row houses with, at the east end, Richardson's **North Congregational Church.** The **Maple Street Historic District** is notable for its Greek Revival and Second Empire homes. You can also drive around the **Springfield Armory National Historic Site**—the armory closed in 1968—and see the collection of military small arms, one of the world's largest. (Open: Daily. Free admission. Telephone: 734-8551.)

The **Court Square Historic District** is a grouping of several interesting and handsome buildings around a park. Facing the square is the Federal period **First Church of Christ** (1819), which has a very handsome and intact wood-frame exterior, but the interior was altered several times in the nineteenth-century and has been restored in this century. Just beyond the church is the **Hampden County Courthouse** (1871), another Richardson building, but so altered as to show very little of his hand. Diagonally opposite the square is the **Municipal Group,** which was completed in 1913 and consists of three buildings: City Hall (to the east) and Symphony Hall, with identical columned porticos, and an Italian Renaissance campanile, which has become a landmark of the town as people speed through on I-91.

The **Basketball Hall of Fame,** at 1150 West Columbus Avenue, will be of interest to anyone who has been even remotely connected with basketball. It was Dr. James Naismith who developed the game, because he wanted to provide a stimulating and exciting alternative to the standard—and boring— phys. ed. classes. And it was his Springfield College team that, in 1891, played the first game, using equipment that consisted of a ball and a fruit basket. Every time someone scored, someone else had to climb a ladder to retrieve the ball.

The exhibitions are imaginative, interesting, and fun. In addition to historic items there are several films, including a four-sided one that places you in the middle of a game; something called The Spalding Shoot-Out, which lets you try to score a basket through hoops of varying heights; life-size action blowups of members of the Hall of Fame; and video highlights of great games. Go, and have a really good time.

The Basketball Hall of Fame is open: Daily, 9–5, 9–6, July to Labor Day. Admission fee. Telephone: 781-6500.

Nearby Excursions from the Connecticut River Valley

Old Sturbridge Village   It would be pushing it a bit to say that this and Worcester (see page 184) are in the Connecticut River Valley, but they're too interesting to leave out.

Old Sturbridge Village, 30 miles east of Springfield on Route 20, is probably the most popular of the village-museum complexes mentioned in this book (Deerfield and Shelburne, Vt., are the others), and your heart may sink when you see the rows and rows of cars and buses. The easiest solution is to get there first thing when the museum opens, and then you can enjoy it before it becomes crowded. But I should add that the complex is big enough so that you should be able to see everything in comfort.

In any case, it's well worth the effort, for this creation, really, of a c. 1830 New England village of more than forty buildings has an individual vision—as do the other two—that gives it a unique appeal. Old Sturbridge Village originally was the creation of Albert and J. Cheney Wells, who bought farm buildings, shops, and houses to hold their collection of antiques; it was first opened to the public in 1946. Like the other two, it now is run by extremely capable, professional, and imaginative museum personnel. Here, as in Shelburne, you can wander through all the buildings as you wish, and the costumed interpreters, in this case going about the activities that the residents of the village would have performed, will tell you about what they are doing, or, if you prefer, leave you alone. In gen-

A view across the green in Old Sturbridge Village.

eral, I found their comments to be extremely interesting. In any case, there's much to see here and you will wish to spend a minimum of four to five hours. There are places to eat on the grounds. I should also point out that the setting itself is beautiful, adding enormously to your overall pleasure.

You enter through the Visitors' Center, where you can get a village map that includes specific activities, demonstrations, and performances on that day and other information. The center also offers temporary exhibitions of folk art and a splendid permanent exhibition of clocks in the **J. Cheney Wells Clock Gallery.** I would put off both until you have seen the village, but I would take time to watch the fifteen-minute slide presentation—note the wonderful shop signs hanging in the auditorium—that introduces you to the life of the period and generally orients you to what you will see.

From the Visitors' Center you will take the short walk to the Common, passing your first building, the **Friends (Quakers) Meeting House,** and then, at the head of the Common, finding the oldest building on the Common, the 1704 **Fenno House,** to your left and the lovely Greek Revival **Center Meeting House** directly ahead, with its graceful spire dominating the scene, and its gentle plain interior and clear glass windows setting the mood of rustic simplicity.

Next to the Fenno House is the **Fitch House** (c. 1790–1820), which has stenciled floors and is now furnished as the home of a country printer. Across the Common is a **Law Office** and the **Richardson Parsonage,** with some very attractive country furnishings. (The "parson," the time I last was there, had a guest, another "parson" from Maine. What I thought would be a tour of the house turned out to be a dialogue between the two men, and as both of them had a good sense of humor, what I at first feared might be a painful half hour turned out to be both funny and informative, the most memorable part of that particular visit.)

There is a **Tin Shop** where you can watch the tinsmith at work, the **Knight Store,** stocked with goods of the period, and, my favorite commercial building, the **Bank,** a modest Greek Revival building that's downright cozy.

At the end of the Common is the finest house (with a lovely garden, too) in the village, the Federal **Salem Towne House,** which has good examples of period furnishings and some lovely woodwork. On the second floor, the ballroom has scenes painted on the walls.

That gives you some idea of what you will see. Off the Common to the left of the Towne House there's also a **Cider Mill** and a **Printing Office,** and a wonderful **Herb Garden,** as well as a **Glass Exhibition** that not only has interesting examples of New England glass making but also has excellent sign-age. In the same area are other special exhibits on firearms, spinning and weaving, broom making, basket making, and lighting, with lighting devices from prehistoric times until well into the nineteenth century.

Certainly one of my favorite areas, though, is on the other side of the Common. Take the road to the left of the Friends Meeting House and go past the Town Pond, the District School, and the Pottery to the **Pliny Freeman Farm.** This is the most completely developed part of the village, and, to me, the most fun. Here you can watch the men and women at their seasonal farm tasks, cooking, caring for the animals, and so forth. It's done with a natural air that is delightful. I also like the nearby **Bixby House,** a simple dwelling that is an honest re-creation of how a working-class family—in this case a blacksmith— lived in the early nineteenth century. There's a vegetable garden out back, and the smith's shop is across the street. Then I like to walk down to the **Sawmill** and watch its 1830 patent waterwheel cut logs into lumber, and from there walk by the lovely mill pond and through the covered bridge over the Quinebaug River.

By the time you're ready to leave you will find that your mind has completely abandoned the twentieth century and that it takes a bit of time to come back to the present. That's when you should see the exhibitions in the Visitors' Center; it makes a gentle letdown before you visit the huge gift shop and go back out into the parking lot.

Old Sturbridge Village is open: May–October, daily, 9–5; November–April, Tuesday–Sunday, 10–4. Admission fee. Telephone: 508-347-3362. This museum also has a TDD/TTY number: 508-347-5386.

Worcester and Nearby   The second-largest city in Massachusetts—about 170,000 residents—and near the center of both the state and New England, Worcester, like Springfield, is an industrial center. Also like Springfield, it is a cultural center, home to twelve colleges, including Holy Cross and Clark University. An item of trivia for your collection: Worcester is the only major industrial city in this country not situated on a coast, a lake, or a river.

Worcester Art Museum   It is worth a special trip to visit this splendid major regional museum, which houses more than thirty thousand works of art, some from as early as 3000 B.C., in thirty-five galleries. I'll briefly sketch a little of what you can expect.

One of the most famous—and best-loved—American folk art paintings, *Mrs. Elizabeth Freake and Baby Mary, c. 1671–74,* is here, part of one of the best collections of American paintings in New England, which also has—you guessed it—two excellent canvases by our old friend Ralph Earl and splendid Homers and Stuarts and Copleys and Innesses and on and on. There is a Romanesque French Benedictine priory of the twelfth century, one of the first medieval structures to be brought to this country, and three glorious frescoes, c. 1300, from Spoleto, Italy. The photography collection has over two thousand images. The twentieth-century galleries contain examples of many of the greatest artists of our time. The European paintings galleries display masterpieces ranging from Piero di Cosimo and Andrea del Sarto to Canaletto and Fragonard to Goya and Turner, Cézanne and Monet, Braque and Kandinsky. This museum is a must if you are anywhere near the area.

The Worcester Art Museum, 55 Salisbury Street, is open: Tuesday, Wednesday, Friday, 11–4; Thursday, 11–8. Saturday, 10–5; Sunday, 1–5. Admission fee. There is a café and a museum shop. Telephone: 508-799-4406.

Fruitlands Museums   Not far from Worcester, on Prospect Hill Road in the town of Harvard, lies one of the more interesting small museums of nineteenth-century American art and history. Situated on 200 hillside acres, it also offers spectacular views over the Nashua River Valley to distant mountains, including Mount Monadnock and Mount Wachusett.

Fruitlands was opened to the public in 1914 by Miss Clara Endicott Sears, a member of the old and distinguished New England families of Endicott and Peabody—she was, for instance, descended from both Governor John Endicott, who arrived in 1628, and his successor, Governor John Winthrop, who landed in 1630.

In 1910 she came to Harvard and immediately fell in love with the setting and views. Near her property, at the bottom of the hill, was a derelict farmhouse that, in 1843, had been the site of a seven-month experiment in communal living under the leadership of Bronson Alcott. He, his wife, and four daughters (including Louisa May), and a small group of Transcendentalists had lived here, and they named it Fruitlands in the false expectation of an abundance of fruit from their new orchards—false because they had sited the orchards in a poor location. Miss Sears decided to buy the farmhouse and restore it to the period when Alcott was there and make it a museum honoring Alcott, Emerson, Thoreau, Margaret Fuller, and other leaders of the Transcendentalist movement. It is quite interesting to visit.

Next she became involved with the nearby Harvard Shaker Community, growing particularly close to one of the eldresses, and she watched with sadness as the community was forced to

Someday, no longer able to resist temptation, I will sneak onto the Fruitlands Museums' grounds after midnight and snatch away this most witty and delightful of all birdhouses.

close in 1918. They gave her their journals, and she bought their 1794 office building and placed it on her property. It opened in 1921 as the first Shaker museum in the United States. Today it is a small, appealing museum of Shaker handicrafts and furniture.

The American Indian Museum is the third of the Fruitlands museums. Miss Sears had found arrowheads on her property, and, she wrote, the discovery "fired a desire in me to gather all the relics together that I could unearth." The result is this collection of examples of the arts and industries of the North American Indians, as well as three dioramas—an Indian encampment in the Nashua Valley, the Sun Dance of the Plains Indians, and a depiction of the rescue of the Indian captive Mary Rowlandson in 1676. Outside the building are two lifesize bronze sculptures of Indians.

The fourth collection that Miss Sears established is the picture gallery, a rather delightful mixture of folk-art portraits—she was one of the first to recognize their artistic value—and Hudson River paintings, including such well-known artists as Bierstadt, Cole, and Cropsey.

Finally, there are two lovely trails through various habitats—red pine, white pine, and meadows—and there is a well-stocked museum store and a restaurant in Prospect House, across from the parking lot, where you can enjoy both lunch and the view.

Fruitlands Museums are open: mid-May to mid-October, Tuesday–Sunday, 10–5. Admission fee. Telehone: 508-456-9028.

WHERE TO STAY AND EAT

The Berkshire region offers an extraordinary selection of restaurants and accommodations; most pleasantly and conveniently, the two often are together. As for the Connecticut River Valley, the selection isn't on the same level, but you'll hardly suffer. As always, I have based my recommendations on comfort, attractiveness, and location. If a restaurant or inn is truly outstanding, it is listed under Best in the Region.

It's worth repeating that especially in the Berkshires, it's important to reserve in advance at the restaurants of your choice.

Where to Stay

THE BERKSHIRES

Area code: 413

As previously noted, the Berkshire region is small—about 45 miles north to south and about half that wide—and all the inns listed are within easy driving distance of anything you will wish to see. I have therefore listed them alphabetically rather than by the towns in which they are located.

Best in the Region: Blantyre, Lenox; Canyon Ranch, Lenox; Wheatleigh, Lenox

Blantyre, Box 995, Lenox 01240

This is the most elegant inn in the Berkshires. Its name comes from the name of a town in Scotland, and it is a huge, Tudor-style house built over two years (1901–1903) by Robert Warden Patterson. At its grandest it had 25 acres of lawn and

175 square feet of greenhouse space. Today, the estate has shrunk to a mere 90 acres with four tennis courts, two tournament-size croquet courts, a sauna and hot tub in a former potting shed, and a heated swimming pool. Dining here is an experience. The most expensive—and luxurious—double rooms are in the main house, those in the carriage house are somewhat more reasonable, while those in the two cottages on the grounds are the least expensive. $$$$$. Open: Mid-May through October. Telephone: 637-3556 (in winter, 298-3806). Credit cards.

Canyon Ranch at Bellefontaine, 91 Kemble Street, Lenox 01240

Another grand resort, this time a spa to end all spas, including the original in Arizona. First, the house: This white-marble-and-red-brick behemoth, originally a replica of the Petit Trianon, was built in 1897 by the eminent American firm of Carrere and Hastings, architects of the New York Public Library (which seems only slightly larger), for Giraud Foster, another New York multimillionaire. In 1949, the interior, with the exception of the library, was totally destroyed by fire, and the exterior has also been altered. Today the main house holds the dining room, consultation areas, and the restored library. The $45 million sunk into the estate has gone into a 120-room inn; exercise rooms; indoor and outdoor tennis, racquetball, and squash courts; a suspended indoor running track . . . and on and on and on. The spa owns 120 surrounding acres. The overall effect is that of the ultimate health and fitness resort—something that may or may not appeal to you, but I must say it's done to perfection. The food is excellent, but the dining room is restricted to guests. Double room: Package plans abound and I find the rate schedule harder to read than a train schedule, so call their 800 number for complete information: 800-742-9000. Open: All year. Credit cards.

Egremont Inn, Old Sheffield Road, South Egremont 01258

As I mention in the text on South Egremont, I like this little village and always enjoy exploring the shops, or even taking a longer, country walk out on Old Sheffield Road. That is why I recommend the Egremont Inn, for its location is perfect; it's just beyond the heart of the village. There is a pool and tennis court, and the rooms are comfortable, but it's the village that makes this so pleasant. $$$$$. Open: All year. Telephone: 528-2111. Credit cards.

Federal House, Main Street (Route 102), South Lee 01260

This lovely 1824 inn is small—only seven guest rooms and has been restored and furnished in excellent taste. As in so many of these inns, some of the rooms have fireplaces. Again, there is excellent dining here. $$$$. Open: All year. Telephone: 243-1824. Credit cards.

Gateways Inn, 71 Walker Street, Lenox 01240

Another Berkshires cottage, but this one refreshingly modest—by the standards of Bellefontaine and Blantyre, anyway. It was built by Harley Proctor (as in Proctor and Gamble) in 1912 and was called Orleton. Today this extremely pleasant small inn, with fireplaces in some of the rooms and an absolutely superb dining room downstairs, is ideal if you want quiet luxury and great food. $$$$$. Open: All year. Telephone: 637-2532. American Express only.

Le Jardin, 777 Cold Spring Road, Williamstown 01267

A modest farmhouse-type inn, relaxed and comfortable, with pretty grounds—the backyard has picnic tables, and there's a pond. There is an excellent dining room. $$$$. Open: April–December. Telephone: 458-8032. Credit cards.

The Orchards, 222 Adams Road, Williamstown 01267

You will not be surprised to hear that the site for this rather luxurious inn is a former apple orchard. It is modeled on English inns, and the owners have done an excellent job in providing for the creature comforts of their guests—some rooms have fireplaces, robes are supplied, some rooms have their own refrigerator, and so forth. $$$$$. Open: All year. Telephone: 458-9611. Credit cards.

The Red Lion Inn, Main Street, Stockbridge, 01262

This is the dean of all the Berkshire inns—my-great-grandmother used to stay here. In fact, it has been an inn since the eighteenth century, although the present building (108 rooms) has replaced the original, which burned in 1895. The inn is filled with antiques, the rooms are attractive, the service is pleasant, and the owners make every effort not only to maintain the inn but also to improve it. If you want a classic Berkshires weekend, stay here. My only caveat: It can be a little too popular and therefore can be noisy. My favorite feature: the porch, where you can sit and rock and watch life pass by. $$$$-$$$$$. Open: All year. Phone: 298-5545. Credit cards.

Wheatleigh, Box 824, Hawthorne Road, Lenox 01240
This cottage—yes, we have another one—was built in 1892–1893 for yet another rich New Yorker, Henry H. Cook, in the style of an Italian villa. It has a particularly appealing entrance courtyard with a fountain, and the entrance hall has two handsome Tiffany windows and an enormous fireplace. And so it goes, with the added—and important—bonus of a superb view out over the Stockbridge Bowl and, in the distance, the Berkshire hills. Several of the comfortable bedrooms have fireplaces, and the dining room is one of the best in the region. If you want elegance, but not so much as at Blantyre, this should be your choice. $$$$-$$$$$. Open: All year. Telephone: 637-0610. Credit cards.

Williamsville Inn, Route 41, West Stockbridge 01266
This is one of my favorite inns in the area. Small (nine attractively decorated rooms, two with fireplaces), well off the beaten track in a country setting, this 1797 inn can be summed up in one word: cozy. There are rooms in two cottages and in the old barn, but I prefer the main house. Again, there is a fine restaurant as well as a pool and tennis court. Get lost on some marvelous drives along the nearby side roads. $$$$. Open: All year. Telephone: 274-6118. Credit cards.

Windflower Inn, 684 South Egremont Road, Great Barrington 01230
I like this inn. It's comfortable and relaxed, attractively furnished without ostentation, and beautifully situated. Some of the bedrooms have fireplaces, too. There is a swimming

pool, and guests can use the country club across Route 23 for golf and tennis. For a quiet country weekend, this is ideal. $$$$$. Open: All year. Telephone: 528-2720; reservations, 800-992-1993. American Express only.

THE CONNECTICUT RIVER VALLEY

Area code: 413, except where noted

This region, too, is small, and distances between sites, with the exception of Sturbridge, are insignificant. Therefore, as in the section on the Berkshires, the inns are listed alphabetically. One note: The inns are not of the same quality as the best in the Berkshires.

Deerfield Inn, Main Street, Deerfield 01342
This would be my first choice of a place to stay in the region. Deerfield is the prettiest and most interesting village in the valley, and I also would give the edge to the inn itself for the best accommodations, as the rooms are attractively furnished and comfortable, and the surroundings are quiet. The public rooms, too, are intimate and pleasant. $$$$. Open: All year. Telephone: 774-5587. Credit cards.

Lord Jeffrey Inn, 30 Boltwood Avenue, Amherst 01002
The location is beautiful, on the common and surrounded by the handsome buildings of the village and college. The inn fits right in and is quite pretty. The common rooms are also pleasant, but the guest rooms are less than memorable, although comfortable enough. $$$–$$$$. Open: All year. Telephone: 253-2576. Credit cards.

Hotel Northampton, 36 King Street, Northampton 01060
This is about as close to dead center in the valley as you can get, and it is for that reason, and the fact that I like Northampton, that I list it. The rooms, the management notes, are filled with "antique collectibles," whatever that means, and are "tastefully finished with feather duvets and Laura Ashley linens and draperies." I have yet to decide which are the an-

tique collectibles, but the rooms are comfortable. Rates vary, but at the most expensive period, September–October, $$$$. Open: Year round. Telephone: 584-3100. Credit cards.

Publick House, Sturbridge 01566

Actually, this is two in one—the Publick House, which includes the inn and what the management calls a country lodge and I call a motel; and the Colonel Ebenezer Crafts Inn, two miles away in a 1786 house with six rooms. The Publick House is nondescript and the rooms are not very attractive, for the most part, but it is convenient to Old Sturbridge Village. The Ebenezer Crafts Inn, on the other hand, is much fancier, quieter, and more comfortable. In the Publick House, during the most expensive season, July–December, $$$$. In the Colonel Ebenezer Crafts Inn, $$$$$. Open: Year round. Telephone: 508-347-3313. Credit cards.

Swift River Inn, 151 South Street, Cummington 01026

This inn, a renovated nineteenth-century dairy farm set on 600 acres, is a sportsman's paradise. In the summer, it's for rock climbers, fly fishermen, and mountain bikers. In the winter, cross-country skiers take over, and classes and instructors are available for beginners. The public rooms and the bedrooms are pleasant and the service is warm and considerate. Double room: Packages are available, and special rates are available. Open: All year. Telephone: 634-5751. Credit cards.

Where to Eat

THE BERKSHIRES

Area code: 413

Best in the Region: Gateways Inn, Lenox; Wheatleigh, Lenox

Blantyre, Off Route 20, northwest of Lee. Open: Dinner, mid-May through November. Reservations required. $$$. Phone: 637-3556. Credit cards.

The restaurant here is so fancy that it borders on the pretentious. But never mind; the food and, especially, the wines make this one of the best places to dine in the region, and if you are celebrating a special occasion, this should be one of your top contenders. First you have your drinks and hors d'oeuvres in a reception area, often with live music in the background; then you select your dinner and wine before entering the paneled dining room. The three-course dinner is prix fixe. Coffee is served in the drawing room.

Castle Street Café, 10 Castle Street, Great Barrington. Open: Dinner. $$. Phone: 528-5244. Credit cards.

The chef, an escapee from New York, has made this a refreshingly good bistro whose menu is based on whatever local produce is available, backed by excellent breads, cheeses, and so forth. They make cassoulet here, one of my favorite dishes in the world, and it rates an A. But there are also Italian and American dishes, including a delicious apple crisp. Lively and fun, and there's a terrific bar at the back of the dining room.

Church Street Café, 69 Church Street, Lenox. Open: Lunch, dinner. $$. Phone: 637-2745. Credit cards.

I like this restaurant very much, for the ambiance, for the moderate prices, and for the consistently good food and pleasant service. I would call it creative American in style, with something of a Southern bias.

Federal House, Main Street, South Lee. Open: Dinner. $$$. Phone: 243-1824. Credit cards.

There are three dining rooms, all with handsomely appointed tables, and the food has what I call vigor. None of your bland sauces here—instead, a delicious horseradish-and-soy sauce for the seared yellowfin tuna, or a fresh peach chutney that avoids the cloying sweetness this condiment too often displays. Very good.

Gateways Inn, 71 Walker Street, Lenox. Open: Lunch (June–October), dinner. Reservations required. $$$. Phone: 637-2532. American Express only.

Like Blantyre, this is formal and elegant, but it is not quite so formal, and the food is better. Blantyre is the kind of place you would go to mark a special occasion; this is where you would go on the last night of a marvelous vacation.

Joe's Diner, 63 Center Street (Main and Center), Lee. Open: Breakfast, lunch, dinner. $. Telephone: 243-9756. No credit cards.

This is a *real* diner that offers everything, soup to nuts, at prices that also seem to come from another era. If you're in Lee and want a delicious meat-and-potatoes meal, head for Center Street and Joe's.

Le Jardin, 777 Cold Spring Road, Williamstown. Open: Dinner. $$. Telephone: 458-8032. No credit cards.

A good restaurant in an attractive setting with a standard, rather old-fashioned menu—when was the last time you saw frog's legs as a selection? On the whole, however, I prefer The Orchards (see below), even though it is more expensive.

The Old Mill, Route 23, South Egremont. Open: Dinner. $$$ Telephone: 528-1421. Credit cards.

The old mill in question is a restored 1797 grist mill, simply but imaginatively decorated, serving excellent food. Nothing fancy, mind you, just satisfying-to-the-soul good meals in an informal candlelit atmosphere.

The Orchards, 222 Adams Road, Williamstown. Open: Breakfast, lunch, Sunday brunch, dinner. $$$. Phone: 458-9611. Credit cards.

The best restaurant in the Williamstown area, and beautifully, even lavishly, appointed. Coffee and 4:00 P.M. tea are served upstairs in the inn's living room. Dinner here can become a special occasion.

The Red Lion Inn, Main Street, Stockbridge. Open: Breakfast, lunch, dinner. $$$. Telephone: 298-5545. Credit cards.

There are several places to eat here: *The Lion's Den,* downstairs, has entertainment nightly and also is a good, informal place for lunch, with hearty sandwiches and salads. Upstairs is the *formal dining room*—jackets are required—where the food is good, featuring such old favorites as chicken pot pie and roast turkey, steaks and chops. And outside, in the back, in a courtyard filled with flowers, is another eating area called the *Back of the Bank Bar.*

Village Inn, 16 Church Street, Lenox. Open: Breakfast, lunch, tea, dinner. $$$. Telephone: 637-0020. Credit cards.

I come here for one excellent reason: The Village Inn serves a real English tea from 2:30 to 4:30 each day—homemade scones with clotted cream, delicious finger sandwiches, a lovely selection of teas, and a dessert tray.

Wheatleigh, Hawthorne Road, Lenox. Open: Dinner. Reservations required. $$$. Phone: 637-0610. Credit cards.

If I were forced to choose the best restaurant in the Berkshires in terms of consistent quality and imaginative preparation, this would be it. For serious, extremely pleasurable dining in a lovely atmosphere and complemented by a brilliant wine list, go here.

Williamsville Inn, Route 41, West Stockbridge. Open: Dinner. $$$. Phone: 274-6118. Credit cards.

This is a very cozy place to eat, with a country view and a wonderful fireplace, and do be sure to save time for a drink in the tiny stenciled bar. As the inn is one of my favorite places to stay, the restaurant is one of my favorite places to eat.

Windflower Inn, Route 23, Great Barrington. Open: Dinner. Reservations required. $$$. Phone: 528-2720. American Express only.

This restaurant offers a choice of entrees and you must order by noon of the day you plan to go. I find this a major inconvenience, but if you're willing to put up with it, the results are very good—simple food cooked with a special flair. The duck and the salads—greens and vegetables are from their own garden—are particularly good.

THE CONNECTICUT RIVER VALLEY

Area code: 413 unless otherwise noted

Alas and alack, not an outstanding place to eat for love nor money.

Deerfield Inn, Main Street, Deerfield. Open: Breakfast, lunch, dinner. $$–$$$. Phone: 774-5587. Credit cards.
   As this is the only game in town, I am happy to say the food is fresh and reasonably good. There is also a coffee shop for snacks, and a garden just beyond.

Lord Jeffrey, 30 Boltwood Avenue, Amherst. Open: Breakfast, lunch, dinner. $$–$$$. Phone: 253-2576. Credit cards.
   Again, the only game in town, but here the food is only passable, and I would stick with simply prepared old standards. On the plus side, one dining room has a fireplace and both are attractive. In summer you can eat lunch outside on the terrace.

Hotel Northampton, 36 King Street. Open: Breakfast, lunch, dinner. $$–$$$. Telephone: 584-3100. Credit cards.
   The food here is adequate, and you might try the **Eastside Grill,** 19 Strong Avenue, phone 586-3347, which serves lunch from 11:30, dinner to 10:00 P.M., is good and reasonably priced, and offers food with a vaguely Cajun twist. Credit cards.

Publick House, Route 131, about 1 1/2 miles south of Exit 3 on the Mass. Turnpike. Open: Breakfast, lunch, dinner. $$–$$$. Phone: 508-347-3313. Credit cards.
   This restaurant is characterized by large portions of uninteresting food. What's good: the relish tray and the breads.

The Whistling Swan, 502 Main Street in Sturbridge, phone 508-347-2321, which is open for lunch from 11:30 A.M. to 2:30 P.M. and for dinner from 5:30 to 9:30, Saturday to 10:00, has a standard menu with the emphasis on seafood and steak. Upstairs, in the **Ugly Duckling,** which is open from 11:30 A.M.

to 11:00 P.M. (11:30 on Friday and Saturday), dining is more informal, and so is the menu. Both accept credit cards.

Swift River Inn, 151 South Street, Cummington. Open: Breakfast, lunch, dinner. $$–$$$. Phone: 634-5751. Credit cards.

The food is good, it's reasonably priced, and the portions are abundant. If you're in the area, try it. If you're staying here, you'll be perfectly content.

Connecticut

O<small>NLY</small> Rhode Island and Delaware are smaller than Connecticut—it could be contained in Texas fifty-three times over, I've been told. More specifically, it is only about 95 miles wide, from east to west, and 55 miles from north to south. It has roughly 3,300,000 residents, most of whom live along the coast or the navigable parts of its rivers, and its capital is Hartford, with just under 140,000 people.

For such a small state, Connecticut is extraordinarily diverse. The Connecticut River, for which it was named, divides it roughly in half, and its rich and fertile valley was what attracted colonists here in the first place. They created a valley culture that still resonates in our history.

Its coast, which lies mainly on Long Island Sound, is dotted with important urban centers—Stamford, Greenwich, Bridgeport, New Haven, New London—as well as small villages of great charm—Guilford, Madison, Essex, Old Lyme, Mystic, and Stonington come immediately to mind.

To the northeast and northwest the state is rural and extremely beautiful. The Litchfield Hills region, for example, is as lovely as its better-known sister just to the north, the Berkshire Hills of western Massachusetts, and is less developed and much less touristy. In southwestern Connecticut, which incorporates Greenwich, New Canaan, Ridgefield, and other wealthy communities, part of the area often called the Gold Coast, there are lovely villages, but they are essentially bedroom communities for New York City, and for me, they have little to do with what gives Connecticut the special characteristics that make it worth visiting.

In brief, Connecticut is a state that offers easily accessible diversions that range from country roads to sophisticated museums, from hiking in the state forests to basking on a beach along Long Island Sound, from exquisite New England greens to you-can-see-them-anywhere shopping malls.

Today, Connecticut, although deeply affected by the recession of the early nineties, maintains its position as first in the nation in terms of per capita income. Electrical and aerospace goods, chemicals, and machine tools provide it with a strong industrial base. Many corporate headquarters are here, too, such as those of Xerox and Union Carbide, and Hartford is still a major insurance center. Agriculture continues to play a major role; the broadleaf tobacco used for cigar wrappers is grown in the Farmington and Connecticut valleys, dairy farming and poultry and fruit raising also are prominent, and in recent years horse breeding has become popular.

Over my lifetime I have spent a great deal of time here, yet each time I return it offers me a new surprise. Perhaps that's why it occupies a place of such special affection in my heart.

History

On a spring day in 1614, Adrian Block, a Dutchman sailing from New York, became the first white man to sail up the Connecticut River. But it wasn't until 1633 that the first Dutch settlers established a trading post near what is now Hartford.

The English were not far behind, though, arriving two years later, attracted by the richness of the valley and the abundant supply of furs, fish, and timber. They rapidly displaced the Dutch, who left the area by 1654.

In 1636, the Reverend Thomas Hooker (1586?–1647) and his band of followers appeared on the scene—Mrs. Hooker came later, by litter—from the Massachusetts Bay Colony, where they had found the rule of the church leaders too conservative. Very quickly, settlers in the river towns of Hartford, Windsor, and Wethersfield began to govern themselves, and just as quickly Hooker stood out as their principal leader.

It was at this time that Hooker preached a sermon in which he outlined what he felt should be the form and purpose of government. This sermon has been recognized as a major step in the evolution of our national government, for it emphasized for the first time such doctrines as the people's right to elect their leaders and to restrict the powers of those they elect. In short, for the first time it was stated that authority lay with the people. By January 1639, this doctrine had been codified in a document known as "The Fundamental Orders of Connecticut," and nowhere in it can be found a mention of fealty to England, or to anyone else, for that matter.

One of the things I like best about New England houses is their add-on quality. Having another baby? Add a wing. Need a new kitchen? Stick it on the side. The results, somehow, are always delightful.

By the time Hooker died, in 1647, Hartford and the other river towns were prosperous. In 1662, Charles II, thanks to petitioner Governor John Winthrop, Jr., presented the Connecticut colony with an unusually generous charter that not only gave the colony legal standing but also recognized its self-government. (Winthrop was a particularly adept negotiator; one of his admirers said that he "noiselessly succeeded in all that he undertook.")

Then, in 1687, occurred one of the most famous events of the colonial period. James II, Charles II's brother and successor, decided that his brother had been far too generous to New England and that he would reassert the royal authority. To that end, he appointed Edmund Andros as his agent. Andros soon came to Hartford to take back the royal charter, which was placed on the table before him. A long debate ensued, drawing on into the darkening evening. Candles were brought, and the discussions were continuing, when suddenly the light was extinguished. When order was restored, the charter had disappeared, and it would stay hidden until William and Mary, in 1715, once again restored the rights of the Connecticut colony. And where had it been hidden? In a hollow of a great oak tree, ever after known as the Charter Oak, which survived until it was felled by a storm in 1856. There's a plaque to mark the spot on Charter Oak Avenue. (After its destruction, so many souvenirs were said to be made from the tree that Mark Twain, onetime resident of Hartford, commented that "a walking stick, dog collar, needle case, three-legged stool, bootjack, dinner table, tenpin alley, toothpick and enough Charter Oak [were all that was needed] to build a plank road from Hartford to Salt Lake City.") As for the charter, it and "The Fundamental Orders of Connecticut" are now housed at the Raymond E. Baldwin Museum in Hartford.

In the meantime, two other settlements had been made in what is today Connecticut: Saybrook, in 1635, and New Haven, in 1638. New Haven extended its authority over other Sound communities and set up an independent New Haven colony, but in 1662, Charles II essentially forced it to merge with the rest of Connecticut, and the state was established pretty much as we know it today.

Since then Connecticut has had a rather quiet history, developing from an agricultural state at the end of the Revolution into the highly complex industrial and financial center we know today.

For Information

The Connecticut Department of Economic Development, Tourism Division, 865 Brook Street, Rocky Hill, Conn. 06067, publishes a Vacation Guide and an excellent free map that includes information on public recreation facilities, state parks and forests, rail and airport facilities. It is invaluable. Telephone: 800-282-6863.

HARTFORD AND THE CENTRAL CONNECTICUT RIVER VALLEY

Hartford

In the eighteenth century Hartford's prosperity was primarily due to shipping, but as early as 1794 the industry began to appear that would dominate Hartford to the present day: insurance. In 1810, the Hartford Fire Insurance Company was founded. Today the city is home to more than thirty-five insurance companies. The reason for this growth is simple: The Hartford companies, from their earliest days, established an impeccable reputation for quickly honoring all justified claims. For example, after the famous fire of 1835 that destroyed hundreds of buildings, with losses the well-known diarist George Templeton Strong estimated at $30 million, a huge sum in those days, the president of the Hartford Fire Insurance Company went to New York to assure policyholders personally that claims would be honored and honored promptly. Business practices like this make the title Insurance Capital of the Nation seem thoroughly justified.

But insurance wasn't—and isn't—Hartford's only important business. Another was established in 1848, when Samuel Colt (1814–1862), inventor of the revolver, built a factory to produce it. The Colt would be made famous by General Zachary Taylor during the Mexican-American War. (The blue onion dome of the 1867 Colt Armory, topped with the statue of a colt, is visible from both I-84 and I-91 and must mystify many a driver.) His Italianate house, Armsmear, at 80 Wethersfield Avenue, was completed in 1857; now, with later additions, it is a rest home.

Hartford is a very handsome city. It has undergone a building renaissance that has brought it national attention through such projects as Constitution Plaza, an agglomeration of buildings set in the downtown area; the Hartford Civic Center; and **Travelers Tower,** Connecticut's tallest building, which has an observation deck offering extensive views of the city and the valley (Phone: 277-2431). But the city has not ignored its significant architectural history, much of which is described below.

The Wadsworth Atheneum   This alone is worth the trip to Hartford. New England is famous for the quality (and quantity) of its museums, but even in such distinguished company, the Atheneum stands out. It is one of the finest regional museums in the country and has long been included among my favorite institutions. It should be noted that its founding date in

1842, by Daniel Wadsworth, makes it the oldest public art museum in America. When it opened, it held seventy-eight paintings, one miniature, two marble busts, and a sculpture. *The Hartford Courant*—founded in 1764, it claims to be the oldest continuously published newspaper in the country—rhapsodized that the pictures alone were "an attraction probably unsurpassed by any similar collection in the country." And they were right. It is astounding what has happened on the museum scene in this country in 150 years.

Daniel Wadsworth was a descendant of settlers who had come to Hartford with Thomas Hooker. One of his ancestors hid Connecticut's charter in the Charter Oak. His father, Jeremiah, created a large fortune, and a portrait of father and son by John Trumbull is in the galleries. Nine years after the portrait was painted, Daniel married a niece of Trumbull, and the painter sparked Wadsworth's interest in art and introduced him to many contemporary artists, including Thomas Cole. It was Wadsworth, in fact, who prevailed upon Cole to take on his one and only apprentice, Frederic Church, who was born in Hartford.

But it isn't just the collections that make this museum so interesting; it's also the five buildings in which they are housed, and the fact that during an absolutely fascinating period of its history, from 1927 to 1944, the museum was headed by one of America's most creative museum directors, A. Everett (Chick) Austin, Jr. (1900–1957).

The buildings that compose the Atheneum cover a city block and deserve special recognition. The original one, and my favorite, was the result of a collaboration of two of the most famous architects of mid-nineteenth-century America, Alexander Jackson Davis (whose masterpiece is the magnificent Gothic Revival mansion of Lyndhurst in Tarrytown, N. Y.) and Ithiel Town. Their contribution is instantly recognizable as the massive creamy-beige granite Gothic Revival building (1844), complete with battlements and towers. Other buildings in the complex include the Colt Memorial, given by Samuel Colt's widow, one of the first great female patrons of the arts (1910); the 1910 Morgan Memorial (J. P. Morgan was a major benefactor); the Avery Memorial from 1934; and the most recent addition, the Goodwin Wing, completed in 1969. They work together amazingly well, forming an extremely interesting complex that you may well wish to examine before entering the interior.

As for Chick Austin, he was among the most fascinating museum directors this country has ever produced. His eye was impeccable, and some of the museum's greatest works of art entered the collections during his tenure: works by Cranach, Rubens, Caravaggio (he bought the first of this artist's works to enter an American collection), Claude, Poussin, Murillo, Salvator Rosa, and, from the twentieth century, the great surrealists Miró, Dalí, Ernst, Tanguy, and de Chirico, as well as Mondrian, Balthus, Picasso, and others.

But it is other aspects of Austin's diversified career that make him so absorbing. Just a few highlights: It was he who gave the world premiere at the Atheneum of the Virgil Thomson–Gertrude Stein opera *Four Saints in Three Acts,* one of this country's more important cultural events in the first half of the twentieth century, with its all-black cast (a first); its choreography by Frederick Ashton, in his American debut; its set incorporating hundreds of yards of cellophane; its direction by John Houseman, making his debut in the theater; and a libretto and score that have made the opera an abiding American masterpiece. And it was he who originally arranged to have George Balanchine create his ballet school and give performances in Hartford at the museum, although Balanchine almost immediately decided that he would rather be in New York than Hartford. His interests, obviously, took in many other art forms, and he was influential not only in music, dance, and painting but also in film, photography and theater. He made the Atheneum one of the most exciting museums in the country.

Fortunately, you can visit **Chick Austin's house,** at 130 Scarborough Street (one of Hartford's more conservative addresses), for it was given to the museum in 1985 by the Austin family. (Call the museum in advance for an appointment.) This truly extraordinary two-story building is a brilliant and witty Palladian "stage set," 86 feet in length and only 18 feet wide. George Gershwin, Lincoln Kirstein, Virgil Thomson, Aaron Copland, Gertrude Stein, Alexander Calder, Salvador Dalí, and many other great artists visited here. The interior, eclectic and fascinating, ranging from Rococo to Bauhaus to Art Deco, is much as it was when Austin built the house. It shouldn't be missed by anyone with an interest in architecture or, for that matter, by anyone who wishes to see the home of one of the more interesting minds and personalities of this century. In his autobiography Virgil Thomson gave the most penetrating summation of Austin's character: "He considered," Thomson wrote, "and said so, that a museum's purpose was to entertain its director." In so doing, he entertains us all.

The collections comprise 45,000 works of art that cover 5,000 years, but particularly strong are the American collections, both decorative arts and paintings; European decorative arts; and European paintings of the sixteenth, seventeenth, and nineteenth centuries. A few favorite paintings to give you an idea of the quality and variety: Church's *Vale of St. Thomas, Jamaica,* in which a storm, sweeping away to the left like a giant curtain, leaves a rising sun of gold and orange to outline the lush vegetation (this is one of a spectacular grouping of Hudson River works); Ralph Earl's splendid *Oliver Ellsworth and Abigail Wolcott Ellsworth,* whose subjects epitomize the rising American middle class in their bold, assured gaze and the prosperity they wear like a mantle (their home, depicted in the painting, is nearby and can be visited); the sensuously sinister and cynical *Nirvana* by Gaugin (from the Atheneum's major collection of nineteenth-century French masterpieces); the Sebastiano del Piombo *Portrait of a Man in Armor,* a depiction of the quintessential Renaissance soldier in which the artist almost brazenly displays his ability to use light and shadow; the Balthus *Bernese Hat,* a disturbing picture in which the enormous eyes of the model express a grave, almost hurt, intimacy—an image that will stay with you long after you have left the museum. . . . It is a collection to savor.

The **decorative arts** collections include J. P. Morgan's brilliant legacy of over 1,000 objects, among them ancient bronzes, Italian Renaissance majolica, baroque ivory and silver-gilt pieces, and eighteenth-century porcelains; textiles from the sixteenth century to today; and a superb collection of English and American silver. As for furniture, one of the stars of the extensive collection is the early colonial Wallace Nutting

Collection, given by J. P. Morgan, Jr., and some superb examples of later eighteenth-century American pieces.

The Wadsworth Atheneum, 600 Main Street, is open: Tuesday–Sunday, 11–5. Admission fee. There is an excellent gift shop and a pleasant museum café, with outdoor seating in the summer. Telephone: 278-2670.

The Mark Twain House and the Harriet Beecher Stowe House

These two houses are located quite close to each other in a 140-acre area called Nook Farm, so called because the houses are in a woodland nook. They are interesting to visit as much for what they say about their most famous residents as for the buildings and furnishings themselves.

Samuel Clemens (1835–1910), alias Mark Twain, bought his lot at Nook Farm in 1873, after deciding that Hartford was one of the most beautiful cities he knew—"a vision of refreshing green," he called it. He lived here until 1891, years during which he wrote *The Adventures of Tom Sawyer, The Adventures of Huckleberry Finn, The Prince and the Pauper,* and four other works.

He first came to Hartford in 1868 to bring a manuscript to Elisha Bliss, the head of the American Publishing Company. (It was thanks to this company that Hartford became something of a publishing center.) Bliss agreed to publish Twain's manuscript, *The Innocents Abroad.*

When Twain decided to build a house in Hartford, Nook Farm was a natural choice as it already had an established literary community, which included Harriet Beecher Stowe. Twain hired a local architect, Edward Tuckerman Potter, to build his house for the enormous sum of $100,000, and the result was hailed as "one of the oddest-looking buildings in the state." Said another critic in reference to the house: "American humor had never found its full expression except in architecture."

What Potter did, it sometimes seems, was everything he could think of. The flamboyantly High Victorian exterior has vermilion-and-black brick bands and intricate wooden stickwork. The slate roof is done in a diamond pattern in three colors. The house has a veranda, seven balconies, and three bays, a semidetached kitchen wing, and prominent gables. It all hangs together and is really a very sophisticated design, but even for High Victorian, it goes awfully far. Twain, although he was never really involved in the general design of the house, seems to have been extremely pleased with the results.

The interiors are fascinating. The house is large—there are 19 rooms—and is filled with ornamentation and color and the obvious expenditure of a great deal of money. Louis Comfort Tiffany and other designers redid the first-floor interiors in 1881, and you see silver stenciling and colored glass, carved woodwork, oriental rugs, and splendid wall coverings. *Sybaritic* is too conservative a term; Twain referred to it as a "delicious dream of harmonious color [with an] all-pervading spirit of peace and serenity and deep contentments."

A few items of trivia: Twain's bed had such an elaborately carved headboard that he slept with his head to the foot of the bed so that he could see the headboard when he awoke; he loved gadgets and had the first telephone in Hartford; his dressing room was designed to look like a Mississippi riverboat wheelhouse; he set a window over his fireplace in order to see flames and snowflakes at the same time. How sad that after all the pleasure he took here he would be forced to move because unwise investments left him unable to afford the maintenance.

Fortunately for us, the house has been brilliantly restored. It is a unique piece of Americana and makes a breathtaking contrast to the nearby Stowe house, which was built in 1871 and purchased by Harriet Beecher Stowe in 1873. This simple Victorian cottage, with a central hall, a parlor on the north and a dining room on the south, is both homey and homely. Its primary interest lies in the Stowe memorabilia, including her own paintings.

Guided tours to the Twain and Stowe houses are available at their respective Visitors' Centers, at 351 Farmington Ave. and 77 Forest St. Both houses are open: Daily, June–Columbus Day and the month of December; closed Monday (the Stowe house) and Tuesday (the Twain House) the rest of the year. Telephone: (Stowe) 525-9317, (Twain) 493-6441 or 247-0998. A word about the Stowe Visitors' Center: This very handsome Queen Anne house (1884) also contains the Stowe-Day Library, which "focuses on the architecture, decorative arts, history, literature and woman suffrage movement of the nineteenth century." Both houses charge admission fees.

State Capitol   This Gothic Revival fantasy is the work of none other than Richard Upjohn (1802–1878), whose most famous building is Trinity Church in New York City. The only High Victorian Gothic state capital in America, it was completed in 1879 at a cost of $2.5 million. It was completely restored between 1979 and 1989 for about $40 million. Outside, it's all turrets and gables and porches and towers, topped by a gold-leaf dome. Inside, brilliant painted columns, stenciling, colored glass, white and colored marble, red slate floors, and brass create a brilliant effect. There are two rather strange artifacts in the Hall of Flags just beyond the west arcade. The first is Lafayette's bedstead, the second Israel Putnam's tombstone. I really don't want to know how they got here. I'd rather speculate.

The whole is quite extraordinary; Frank Lloyd Wright supposedly called it "the most ridiculous building I know of," which it may well be, but it's also dazzling in its own way, and I can't imagine anyone not enjoying a visit.

The State Capitol, 210 Capitol Avenue, offers guided tours and is open: February to mid-November, Monday–Friday. Free admission. Telephone: 240-0222.

Old State House   This handsome, elegant Federal-style building was completed in 1796, the first major public building to rise in the Connecticut Valley after the Revolution. It was designed by Charles Bulfinch (1763–1844), our first native-born architect, who also designed the Massachusetts State House and the Maine State House and was involved in the completion of the United States Capitol. His use of a dome and frontal columns has influenced almost every capitol building throughout the country, and his work in Boston made it the most beautiful city of its time in the United States. Connecticut's Old State House can be visited and houses a tourist information center on the ground floor and, on the second floor, the restored Senate chamber.

The Old State House, 800 Main Street, is open: Daily. Free admission. Telephone: 522-6766.

The Surrounding Area

Those are the most interesting aspects of Hartford itself. What is too little known is that in the surrounding countryside there are beautiful towns with fascinating architecture, a museum of American art that ranks among the best collections in the country, and other unusual and unique sites. You will be constantly—and pleasantly—surprised to discover that a great deal of America's history is here, and making Hartford your headquarters for a few days of sightseeing will be extremely rewarding. Below, then, in alphabetical order, are descriptions of the most interesting of these easy-to-visit locations.

Farmington and Avon   Farmington, one of the loveliest suburbs in New England, is exquisite in a way that only great quantities of money can create. Come here and spend time walking and driving about the village and enjoying the perfectly restored eighteenth- and nineteenth-century homes. And be sure to note the First Church of Christ Meeting House (1771). It has been greatly altered since its original construction, but it is still an especially handsome building.

There also are two splendid house museums that in themselves are worth a trip.

Avon Old Farms School has a unique and fascinating campus that was designed by Theodate Pope Riddle in the English Cotswolds tradition. Well worth visiting.

Hill-Stead Museum is of interest for several reasons. The inviting Colonial Revival house (1901, with a later addition) was designed by McKim, Mead, and White with the active participation of the daughter of the owner, Theodate Pope Riddle, who was one of the first important female architects this country produced. (She also was responsible for Avon Old Farms School—see below.) The house is set on 150 acres of grounds. Beatrix Jones Farrand, a niece of Edith Wharton (see page 141) and one of the greatest landscape architects this country has produced, designed the Sunken Garden (post 1916), which was restored in 1986.

It is the interior, though, that makes this a house to visit. Among the comfortable furnishings and very fine European and Oriental decorative arts brought together by Theodate's father, Alfred Atmore Pope, is a **collection of paintings** that includes superior examples of Manet, Monet, Whistler, Cassatt, and Degas. Mr. Pope was one of the first American collectors of French Impressionist paintings, and it becomes increasingly clear as you look at his collection that he had a very fine eye. Visiting here is as relaxed and pleasant an experience as anything I can think of.

The Hill-Stead Museum, at 35 Mountain Road, is open: Year-round, Tuesday–Sunday. Because hours are limited, it is a good idea to phone ahead: 677-9064. Admission fee.

From the museum you should go to see Mrs. Riddle's most important contribution as an architect, the nearby **Avon Old Farms School,** a boys' prep school set on 1,000 acres. She began to buy the land in 1913, construction began in 1921 (by 1925 more than 500 workmen, many of them craftsmen imported from England, were at work on the campus), and by 1930 it was essentially finished. Her inspiration came from England's Cotswolds; she insisted that traditional sixteenth-century tools be used and she forbade the use of levels and straight edges. (Her one stylistic exception was the campus bank, which is Greek Revival.) The result is one of this country's more unusual and lovely campuses.

The **Stanley-Whitman House** (c. 1720) was the first building in Connecticut to be designated a National Historic

Landmark. It has been painstakingly restored and is, in construction and detail—notably the overhang created by a second floor larger than the first—something of a throwback to the Jacobean and Elizabethan periods. That is certainly one of the reasons that for many years it was thought to have been built c. 1660. Great care was taken to establish accuracy in the restoration and in the seventeenth- and eighteenth-century furnishings. For example, in deciding how to furnish the kitchen and the room above it, an analysis was undertaken of twenty-nine Farmington inventories done for probate between 1725 and 1735; there existed as well a listing of possessions that belonged to the wife of the 1725 owner—an extraordinary piece of research.

The Stanley-Whitman House, at 37 High Street, is open: May–October, Wednesday–Sunday; March–April and November–December, Sunday. Admission fee. Hours are variable, and it is a good idea to call in advance: 677-9222.

Granby   Granby, a major center of tobacco production, has a significant curiosity, Old New-Gate Prison and Copper Mine in East Granby.

Copper was discovered in East Granby in 1707, but by the time of the Revolution the owners of the mine had run into financial problems, and sold it to the colonial government. It was converted to a prison, first for ordinary criminals and then for native Tories and American military prisoners. Later it served as a state prison, until it was closed in 1827.

Today the ruins—picturesque—can be visited, as can the mine tunnels—gruesome—where prisoners were forced to sleep. You will gain a perspective on the country's early days that is quite different from the ordinary. You might carry a sweater; temperatures are considerably lower in the tunnels.

Old New-Gate Prison and Copper Mine is on Newgate Road, which is off Route 20 East. It is open: Mid-May to October, Wednesday–Sunday, 10:00–4:30. Admission fee. Telephone: 653-3563.

Middletown   Settled in 1650 at a great bend on the Connecticut River, the town received its name because it is halfway between Hartford and Old Saybrook. It achieved its greatest prosperity in the latter part of the eighteenth century—from about 1750 to 1800 it was Connecticut's richest town—thanks to its trade with the West Indies and the fact that it was a shipbuilding center. Middletown is the home of **Wesleyan University,** which was established by the Methodists in 1831 but was always a nonsectarian institution. And it is the campus of Wesleyan that one visits today, to see two unusually magnificent houses.

The first is the **Samuel Russell House** (1829) on High Street, a large and splendid Greek Revival house that once dominated the village below it.

Samuel Russell was a shipowner, as were his father and grandfather before him. His firm, Russell and Company, was one of the most successful and famous in the China trade, and several of its clippers set world speed records.

It was while he was away in China that his wife built this house. He had originally sent plans for a rather modest home. She hired Ithiel Town, one of the most famous architects of the day, who used Corinthian columns that had been intended for a bank in New Haven that failed, bought black marble mantels, imported glass from Hamburg, and chose the most elegant hardware. Eventually, the house contained 42 rooms. Samuel must have been amazed as he sailed up the Connecticut to see this splendid Greek temple that was his home.

The other house, also on High Street but on the other side, is one of the most elegant houses in this part of New England. (Interestingly, Samuel Russell superintended the construction of this house as the owner, a friend, was living in Philadelphia.) It is the Greco-Italian **Richard Alsop IV House** (1840). You can't miss it—you will see the exterior frescoes on the veranda facing High Street. The interior is glorious—do note the staircase and detailing, and the exquisite frescoes throughout. Unfortunately, no one knows anything about the artist who did them. My favorite rooms are the conservatory and the morning room, which is delicately painted with ravishing birds and flowers.

It is worth a special trip to see these two houses; because they are part of the university, it is wise to call ahead to make sure they will be open: 347-9411.

Also of interest on the campus, and easily accessible from

High Street, is the Center for the Arts (1973), designed by Kevin Roche/John Dinkeloo & Associates.

New Britain   Known as Hardware City because of the farm tools, locks, and builders' hardware it once produced, this is not, as you might have guessed, the garden spot of New England, although the 90-acre Walnut Hill Park, designed by Frederick Law Olmsted, is a splendid oasis.

It is here, in a relatively nondescript stone house overlooking the park, that you find what New Britain does have that makes a visit worthwhile: the **New Britain Museum of American Art,** a collection of more than 5,000 works by American artists from 1740 to the present. One of the finest American art collections in the country, it is, in a word, wonderful. There are first-rate works by artists ranging from Benjamin West, Gilbert Stuart, and John Singleton Copley to Albert Bierstadt, Winslow Homer, John Singer Sargent, and George Inness, to Edward Hopper, George Tooker, Marsden Hartley, Charles Demuth, Romare Bearden, Jacob Lawrence, Sam Francis, Thomas Hart Benton . . . and that is only the beginning.

Because it is in a house, with unobtrusive gallery additions, the museum has great charm and a sense of intimacy that larger, better-known collections lack—at the entrance, for example, a grandfather clock chimes on the quarter hour. Viewing the art is an exceptionally pleasant experience. Some of my favorites: the five Thomas Hart Benton murals, *The Arts of Life in America,* teeming with angular muscularity; the Eastman Johnson *Hollyhocks,* a rather extraordinary genre painting of women in an enclosed garden that constricts them in an almost unpleasant way, so that they seem just as artificially cultivated and groomed as the plants they admire; a stunning early Georgia O'Keeffe, *The East River from the Thirtieth Story of the Shelton Hotel;* George Tooker's *The Bird Watchers,* with its surreal overtones of a medieval scene at the foot of the cross; and Edward Hopper's sublime *Monhegan Island.*

In addition, a gallery on the second floor of the museum displays part of the Sanford B. D. Low Memorial Illustration Collection, which consists of over 1,400 works covering the history of American illustration from the nineteenth century to the present. It is the first such collection in a museum, and when I was there last, the artists on view included N. C. Wyeth, Norman Rockwell, John Held, Jr., Howard Pyle, and Steven Dohanos. Every single one of us will have some association with at least one of the works on view, whether it be from *Treasure Island* or *The Saturday Evening Post* or any one of a dozen other remembered joys of life. It is a delight to visit.

I cannot stress enough, then, that anyone interested in painting and art in America must come here. Everyone will gain pleasure from the collection.

The New Britain Museum of American Art, at 56 Lexington Street, is open: Year-round, Tuesday–Sunday, 1–5. Free admission. There is a pleasant, small shop and a museum library. Telephone: 229-0257.

Suffield Suffield is in what is left of the Connecticut tobacco country. The area is called Tobacco Valley, and the crop has been grown here since the mid-seventeenth century. The first cigar factory in the country opened in 1810 in West Suffield, and many of the houses along Main Street in Suffield itself

We've all seen beautiful houses, but surely a carriage house as elegant as this one in the lovely "shaded, cool oasis" of Suffield deserves a special mention.

were built with tobacco money. Today, the tobacco grown is the broadleaf variety that is used to wrap cigars. The netting that you see above the plants is part of the effort to duplicate the temperature and humidity of the tropics, where the plant originated.

But back to the village. I once read a description of it that called it a "shaded, cool oasis in the midst of wide stretches of reddish, fertile loams," and that is exactly what it is. It was founded in 1670, and Main Street (then called High Street) was laid out in that year. Everything went along just fine in this pretty New England town until the 1960s, when redevelopment, that curse of the time, began to tear down some of the better buildings. As a result, the Main Street Historic District was established in 1963 to protect the important heritage of the village, and now it is listed on the National Register of Historic Places.

The entire village is worth an extended stroll, and there is an excellent brochure, "A Tour on Main Street," that takes you on a 1 1/2-mile circuit. It is available throughout the village and describes succinctly and well the houses and buildings that you will see.

The most interesting house by far is the **Hatheway House,** which has been called the "most important pre-1820 dwelling standing in the Connecticut Valley today." It is another of those extraordinary buildings that contain a unique surprise.

The main structure was built in 1761, but it was extended and remodeled in 1794. Today this handsome, white clapboard Federal house with its central chimney, gambrel roof, and elegant proportions, has finely restored interiors with good examples of eighteenth-century furniture, paintings, and the decorative arts. Of particular interest is the north wing, added in 1794, which includes a stair hall and formal dining room with lovely Federal-period decoration. The surprise is a collection of exquisite eighteenth-century French wallpapers in the entrance hall and second-floor hall, bedchambers, and sitting room. The wallpaper in the entrance hall, Pompeian in inspiration, is as brilliantly colored today as on the day it was hung. The overall effect is oddly exhilarating. The Hatheway House is located at 55 South Main St. and is open: Wednesday,

Saturday and Sunday, 1–4. Admission fee. Telephone: 668-0055.

The King House Museum   Built in 1764, this house, now the museum of the Suffield Historical Society, has some good examples of period furniture, decorative arts (including a nice collection of Bennington pottery, bottles, and Civil War surgical instruments), and paneling, as well as a gallery of local tobacco and cigar memorabilia. It is located at 232 South Main Street and is open: May–September, Wednesday and Saturday, 1–4. Admission fee. Telephone: 668-7256.

Wethersfield   In 1634, ten followers of Thomas Hooker settled on land that now is part of Wethersfield. With Windsor and Hartford, it was one of the three original towns of Connecticut, and in the seventeenth and early eighteenth centuries, this town, only 40 miles from Long Island Sound, was the center of commerce for the Connecticut River Valley. When floods changed the course of the river, its trade declined and farming replaced trade as the center of the economy. (Red onions from Wethersfield were produced in such profusion and enjoyed such a good reputation that it became known as the land of onions. You can still pick up a packet of red onion seeds from Comstock, Ferre & Co., the oldest continuously operating seed company in the United States.) Good news for us, for the lack of industrial development meant that there was no need to destroy the early buildings, and the Wethersfield of today still contains roughly 150 buildings that date from before 1850. Consequently, it is a village of great charm and an unusually accurate window into the past, and you can easily spend a half day here.

For an overall feel of the village, begin on **Main Street,** enjoying the beauty of the place. The excellent brochure "A Tour of the Old Village," available from the Webb-Deane-Stevens Museum (see page 220) and the Wethersfield Historical Society, will give you some idea of the history of the buildings you will see. Stop first at the brick **First Church of Christ,** built between 1761 and 1764, with its lovely belfry and slender spire. It is one of the earliest and finest brick churches in New

England, and both George Washington and John Adams worshiped here. Inside, the church has been sensitively restored and is worth seeing. (Telephone: 529-1575.) You also may wish to examine the graveyard, known as the Ancient Burying Ground, the resting place of many of the earliest settlers—the oldest stone is dated 1648. (I also like Trinity Episcopal Church at 300 Main, a charming Gothic Revival building with some very pretty Tiffany windows.)

Next, visit Cove Park, which was originally a bend in the Connecticut River and the site from which the ships sailed that brought the town its original prosperity. A flood in 1692 changed the course of the river and created the cove. Here you will find the **Cove Warehouse,** built in the 1690s. It is the only one of its kind from the seventeenth century remaining in this country. Cared for by the town and the historical society, it is currently not open to the public.

Now you are ready for lengthier visits to special buildings in the town that are open to the public.

The Webb-Deane-Stevens Museum   This is a grouping of three houses from the mid-eighteenth century to the early nineteenth. But before beginning your tour here, look across the street to 212 Main, the brick **Hurlbut-Dunham House,** a particular favorite of mine. It was built in 1804 by a captain whose ship was the first from Connecticut to sail around the world, in 1796. About 1860, Italianate features—a piazza, portico, and belvedere—were added to the Federal structure in such a sensitive manner that the whole has great charm and individuality. It now is owned by the Wethersfield Historical Society.

Now back to the business at hand. I should point out at once that the most painstaking care has been taken in restoring these houses, ranging from intensive study of the paints used on the interiors to examination of probate records of the time to ensure that furnishings are accurate. The result is a fascinating look at three families in an eighteenth-century Connecticut River Valley town and how they saw themselves in their time and their society.

The earliest building in this grouping is the Georgian **Joseph Webb House,** built in 1752 and distinguished by its handsome gambrel roof. This is the house of a rich man of the period; indeed, the Webbs, father and son, were not only successful but also very hospitable. This is one of the places in which George Washington really did sleep, in May 1781, and the red wool-flock wallpaper in the bedroom in which he stayed remains there today. (Washington was in Wethersfield to meet with the commander of the French forces, the Count de Rochambeau.) The house is handsomely furnished and displays some Webb family pieces and pieces from other families in the area. Behind the house is a handsome Colonial Revival formal garden.

When Joseph Webb, Sr., died in 1761, he left his affairs in some disarray, and his widow, Mehitable Nett Webb, went for help to Silas Deane, a Yale graduate who would later achieve fame in the Revolution, first as a negotiator with the French and then as a falsely accused profiteer. She married him two years later, and Deane built the **Silas Deane House** next door to her original home. It has an unusual exterior for its time; an off-center entrance door leads into an unusually wide hall, which sets the mood of spaciousness that is the hallmark of this house. The elegantly turned balusters of the staircase, the paneling of the front parlor, and the oversize (12 over 12) windows give this house a quiet, rich elegance that is matched by its furnishings.

The third house, the **Isaac Stevens House,** is a conservative Georgian building completed in 1788. This house is distinguished by the fact that when it was taken over by the Colonial Dames, they also received the possessions that the family had accumulated over almost two hundred years. Stevens was a leather tanner and saddler, and his house lacks the rich sophistication of the other two. It shows how a middle-class family lived at the time, which makes it an extremely interesting point of comparison.

The Webb-Deane-Stevens Museum, at 211 Main Street, is open: May–October, Wednesday–Monday, 10–4; November–April, Saturday–Sunday, 10–4. Admission fee. Telephone: 529-0612.

The Buttolph-Williams House (c. 1720), with its overhanging second story supported by brackets, cedar-shingled roof, and small, diamond-paned casement windows, is typical of its time. It has been called the most faithful restoration in Connecticut of a house of this period.

The interior features a hall-and-parlor plan, with a narrow entryway allowing only 4 1/2 feet between the door and the stairs. The rooms are furnished as they would have been in the late seventeenth century, and the furniture, tools, and other decorative objects are first-rate examples of their period. The house, then, is fascinating to visit not only because it is a relative rarity but also because it has been extremely sensitively restored.

The Buttolph-Williams House is at 249 Broad Street. It is open: Mid-May to mid-October, Tuesday–Sunday, 12–4. Admission fee. Telephone: 247-8996.

Nearby, in **Rocky Hill,** the chief port for Wethersfield after the river changed its course, is **Dinosaur State Park,** a 70-acre area with 2,000 dinosaur tracks made in the mudflats that existed about 200 million years ago. A geodesic dome has been set up over parts of the area to protect the tracks. Open: Daily, except Monday. Admission fee. Telephone: 529-8423.

Windsor   Windsor, founded in 1633, vies with Wethersfield for the title of oldest permanent English settlement in Connecticut. Today it is more a suburb of Hartford than an independent town, but it still has enough of its original flavor to remain distinct.

It was established as a trading post at the mouth of the Farmington River by a group from the Plymouth Colony, who had brought with them the frame of a building that they could immediately put up for habitation.

In 1637, a "Pallizado" was built—a stockade fort strong enough to withstand any attack from the Indians. Today, there is a walking tour of the area—the brochure guide is available from the Windsor Historical Society at 96 Palisado Avenue— that includes such sights as the First Church in Windsor, built in 1794 but remodeled in 1844 to a classic Georgian structure (the key is at the church office, 107 Palisado Avenue, telephone: 688-7229), the Old Burying Ground, several eighteenth- and nineteenth-century houses, and the green.

On this tour you can see the 1640 **Fyler House** and the 1765 **Chaffee House,** part of the Windsor Historical Society. The Fyler House is one of the oldest surviving frame houses in Connecticut; the earliest part was built before 1640. It is owned and operated by the Windsor Historical Society, which saved it from becoming a gas station in 1925. Both houses have been restored and are filled with period furnishings. The museum, connected to the Fyler House, displays artifacts from the colonial period and a genealogical and historical research library.

The Windsor Historical Society is open: April through November, Tuesday–Saturday, 10–4, December through March, Monday–Friday. Admission fee. Telephone: 688-3813.

The real purpose of coming to Windsor, though, is to see the **Oliver Ellsworth Homestead** (1781). Oliver Ellsworth (1745–1807) was a member of the Continental Congress and a framer of the Constitution; he served as Connecticut's first senator, drafted a bill organizing the federal judiciary system, and was appointed by Washington to be the third Chief Justice of the U.S. Supreme Court. As if that weren't enough, he was appointed Envoy Extraordinary to Paris, where he successfully negotiated a treaty with Napoleon, who liked him well enough to give him a Gobelin tapestry that still hangs in the house. He was the wealthiest man in Connecticut by the end of the Revolution, and his house, still filled with many of his possessions, reflects his splendor.

The Wadsworth Atheneum has a monumental and magnificent portrait of him and his wife, Abigail, painted by Ralph Earl in 1792. There they sit, absolutely self-assured, in the Palladian-style office-parlor. He is holding a copy of the Constitution. Their house (illogically enough, as they're sitting in one of its rooms) can be seen through an open window, surrounded by thirteen elms Ellsworth planted to commemorate the original thirteen states. These are proud republicans, boldly representative of the nascent power and wealth of their new country.

The Oliver Ellsworth Homestead is open: May 15–October 15, Tuesday–Saturday, 1–5. Admission fee. Telephone: 688-8717.

Woodstock   This quiet rural town on Route 171 in the northeastern part of the state is the farthest from Hartford and is surrounded by lovely rolling countryside. It has a particularly lush village green and the usual lovely New England houses, but what makes it special is **Roseland Cottage,** on the main street, a joyous Gothic Revival, board-and-batten building, bright pink and multigabled, in delightful contrast to its prim New England village neighbors. Its trellis work, bays, fleur-de-lis crests, chimney pots, and other features make the exterior a study in itself, one you will want to spend some time examining.

It was built in 1846 for Henry C. Bowen of Brooklyn, N.Y., as a summer residence and is the central building of a group that includes a barn with one of the oldest surviving indoor bowling alleys in this country and a beautiful Victorian boxwood parterre garden, the only one in New England, which was originally laid out in 1850. It was designed by Joseph C. Wells, but in every aspect it was heavily influenced by the theories of Andrew Jackson Downing; because it is virtually intact, it is one of the best-preserved examples of Downing's ideas about buildings, furnishings, and grounds.

The interior retains its original Gothic Revival furnishings, and the painted glass windows (made by a process very different from staining), as well as the Lincrusta wall coverings (Lincrusta, invented by Frederick Walton, who also invented linoleum, is a thick and embossed wall covering that imitates leather) in three of the rooms done in 1880, make this an unusually complete and interesting period house.

One final note: Mr. Bowen gave extravagant July 4 celebrations, accompanied by fireworks, speeches, and parties. Four presidents—Grant, Hayes, Harrison, and McKinley—were his guests at these events. President Grant bowled a strike with his first ball and then retired to the outdoors to enjoy his cheroot.

Roseland Cottage is open: Memorial Day weekend to Labor Day weekend, Wednesday–Sunday, 12–5; Labor Day weekend to mid-October, Friday–Sunday, 12–5. Admission fee. Telephone: 928-4074.

THE CONNECTICUT SHORE

FROM STONINGTON TO NEW HAVEN

The Connecticut shoreline is very different from the other sections of the state. From the beginning, this was a seafaring area, and with the exceptions of New London and New Haven, industrialization passed it by. Then, after the Civil War, when sailing vessels began to disappear and whaling faded into a memory, the towns remained intact, sleepy little villages time seemingly passed by.

Today, though, the beauty and rich heritage of the Connecticut shoreline has been rediscovered, and weekenders, retirees, and tourists have brought a new kind of prosperity to the area.

Stonington and Mystic

Stonington is one of the prettiest villages on the Connecticut coastline and one of the few that is far enough east to be on the Atlantic Ocean. It's always been a maritime center; a ship from here, the *Betsy*, was the first ship flying the American flag to circle the globe, and the town was known as a nursery for seamen. At first, it was a center for whaling and sealing and shipbuilding. Today, it is an active fishing village and a favorite weekend and summer resort. After the crowds of Mystic, it is extremely pleasant to come here and wander on the lovely old streets lined with beautifully restored houses and attractive shops.

There's a charming old (1823) stone lighthouse, now the aptly named **Old Lighthouse Museum,** which has a somewhat eclectic collection of whaling tools and scrimshaw, portraits, ship models, and stoneware. The museum, at 7 Water Street, is open: May–October, Tuesday–Sunday, 11–5. Admission fee. Telephone: 535-1440.

At Cannon Square you will see two cannons, a 6-pounder and an 18-pounder, that, in the War of 1812, held off five British warships with 140 guns that were under the command of Captain Thomas Hardy, a favorite of Admiral Nelson's. The story goes that the British appeared off Stonington and sent a message to the people that they must leave within one hour or shelling would commence. "We will defend," the villagers proudly replied, and defend they did. Over three days the British fired more than fifty tons of metal and wounded one person. The two cannons, on the other hand, killed almost two dozen British mariners, wounded another fifty or so, and came close to sinking one ship, the *Despatch.* The British gave up and left. Not one of Albion's finest hours.

Mystic Seaport Museum   The first time I went to Mystic Seaport it was late in the morning. Mistake number one, for it was packed, and I thought, "Another time." The next time I went, I arrived first thing in the morning, and I was able to enjoy everything before the place became too terribly crowded. And I didn't rush, either. I was there about three or four hours, which is my limit for just about anything. This is a routine that I still follow, with one addition—I try and get there on a slightly cloudy day to avoid the glare from the water. And the bottom line to all this? Mystic Seaport is wonderful.

Ship masts . . . A view such as this in Mystic epitomizes the romance of the 19th century, and you feel you have passed into the world of Moby Dick *or* Two Years Before the Mast.

Mystic Seaport Museum, a collection of more than 60 buildings and more than 300 ships and boats on 17 waterfront acres fronting upon the Mystic River, is the largest maritime museum in the country. It was founded in 1929 to "actively pursue the collection, preservation and exhibition of artifacts and skills related to maritime history and its influence on American life." (The name Mystic, by the way, is from the Indian word *mistick,* which means "tidal river.")

Mystic Seaport is located in the town of Mystic. This small coastal community, the scene of shipbuilding since the end of the Revolutionary War, is just a few miles from Long Island Sound, but because it had no real harbor or significant population base, it never became a major commercial port. Instead, the people turned to shipbuilding. They built every kind of ship imaginable, from clippers and steam ships to yachts and Civil War transports, and Mystic became one of the great shipbuilding centers in the country. (You can see what the town was like between 1850 and 1870 by examining the **Mystic River Scale Model,** in its own building in the Mystic Seaport. With over 250 small-scale models, which took the curatorial staff more than three years to create, it gives a wonderful bird's-eye view of the town and helps you to place yourself in context.)

But after the Civil War, and as the nineteenth century waned, the shipyards went into decline, although they continued to produce sailing vessels up to the end of World War I. To save this heritage, what was originally called the Marine Historical Association was founded in 1929, and when they received the land and buildings of the Mystic Manufacturing Company in 1931—the buildings are known today as the Stillman, Packard, and Wendell buildings—they were on their way.

Perhaps the single most important event at the museum was the arrival of the only surviving ship from this country's great nineteenth-century whaling fleet, the *Charles W. Morgan,* in 1941 (see page 228). That event precipitated the decision to turn Mystic Seaport into an outdoor museum, and to move appropriate nineteenth-century buildings here to provide a proper setting for this centerpiece of the collection. I should point out that Mystic Seaport is not meant to be an exact replication of a New England seaport village. Rather, it is a collection meant to show various industries, activities, and shops that might have been found in such a community. Today, Mystic Seaport has evolved into a serious architectural and ship restoration center with major maritime collections.

You will get a map of the village when you pay for your ticket, so what I describe below will be very easy to follow.

I like to begin my visit by going directly to the waterfront and then to the Dock Office to check out the schedule of the only extant coal-fired, steam-powered passenger ferry in this country, the **Sabino,** which once served the Maine coast and islands. I sign up for the first available run because it is a superb way to get an overall impression of the Mystic Seaport Exhibit *and* the surrounding town of Mystic, and a good narration is provided. In short, it's like being part of a living video, and much more pleasant.

If I can't board right away, or when I am back after the run, I walk around the perimeter of the village, selecting on the spur of the moment the buildings I want to see that day. Perhaps it will be the Whaleboat Exhibit or the Rigging Loft. Or maybe the Mystic Bank or Tavern or Sailors' Reading Room or Smoke House or Drug Store. But I also like to see the Burrows House and the Shipcarver's Shop . . . and so it goes. The good thing is that you can pop your head in and out of buildings, get an idea of the demonstrations available, and either explore further or decide to come back later.

Of course, there are several musts. The first of these is a visit to the **Charles W. Morgan.** Built in 1841 in New Bedford, Mass., she was named after her principal owner, a Philadelphia Quaker. She sailed as a whaler until 1921, and it is claimed that over that period she covered more miles of ocean and made greater profits than any other whaleship. She even was a movie star and was featured in two silent films: *Down to the Sea in Ships,* with Clara Bow, and *Java Head.* Then a grandson of one of the ship's owners bought her and put her on view on his estate in South Dartmouth, Mass.

Although she arrived at Mystic Seaport in 1941, restoration work was not begun until 1968, and the ship was kept out of the water during that time. The continuing process of restoration allowed her to be put back in the water in 1974, and today she can be boarded at her berth. The sailors' living quarters, incredibly claustrophobic, and the dark hold, with its giant oak casks, linger in my mind, in sharp contrast to the beautiful yellow pine deck and intricate rigging.

My single favorite exhibition, though, is the **Wendell Building,** the first exhibit building of the Seaport and part of the original Mystic Manufacturing Company. There, in a room of dramatic space, you will see the museum's collection of nineteenth-century figureheads—exuberance, drama, fierceness, piety . . . so many emotions so straightforwardly (and skillfully) displayed.

The **Stillman Building,** on the other hand, houses the most informative exhibition, entitled "A Reflection of America," which traces the history of the *Charles W. Morgan* and its representative role in American history from 1841 to the present and which manages to be scholarly yet maintain the viewer's interest by the ingenuity of the presentation. On the second floor is an exhibition of scrimshaw and—after the figureheads my favorite exhibit—ship models, including some of the finest examples in this country.

From here, walk to the end of the Seaport to see the **New York Yacht Club Station #10** (1844), the first headquarters of this yacht club, and a wonderful building that has been attributed to A. J. Davis. It was in this building that the foundations were laid for the America's Cup race.

I also am very fond of the **Henry B. duPont Preservation Shipyard.** Here, from a second-floor balcony, you can watch Mystic Seaport staff preserving and restoring the vessels in the collection. This is the only exhibit of its kind in this country.

There is, of course, more that I could tell you about, but the above should give you an idea of the diversity and fascination of the collections. Just remember—get there early.

Mystic Seaport is open: Daily, 9–5. Admission fee. Telephone: 572-0711. Mystic Seaport has two places to eat, The Galley, on the Village Green, for sandwiches and light food, and the Seamen's Inn, at the north entrance, which is more formal. There is a very large gift shop offering everything from paintings and other works of art and posters to foodstuffs and books to wastebaskets and Christmas tree ornaments, and there is a variety store, also on the Village Green.

Mystic Marinelife Aquarium   The first few times I was in Mystic I always passed by this aquarium for one reason or another. When I finally did go, I had a great time. But again, be aware that it can get very crowded, and get there as early as possible in order to enjoy the exhibits.

Inside the aquarium, huge glass exhibits in darkened rooms present endlessly fascinating marine animals. You can watch more than 6,000 specimens from all over the world. It has been said that watching fish in an aquarium lowers the blood pressure, and indeed there is something very relaxing about some of these beautiful and graceful creatures. Watching the sharks, on the other hand, put my blood pressure right back up there.

There is also a 1,200-seat marine theater featuring daily demonstrations of dolphins and whales, and Seal Island, a 2.5-acre home to four different species of seals and sea lions. Finally, there is Penguin Pavilion, home to a breeding colony of African black-footed penguins. It's great fun, especially for kids. Plan on making it part of your visit.

The Mystic Marinelife Aquarium is open: Daily, except for Thanksgiving, Christmas, New Year's Day and the last full week in January. Admission fee. Telephone: 536-3323.

New London

Founded in 1646, this small city of under 30,000 people sits at the mouth of the Thames River. Its harbor, a drowned valley, is one of the deepest on the Atlantic Coast, and consequently New London has always been an important seagoing center. In the nineteenth century it became a major whaling port; by 1864, New Bedford was its only rival, and it was a ship from New London that captured the largest recorded whale, which yielded 362 barrels of oil and 40,000 pounds of bone. The last whaler sailed in 1909, but many houses that were built from whale-oil money still stand in the city. Whale Oil Row, a very handsome grouping of four white Greek Revival mansions at 105-199 Huntington Street, will give you an idea of the wealth that poured into this city. Today New London is the home of the United States Coast Guard Academy, and Groton, just across the Thames, has a huge submarine base.

The architecture of New England often offers gentle pleasures—the almost harsh simplicity of these coastal buildings, for instance, softened by that lovely S-curve of the bracket on the left.

There are four interesting sites: the Joshua Hempsted House, the Shaw-Perkins Mansion, the Lyman Allyn Art Museum, and Monte Cristo Cottage.

The most interesting of these is the **Joshua Hempsted House** (1678) at 11 Hempsted Street, for it is an excellent example of seventeenth-century architecture in America. Low ceilings, tiny leaded casement windows, seaweed insulation, excellent furnishings of the period . . . all this makes for an interesting visit. It is open: Mid-May to mid-October, Tuesday–Sunday, 1–5. Admission fee. Telephone: 443-7949. On the grounds, too, is the stone Nathaniel Hempsted House, built in 1759, whose seven rooms with period furnishings can also be visited by the public.

The **Shaw-Perkins Mansion,** at 11 Blinman Street, was built in 1756. During the Revolution it was the naval headquarters for Connecticut, and both Washington and Lafayette came here. Open: All year, Tuesday–Saturday. Hours are limited, and you should telephone in advance: 443-1209. Admission fee.

The **Lyman Allyn Art Museum,** 625 Williams Street, is of primary interest for its collection of Connecticut painters and

the decorative arts of the state. Open: All year, Tuesday–
Sunday. No admission fee. Telephone: 443-2545.

Anyone who admires Eugene O'Neill will be interested in
Monte Cristo Cottage at 325 Pequot Street, his boyhood
summer home, which is the setting for both *Long Day's
Journey into Night* and *Ah, Wilderness!* Open: April to mid-
December, Monday–Friday. Admission fee. Telephone: 443-
5378.

You also may be interested in knowing that H. H. Richardson (1838–1886), one of the greatest American architects of
the nineteenth century, the creator of the magnificent Trinity
Church in Boston and Allegheny County Courthouse and Jail
in Pittsburgh, seminal buildings whose influence was felt well
into the twentieth century, designed New London's **Union
Station** (1887). And you might want to take a look at **Ye
Antientiest Burial Ground** (a name too cute to live), on
Huntington Street, which has a great many early, carved
stones, and the **Custom House** (1833), which was designed by
Robert Mills (1781–1855), who is best known for the Wash-
ington Monument.

Finally, if you are interested in the development of the
United States Coast Guard Academy, the entrance of
which is on Mohegan Avenue, the Coast Guard Museum and
the Visitors' Pavilion should be on your list. Admission is free,
but you should telephone 444-8270 for hours.

A Perfect Weekend: Essex, East Haddam, and Other Villages

This is my favorite area of the coast, and if you would like to
plan a weekend in the region—which I strongly recommend—
this is the place to be, for you can conveniently visit any of the
coastal sights or enjoy this very beautiful area while staying in
comfort at a good inn and dining well. What follows will more
than fill your weekend.

Essex, established in 1645 and one of the oldest settlements
in Connecticut, is a lovely old river town and, thankfully, is the
home of one of the better inns in the region, the Griswold (see

Where to Stay). Because of its beauty, it attracts a well-heeled summer crowd; therefore, its homes are well maintained, its shops are well stocked, and its marina holds handsome yachts and cabin cruisers.

Essex was a shipbuilding center—it has the honor of having launched America's first warship, the *Oliver Cromwell*, in 1776, and in the War of 1812 the British saw it as enough of a threat to raid it and burn 28 ships. It reached its peak about 1840, when it was building everything from transatlantic packets to ships that carried cotton from the South to the great mills of Europe. As shipbuilding declined, nothing replaced it, luckily for us, and the town stayed the same.

Whether you stay in Essex or not, you certainly will want to spend a few hours wandering its streets and visiting the delightful **Connecticut River Museum,** located on the river in the warehouse at the Essex Steamboat Dock at the foot of Main Street. Its collection of ship models, paintings, and prints concerning the river is interesting; there is a reproduction of the first submarine built in this country, the *American Turtle,* built by David Bushnell in 1775; and the Boat House exhibits small craft and explores Connecticut's boat-building tradition.

But what makes this little museum particularly interesting is the quality and imagination of its special exhibitions. For example, the Connecticut River Valley had a thriving trade in the eighteenth-century with the West Indian islands of Trinidad, Barbados, and Jamaica, and this brought a great deal of money into the valley's economy. The valley farmers would send their horses, goats, and cattle to the islands and, in return, would receive fruit, molasses, rum, and sugar. Around these facts, the museum created a fascinating and clever exhibition that kept me interested for the better part of an hour. The Connecticut River Museum is open: Year-round, Tuesday–Sunday, 10–5. Admission fee. Telephone: 767-8269.

From Essex you can easily take my favorite little trip (2 1/2 hours) in the Connecticut River Valley. Offered by the **Valley Railroad Company,** it is a combination steam-train and steamboat trip. You leave from Essex on a 1920s restored train and go to Deep River. There you transfer to the steamboat and go upriver to East Haddam, and then back. There is a very

The Goodspeed Opera House in East Haddam, right on the Connecticut River and home to an excellent regional musical theater, is also a Victorian extravaganza—as you may already have noted.

good commentary on the boat, and the ride is an excellent way to enjoy both the countryside and the river. For fare, timetable, and reservations information, telephone 767-0103.

Gillette Castle, one of the ugliest houses I have ever seen, now part of the 184-acre Gillette Castle State Park, commands some of the best views of the Connecticut Valley, for it stands 200 feet above the river. You can—and perhaps should—see the views without entering the house, but its ugliness does hold a certain fascination and I'm glad I have exposed myself to it. I would approach it from the opposite bank and take the **Chester-Hadlyme Ferry,** which has been operating since 1769 and currently runs from April through November. The five-minute ride is delightful; you will see a handsome grouping of houses and the castle looming above you, its rough-hewn stone making it look as if it were growing carbuncles.

Gillette Castle was built in 1917 by William Gillette (1853–1937), an actor who made a fortune playing Sherlock Holmes and writing melodramatic plays. Heaven alone knows where his taste came from, but I am glad to say that it is unique. Let me simply comment that the interior of the house—all two dozen rooms were designed and decorated by

Gillette—lives up to the promise of the exterior. Please be sure to note the ceramic frog troubadours on the mantelpiece and the gadgets Gillette adored, such as the metal track designed to carry furniture. And then, of course, there's the Sherlock Holmes chamber. . . . The Castle is open: Daily, late May to mid-October; Saturday and Sunday, mid-October to mid-December. Admission fee. Telephone: 526-2336.

Another attraction, this time in Higganum on Brault Hill Road, is the **Sundial Herb Garden,** which actually consists of the main garden with a sundial in the center, a topiary garden, and a knot garden. There is also an herb shop and tearoom. The whole is the creation of Ragna Tischler Goddard, a fascinating woman whose knowledge of herbs is boundless. For visiting hours of both gardens and shop, telephone 345-4290.

East Haddam, another lovely river village, has gained a certain amount of fame as the home of the **Goodspeed Opera House** (1876), where American musicals are revived and performed from April through December, often to such acclaim that they are taken to Broadway. The opera house, a delightful Victorian affair right on the river, was built by William Goodspeed during the era when Connecticut–New York steamers stopped here. For schedule and reservation information, telephone 873-8668.

An oddity: In St. Stephen's Episcopal Church hangs a bell cast in A.D. 815, which makes it the oldest bell in America. The story is that the church housing it in Spain was destroyed when Napoleon invaded the country. In 1834, needing ballast, a sea captain brought it to New York, and eventually it made its way here.

Across the river, in Marine Park, the **New England Cruise Line** offers Connecticut River cruises and other excursions. To reach it you cross the river just beyond the opera house on what is reputed to be the longest swinging bridge (899 feet) in the world. For complete cruise information, telephone 345-4507.

From here it's a short drive to **Moodus,** whose very pretty green holds the **Amasa Day House** (1816), which has some interesting stenciling, done over a century ago, on floors and stairs, as well as some period furnishings. The house is supposedly open daily, from mid-May to mid-October, but I have found the visiting hours erratic and would suggest you call in advance (873-8144) to make sure it's open. Admission fee.

And do visit **Old Lyme.** You might even consider staying here (see Where to Stay), but certainly you will wish to explore the streets and art galleries. My favorite: **The Cooley Gallery,** at 25 Lyme Street (434-8807), which specializes in nineteenth-century artists and particularly those of the Connecticut River Valley.

You should also consider visiting **Guilford** (1639), farther west along the coast, but well worth the little extra effort it would take to get there because this village, with more than 400 houses from the eighteenth and nineteenth centuries and a splendid green, has one of the most varied collections of early houses in New England. (Two bits of trivia: Do you know the expression "running like Sam Hill"? Samuel Hill was born in Guilford in 1677 and ran for office so many times that he inspired the expression; at the time of his death he was a representative in the state legislature, town clerk, probate judge, and clerk of the Proprietors. The other item: Granite from Old Lyme was used for the foundations of the Brooklyn Bridge and the Statue of Liberty.)

Obviously, this is a town in which you will want to take a

This delightful 1639 stone house in Guilford is the oldest of its kind in New England.

long stroll. There are three houses open to the public, the Henry Whitfield Museum, the Hyland House and the Thomas Griswold House.

The **Henry Whitfield Museum** (1639) is a stone dwelling, the oldest in New England, and the first building to be erected in Guilford. It also served as church, garrison, and meeting hall. Although it has been considerably modified since it first was built, I think it's very lovely, and it contains some excellent and rare seventeenth- and eighteenth-century furnishings. The Henry Whitfield Museum, on Whitfield Street, is open: Wednesday–Sunday, 10–5. Closed: Mid-December to mid-January. Admission fee. Telephone: 453-2457.

The **Hyland House** (1660), a saltbox with a beautifully carved overhang, is furnished with period antiques and has fine paneling in the parlor. In 1727 Ebenezer Parmelee, who lived here, built one of the first town clocks in this country and installed it in the First Congregation Church on the green. You can pick up a map of Guilford's historic homes there. The Hyland House, at 84 Boston Street, is open: Early June to Labor Day, Tuesday–Sunday; Labor Day to Columbus Day, Saturday and Sunday. Admission fee. Telephone: 453-9477.

The **Thomas Griswold House** (c. 1774), also a saltbox, encompasses the period from the late eighteenth century to the mid-nineteenth. There also is a Farmers' Museum and a working blacksmith shop. It's worth a stop. The house, at 171 Boston Street, is open: Mid-June through mid-September, Tuesday–Sunday, 11–4. Admission fee. Telephone: 453-3176.

New Haven

In 1614 the Dutch navigator Adrian Block sailed into the harbor here and named the place Rodeberg (Red Mount Place), presumably after the red basalt ridges, East Rock and West Rock, that still serve as landmarks for the city.

Then, in 1638, after hearing of the excellent harbor, the Reverend John Davenport (1597–1670), a Puritan minister from London, and Theophilus Eaton (1590–1658), a prominent merchant, brought a group of colonists here to settle. They called the city-to-be New Haven, after the Sussex seaport. Because they were more prosperous than other colonists, they made rather grander plans, and they laid the colony out in nine squares, the central one being the common green.

In 1639, they adopted a constitution that ignored not only loyalty to the king but also English common law and the principal of trial by jury. Instead, the word of God was the law. Two groups of seven men, known as the Seven Pillars, were elected by twelve church members to head church and state governments, and Eaton became the first governor of the independent New Haven Colony. (The term *Seven Pillars* comes from Proverbs: "Wisdom hath builded her house; she hath hewn out her seven pillars.") From that time until the colony merged with Connecticut in 1662, it was governed largely by the will of Davenport, and when the merger with the more liberal Connecticut finally occurred, Davenport felt that all was "miserably lost."

Shipping dominated the town's early commercial activity, and industry took over in the mid-nineteenth century, when New Haven produced Winchester repeating rifles, clocks, and carriages, among other things. In addition, from 1701 to 1873, New Haven and Hartford shared the honor of being the state capital.

Eli Whitney manufactured his cotton gin (short for *engine*) here and ushered in the modern period of manufacturing through his technique of making objects with interchangeable parts. Noah Webster compiled his first dictionary here, and innumerable distinguished and famous men—and now women— have graduated from Yale, which moved to New Haven from Saybrook in 1716.

Today, thanks largely to the presence of Yale, with its extraordinary facilities, New Haven has become a major cultural center and is easily worth a day's visit.

The Green This 16-acre plot is all that is left of the original nine-square plan. It is the single most interesting section of New Haven architecturally and, because of its proximity to Yale, makes the ideal starting place for your visit.

The three very handsome churches here are **Trinity Episcopal Church** (1814), **Center Church** (1814), and **United Church** (1815).

Trinity Episcopal Church was designed by Ithiel Town,

one of the primary advocates of Greek Revival. This, however, is a Gothic Revival church, probably the first in America, and therefore of considerable historic interest. Town also designed Center Church, a Georgian building that ranks among the most beautiful buildings of its style in New England, and the Connecticut State Capitol, modeled after a Doric temple, which stood between Center and United but is now gone. The third church, United, in the Federal style, was designed by an architect named David Hoadley.

You would think that buildings in all these disparate styles would compete with each other and create a disharmonious grouping. Instead, they work beautifully together and form one of New England's most distinguished and dramatic ecclesiastical settings. This is thanks primarily to the genius of Town, who, being what has been called a Romantic Eclectic, was able to combine agreeably all these styles of the past.

Of the three, Trinity Church has the least interesting exterior. It is a rectangular building made of traprock with brownstone trim, with a center, attached tower. The interior has been altered—the chancel was not part of the original design; the original was a simple auditorium, with balconies supported by clustered columns—a sort of meeting house with Gothic elements. Not a very promising beginning for what was to be the most popular ecclesiastic style in the nineteenth century.

Center Church was undoubtedly inspired by St. Martin's-in-the-Fields in London. The building materials are brick and wood, and the gracefulness and delicacy of the wooden steeple is immediately apparent. (An interesting note: The steeple was constructed inside the brick tower and, when completed, was raised into place.) The interior, beautifully proportioned and with a gallery on three sides supported by Ionic columns, has a large Tiffany window behind the pulpit that portrays John Davenport delivering his first sermon in New Haven; note the seven columns and seven-branched candlestick at the bottom, which symbolize the Seven Pillars of the church and civil governments.

United Church is more delicate—or perhaps refined—in feel, both on the exterior, with its pilastered projecting portico and three arched entrances, and on the interior, with its fine paneling.

The green, then, is important not only because of its real architectural beauty but also because it represents in such an interesting way a great deal of what makes New England different from other areas of the country: her churches.

The rest of your visit to New Haven will be spent at Yale, so perhaps a little background is in order.

Yale University was founded by a group of clergymen, who made a gift of books "for the founding of a College in this colony." The founders asked the Reverend Abraham Pierson to be the first president, and they selected Saybrook as the college's site. The college moved to New Haven in 1716 and, in 1718, adopted the name Yale to honor a large gift from Elihu Yale, who had been born in America but lived in England.

Since then Yale has had a distinguished history: It was, for example, this country's first college to grant the degree of Doctor of Philosophy (1861) and the first to establish a School of Fine Arts (1869). The claim is made that 10 percent of all this country's primary diplomatic posts since 1789 have gone to Yale graduates and that every two years fifteen Yale men, on the average, are elected to Congress.

Today Yale, like so many other institutions of higher learning, faces multiple problems. Most notable is that its buildings, many dating from the 1920s and early thirties, have been allowed to deteriorate to an alarming degree. Notwithstanding, it is an institution of absolutely magnificent resources.

Because there is so much to see and do here, I will divide it into two parts: a walking tour of the campus, and then a visit to its two outstanding art gallerys.

Begin by leaving the green and going to Phelps Gate on College Street. Here you will enter the Old Campus, where you will find Yale's earliest buildings, including Connecticut Hall, (1752), the oldest surviving structure. Outside this hall you will see a statue of Nathan Hale, who graduated from Yale in 1773 and lived in this building as an underclassman.

Exit into High Street, and just across the street is Yale's most visible landmark, the neo-Gothic Harkness Tower, built in 1920. Try to examine some of the carvings here and on the other neo-Gothic buildings; the carvers, just like their medieval ancestors, took great delight in portraying various personalities and professional types in the gargoyles. It is one of the most delightful aspects of the campus.

Cross to York Street on the student walk, passing between Branford and Jonathan Edwards colleges. Branford, by the way, has a particularly pretty courtyard with a special view of Harkness Tower. On York you will turn right and pass the neo-Gothic façade of Davenport and the Georgian Pierson college and then, as you pass into their courtyards, all of a sudden the buildings change to Georgian.

Continue down York, perhaps stopping in at one of the excellent men's shops there, and cross Elm Street. The group of buildings to your left are Morse and Ezra Stiles colleges, which were designed by Eero Saarinen (as was the wonderful David S. Ingalls Hockey Rink on Prospect Street, which looks like a cross between a Viking ship and a whale). Within this complex, too, is the Yale Co-op. Supposedly, Saarinen was inspired by Italian hill towns when he created these collages. I don't find them to be among his most inspired works, but walk about them and judge for yourself.

Near Morse and Stiles, on the north side of the Sterling Memorial Library (see below) and beyond it, are the Sterling Law Buildings. Here the stone carvers I mentioned earlier have, appropriately, carved cops and robbers above windows.

Now cross High Street, and you will see the Beinecke Rare Book and Manuscript Library (1963), which I feel is one of the most beautiful buildings on the campus. It is the work of the great architectural firm of Skidmore, Owings, and Merrill and is constructed of granite-covered trusses fitted with gray veined translucent marble panels. Inside the library, the effect is magical, and selections from the superb collection are always on display.

This section of the campus is the most open, and here, too, you will find the cathedral-like Sterling Memorial Library, also worth a visit, and, beyond the Beinecke, the University Dining Hall and Woolsey Hall, where concerts and lectures are held.

Those are just a few highlights, and you can continue wandering to your heart's content, noting, perhaps, some of the college's famed secret societies, such as Skull and Bones and Scroll and Key, or happening upon the 30-foot-long Tiffany window (1890) in Linsly-Chittenden Hall on High Street. But be sure to save enough time for the two brilliant galleries, the Yale University Art Gallery on Chapel Street and, on the opposite side of Chapel, the Center for British Art.

Yale University Art Gallery Established in 1831, it is the oldest collegiate art gallery in America. Today the collection is housed in a 1928 Italian Romanesque building and the 1953 structure of Louis Kahn (1901–1974), who taught at Yale from 1947 to 1957 and who also designed the Center for British Art (1974), his last building.

The Yale University Art Gallery was founded when the painter John Trumbull gave 100 works of art in exchange for an annuity. (His son-in-law, Daniel Wadsworth, had hoped to save some of the paintings for Hartford, and had promised to build a museum for them. Although he never got the paintings, he founded the Wadsworth Atheneum in Hartford nonetheless.)

On the ground floor are the collections of ancient art and that given by the Société Anonyme, which includes such artists as Brancusi, Villon, and Mondrian.

The first floor is primarily dedicated to special exhibitions. The second floor contains Impressionist paintings and other nineteenth-century French schools and includes van Gogh's great *Night Café* as well as wonderful examples of other painters ranging from Millet to Matisse. Here too are found the African and twentieth-century collections, with signature works by Joseph Stella, Ernst, Picasso, Rothko, and others.

The third floor houses the James Jackson Jarves collection of Italian painting from the thirteenth to the sixteenth century and has long been my particular favorite—because it has the first painting I fell in love with, *The Lady with a Rabbit* by Piero di Cosimo, as well as some other wonderful works; and because Jarves was a splendidly eccentric American collector who was among the first connoisseurs in the world to recognize the quality of the early Italian painters. This, then, is not only a beautiful collection but a historically important one.

There are works of other great European artists on this floor, from the thirteenth well into the twentieth century, but the American decorative arts collection found here—silver, furniture, ironwork—must be seen for the brilliance of the display. It is arranged in a manner to teach students the development of different American art forms, and to say it is ingeniously done is understating the case. And then in the last two galleries are works by American artists, including two of Trumbull's masterpieces, *Bunker Hill* and *The Declaration of Independence.*

Finally, the fourth floor is devoted to Far Eastern art, from just before the birth of Christ to this century, and prints, drawings, and photographs.

The Yale University Art Gallery, 1111 Chapel Street, is open: Mid-September to mid-May, Tuesday–Sunday; mid-May to mid-September, Tuesday–Saturday. Free admission. Telephone: 432-0600.

Yale Center for British Art   This museum opened in 1977. It was the gift of Paul Mellon, a Yale alumnus, who gave his great collection of British art to Yale. Today, the collection contains approximately 1,300 paintings, 20,000 drawings, 30,000 prints, and 20,000 rare books, making it the most comprehensive outside Great Britain. In the collection, which focuses on the period 1700–1850 but ranges from the late sixteenth century into the twentieth century, are great works by Turner, Van Dyck, Reynolds, Constable, Gainsborough, Stubbs, and Blake, and, particularly fascinating to me, splendid works by such less well known masters as Fuseli. I should add that the special exhibitions here are usually highly original and informative. Simply put, it is a great center that provides unique insight into English culture.

The Yale Center for British Art, 1080 Chapel Street, is open: Year-round, Tuesday–Sunday. Free admission. Telephone: 432-2800.

One other excellent museum on the campus is of particular interest: the **Peabody Museum of Natural History,** Yale's science museum and the largest museum of natural history in New England. Its collection of dinosaurs is world-famous, and the exhibits of fossils, Indian artifacts, and mammals, not to mention the videos and computerized displays showing evolutionary trends in man and other primates, are extremely interesting.

The Peabody Museum is located at 170 Whitney Avenue. It

is open: Year-round, Monday–Friday. Admission fee. Telephone: 432-5050.

Finally, before leaving New Haven you must drive by the entrance to the **Grove Street Cemetery,** opposite High Street at Grove. It is the oldest incorporated cemetery in this country, the first to be laid out in family plots, and the final resting place of such luminaries as Lyman Beecher (Harriet Beecher Stowe's father), Eli Whitney, Noah Webster, Charles Goodyear, and various Yale presidents. But, for me, the chief interest is the brownstone Egyptian pylon gateway (1848). Egyptian architecture provides perfect symbolism for a cemetery, and combined with a touch of nineteenth-century American Romanticism, it makes a particularly dignified and somber entrance.

WESTERN CONNECTICUT

THE LITCHFIELD HILLS AND THE HOUSATONIC RIVER VALLEY

This unspoiled area of rolling hills and rich valleys, New England towns and pretty drives is, in terms of natural beauty, my favorite in Connecticut. To come here is to escape the crowded scene along the shoreline and the tourist bustle just a little north in the Berkshires. In brief, for a weekend of quiet relaxation during which your major activity is entering an antique shop or dining room or paddling in a pool, all surrounded by lush and special scenery, this is the place to be.

Litchfield

Ideally situated almost at the center of the region on a plateau above the Naugatuck Valley, Litchfield is the prettiest village in the area and one of the prettiest in New England. I would advise you to stay here or near here (see Where to Stay), because visiting other parts of Western Connecticut from here is very easy.

Litchfield was settled in 1720—the town and the surrounding area were bought from the Indians in 1715 and 1716 for a

total of £15—and was named for the cathedral town of
Litchfield in Staffordshire, England. Its long, wide common
was laid out in the 1770s, and during the Revolution, because
the village was protected from the British by its location well
away from the coast and major urban centers, it became a
major storage center for the colonial army. At one point it was
on the major route between New York and Boston.

In the nineteenth century, the railroads bypassed Litchfield,
laying their major lines in the valley below, and what then
seemed to doom its industrial growth actually preserved its
eighteenth-century charm. In addition, the citizens were
shrewd investors whose individual prosperity helped maintain
the town.

Then, in the latter part of the nineteenth century and the beginning of the twentieth, the townspeople decided to get rid of
the Victorian accretions on their eighteenth-century houses
and restore them to their period. They hired Frederick Law
Olmsted (1822–1903), the founder of American landscape architecture and the creator of Central Park, to redesign the common; the overall result of this activity formed the basis of what
you see today.

*An ancient house with almost equally ancient lilac bushes. The two
are resonant of the deepest memories of the New England soul.*

When I visit this delightful town I like to first take a walk, beginning at the nearly perfect **Congregational Church** (1828–1829) facing the common, with its four fluted Ionic columns, shuttered windows, and beautifully proportioned steeple. From here, walk down East Street, enjoying the lovely buildings, to North Street, my favorite in the village because of its spectacular trees and great houses set on deep lawns.

Sheldon's Tavern, at 73 North Street, is mentioned by George Washington as having sheltered him for the night. It was designed by William Spratt, an English architect who served in the British army during the Revolution and who also designed the Lindens, on the opposite side of the street, arguably the most beautiful house here, with its Palladian window, colonnaded entrance portico, and four chimneys. The Lindens was built by Julius Deming, who made his money in the China trade and whose partners were Benjamin Tallmadge and Oliver Wolcott (see below). Their ship, the *Trident,* sailed to China from New Haven for fourteen years.

Also on North Street is the home of the Reverend Lyman Beecher, father of Harriet Beecher Stowe, author of *Uncle Tom's Cabin,* and the Reverend Henry Ward Beecher, whose sermons at Plymouth Church in Brooklyn Heights, N. Y., made him the most famous preacher in America until scandal destroyed his career.

You also should explore South Street, where Ethan Allen was born in 1737, and where you can enjoy poking about the shops along the street and in Cobble Court.

Once you have wandered about to your heart's content, you can visit the buildings open to the public, the most interesting of which is the **Litchfield Historical Society Museum,** where you will meet our old friend Ralph Earl, who worked in Litchfield and painted many of its prominent citizens, including Oliver Wolcott (instrumental in the ratification by Connecticut of the Constitution), his wife, and his daughter, Mariann. This last portrait, painted in 1789, is part of the Society's collection, as are two elegant portraits of Benjamin Tallmadge, his wife, Mary, and some of their seven children. The portrait of Mrs. Tallmadge and two of the children includes a landscape view of Litchfield. The Tallmadge house, by the way, still stands on North Street. Benjamin Tallmadge was chief of the intelligence service in the Revolution, and it was he who identified Major John André as a British spy. In his portrait he wears on his lapel the badge of the Society of Cincinnati.

This excellent collection is a fine hodgepodge of china, store signs, pewter, paintings, photographs, furniture—the materials that make these historical societies treasure troves of regional history. In this instance, the collection is of very good quality, as indicated by the presence of the Earl portraits. There is also a research library.

The Litchfield Historical Society Museum is located on the common at the junction of East and South streets. Open: April–October, Tuesday–Sunday, 10–4; November and December, Saturday and Sunday, 12–4. Admission fee. Telephone: 567-4501.

The Law School (1784) at the **Tapping Reeve House** (1773) was America's first law school, and (a nice bit of trivia) Tapping Reeve's wife, Sally, was Aaron Burr's sister. According to one source, the school, which opened in 1782 and closed its doors in 1833, numbers among its graduates two vice presidents (Aaron Burr and John Calhoun), five Cabinet members, seventeen U.S. senators, fifty-three members of the House, three Supreme Court justices, ten state governors, and two secretaries of state—not to mention college presidents, state attorneys, and so forth. Not bad. The house is handsome and well furnished and has lovely paneling, and the schoolhouse is especially impressive in that so many distinguished leaders of this country studied in this tiny one-room building. The buildings are open: Mid-May to mid-October, Tuesday–Sunday, 10–5. Admission fee. Telephone: 567-4501.

The White Memorial Foundation and Conservation Center was established by Alan C. White and his sister, May, and is dedicated to preserving the environment. It operates a 4,000-acre preserve, about 2 1/2 miles south of Litchfield on U.S. 202. This is the largest nature and wildlife sanctuary in Connecticut, with 35 miles of trails for riding and hiking, access to Bantam Lake, the largest natural lake in the state for fishing and canoeing, and picnicking facilities.

The Whites' home, now the Conservation Center, houses an interesting museum, with mounted birds and animals, and some excellent dioramas; a nature library that ranks as the finest in the state; and a well-stocked gift shop. You can get a map of the trails and wildnerness areas here.

The Foundation is open year-round, the museum from early April through October, Tuesday–Saturday, 9–5; November– March, 8:30–4:30; Sunday, year-round, 11–5. Admission fee. Telephone: 567-0857 for information on the preserve and the Center.

And then there is **White Flower Farm.** Breathes there a man or woman with soul so dead who hasn't at least salivated over the catalogue of this institution? Well, here it is, 3 miles south of Litchfield on Route 63, all 10 acres of cultivated plants—not to mention the greenhouses and the gardening store. If you are a gardener, I defy you to come here and not spend your patrimony.

White Flower Farm is open: Mid-April to late December, Monday–Friday, 10–5, Saturday and Sunday, 9:00–5:30. Free admission. Telephone: 567-8789.

A DRIVE FROM LITCHFIELD

Technically, this lovely little trip encompasses more than the Litchfield Hills, but so what. In a nutshell, you drive out from Litchfield, going south on Route 202 to Bantam first and then to New Preston, where you may wish to take a detour around Lake Waramaug. You then go back to Route 47 and drive south to Washington Depot and Washington, down Routes 199 and 67 to Roxbury and into Southbury. Then head back north on Route 6 to Woodbury, then up Route 132 to Hotchkissville and Bethlehem, then north on 61 to Morris, east on 109 to East Morris, then north again on 63 into Litchfield. Depending on what you wish to see and do along the way, you should plan on spending at least a day.

When you reach **Bantam,** you may wish to take the first of several possible detours. This one, a left on Route 209, will take you around part of the shoreline of Bantam Lake, then on down to **New Preston,** a neat little village where you may want to explore the antique shops and galleries.

From here, take the 9-mile drive around Lake Waramaug,

and then go back to Route 47, where you will take a right and continue to Washington Depot and **Washington.** (If you feel like stretching your legs, visit the Hidden Valley Reservation here; it has easy-to-walk trails and exquisite views.) Washington Depot has some shops—it's the commercial center—but it is Washington you have come to see, with its particularly welcoming green, a delightfully cozy Congregational church, the buildings of the Gunnery School, and other handsome buildings.

Continue to **Roxbury,** first visiting the very interesting **Institute for American Indian Studies** (telephone 868-0518 for hours). There you will find intelligent and well-displayed exhibits of Indian crafts, an Algonquin village, a furnished longhouse, nature trails, and other attractions. Roxbury has the usual pleasant green and houses. Just outside, on Route 67, take a right on Mine Hill Road (it's just over a bridge) and follow the signs to **Mine Hill Preserve,** which I find fascinating in a nineteenth-century romantic way.

The mine was opened in the mid-eighteenth century by men looking for silver. No silver was found, but iron ore was, and a great deal of money later was spent developing the vein. At its height in the nineteenth century, the mine produced 10 tons of pig iron daily, but it went out of business as the huge mines in Minnesota made the labor intensive-work here unprofitable. I find it great fun to wander the trail, exploring the ruined buildings and foundations and enjoying the woods.

Now go on to **Woodbury,** settled in 1674 on land above the Pomperaug River. For me this is the highlight of the trip, and for two reasons: The quality and range of the antique shops found here is superb; and there is a Gertrude Jekyll garden, one of only three in this country created by the great English garden designer—she virtually invented what we now call the English garden—and the only one extant. (Another piece of trivia: Ulysses S. Grant and William Tecumseh Sherman both had family roots here.) If antiques and gardens interest you, you could easily spend half a day here.

First the **antique shops:** There are at least forty shops here, in houses dating from the eighteenth century through the Victorian period, and with wares to match. The range is from major eighteenth-century pieces at prices in five figures to reasonably priced decorative objects and everything in between. (North of Woodbury, on Route 6, is Mill House, an antique shop that now includes eight buildings. Well worth visiting.)

And if you are at all interested in gardens, you will certainly want to visit the **Glebe House** (c. 1750) **Museum and Gertrude Jekyll Garden.** Glebe land is cultivable land that is owned by the parish church and apportioned to the clergyman. This house became a glebe in 1771. It is on this land that the parish house was built. America's first Episcopal bishop, the Reverend Dr. Samuel Seabury, was elected here in 1783, and the house, of no little architectural distinction, is furnished with Connecticut eighteenth-century pieces. It opened as a museum in 1925. The tour focuses on the social history of rural Revolutionary era life.

In 1926, one of the board members visited Jekyll, then a very old lady, and commissioned her to do a garden suitable to an old country house. She designed borders filled with delphinium and lavender, hollyhocks and columbine, lupine and roses, and, at the back of the house, a fragrant garden as well as a kitchen garden. But for some unknown reason, the garden was never actually installed, and it wasn't until many years later that a researcher found the plans among the papers of the brilliant American designer Beatrix Farrand. After much discussion, the board agreed to install the garden, and in 1989 the work began. Today, its great washes of color are as lovely as a dream, and it is the only garden by Miss Jekyll in this country.

The Glebe House Museum and Gertrude Jekyll Garden is open: April–November, Wednesday–Sunday, 1–4. Admission fee. Telephone: 263-2855.

Once you tear yourself away from Woodbury, you can head north for a scenic drive through Hotchkissville and on to Bethlehem, a typical Connecticut hill town that, not surprisingly, goes all-out at Christmas time. From there, meander on to Morris and East Morris, where you can take Route 109 for a lovely excursion past reservoirs and through woods. And then, when you are sated by all this beauty, back home to Litchfield.

A Drive from Litchfield That Includes the Housatonic Valley

Once again, to do this properly will take more than a day, but you can pick and choose, and you can always come back. Let's get the directions out of the way first. From Litchfield go north to Torrington on Route 202. Then go north on 272 to Norfolk, then east on Route 44 through Canaan, Salisbury, and Lakeville, where you will go south on Route 41 to Sharon, then south and east on Route 4 to Cornwall Bridge. Then go north on 7 to West Cornwall, back down 7 to Cornwall Bridge, and continue through Kent Falls State Park, North Kent, Kent Furnace, and Kent. To return to Litchfield, take Route 341 at Kent east to Warren, where you will go south, still on 341, to Woodville. From there, go east on Route 202 into Litchfield.

John Brown, the famous abolitionist who led the attack at Harpers Ferry, was born in the small (33,000 or so people) industrial town of Torrington. It was once known as Mast Swamp because the pine trees that covered the hillsides were used for masts; later it became a center for brass. Near here is the

This rather crisp white building in Cornwall Center has an appropriately Shaker look—appropriate because it is the shop of a cabinetmaker, Ian Ingersoll, who re-creates furniture in the Shaker style.

Paugnut State Forest, a 2,000-acre preserve with a state park at the northern end for swimming, boating, and picnicking.

From Torrington to **Norfolk** is a longish but very pretty country drive. Surrounded by hills, Norfolk is a lovely old town that has attracted people as a summer resort since the 1860s. It is well worth an exploratory walk, and be sure to include the Battell Memorial Fountain on the southern corner of the green, which was executed by Stanford White, and the Battell Chapel in the Church of Christ, which has several Tiffany windows.

Today the village is home to the summertime **Norfolk Chamber Music Festival,** which runs from June through early August and is one of the most delightful festivals in New England. It traces its origins to 1906, when Ellen Battell Stoeckel asked a group of guests to a concert in the music shed of her extremely beautiful estate. Later, the Yale Summer School of Music took over the management of the festival, and today, before you attend a concert, you can picnic on the grounds and enjoy a delightful stroll. The estate is located at the junction of Routes 44 and 272. Telephone: 542-5537 from late May through the summer, 432-1966 at other times.

Route 44 is one of the prettier roads in Connecticut from here west. When you reach Canaan, you may wish to go to the 1872 Canaan Union Station, "the oldest depot in continuous railroad service in the United States," at the junction of Routes 7 and 44 and take a 30-mile round-trip train journey through the Housatonic Valley. The Housatonic Railroad Company operates its scenic trip from May through October. For information telephone 824-0339.

The next town is **Salisbury.** Iron was discovered here in 1732 and was mined until the early 1800s. It is a lovely town that obviously attracts people with money, who can maintain the handsome homes. **Lakeville,** the next town, seems to run right into Salisbury and is equally lovely. It developed around a blast furnace owned by Ethan Allen, which cast cannon used in the Revolution. Later the site would hold the red-brick buildings of the first factory to produce cutlery in this country. The **Holley-Williams House Museum** on Main Street in Lakeville, a Federal building from 1808, which was lived in by the same family until 1971, makes an interesting visit. For hours, telephone 435-2878.

From Lakeville you will begin a particularly pretty drive. Turn south on Route 41, first passing the campus of the **Hotchkiss School,** just down the road. From Hotchkiss to **Sharon,** a popular weekend spot for New Yorkers, is a short distance. Sharon is one of my favorite towns in Connecticut, with its wide, gracious main street lined with solid, handsome houses of stone and brick, some influenced by the Dutch architecture more familiar to the Hudson River Valley, and attractive shops. The street ends at the 1885 clock tower of gray granite trimmed with red sandstone. A walk in this village is particularly appealing.

From Sharon go to Cornwall Bridge, then go north on 7, to **Cornwall Center,** still an idyllic spot even though it has become something of a tourist mecca, with shops and restaurants out of proportion to the needs of the area. Still, tourist spots become meccas for the good reason that they have something special to offer, and in this case it's the natural beauty of the location, with the Housatonic meandering under a covered bridge designed by Ithiel Town. There are two shops here that deserve special mention. The first, at the bottom of the hill near the covered bridge, belongs to the cabinetmaker Ian Ingersoll, who creates furniture in the Shaker style. His pieces are works of art, not copies. (Telephone: 672-6334.) The second, a large gray clapboard house at the top of the hill, is a well-stocked book, print, and map shop owned by Barbara Farnsworth. (Telephone: 672-6571.) Both are open on Saturdays, but, if you are interested in visiting either of them on another day, call in advance to make sure they'll be open.

Now it's time to go back down to Cornwall Bridge, passing through Housatonic Meadows State Park, and then continue south. I like to see the 200-foot falls at **Kent Falls State Park.** Falls have a special meaning for me—I generally will go out of my way to see them—and these are an easy walk from the road.

The next stop is the **Sloane-Stanley Museum.** Eric Sloane (1905–1985) was an artist and writer who also established a notable collection of early American tools. The museum opened in 1969 with a collection of tools donated and displayed by Sloane. The presentation of the tools—chisels, scythes, axes, screwdrivers—is perfection, bringing out the inherent beauty

The waterfall at Kent Falls State Park can be seen from the high-way, but you really should take time to visit it and walk the path that leads to the top.

in each. An addition housing a collection of Sloane's paintings in a re-creation of his studio was added after his death in 1985.

Behind the building, down an incline, are the handsome and romantic ruins of the Kent Iron Furnace, which went into operation in 1826 and continued almost to the end of the nineteenth century. Also on the grounds is the reproduction of a pioneer cabin that Sloan built to show how difficult and devoid of romance the life of a pioneer really was.

The Sloane-Stanley Museum is open: Mid-May through October, Wednesday–Sunday, 10:00–4:30. Admission fee. Telephone: 927-3849.

The village of **Kent** is an art center with some interesting galleries and attractive shops—you'll want to spend time window-shopping here—many in houses with particularly inviting porches. From here go farther south on 7, along the banks of the Housatonic (you may pass students from the Kent School sculling through the waters), to Schaghticoke Road, and turn onto it, going back toward Kent. Here you will go through the reservation of the Schaghticoke Indians, a tribe that furnished more than a hundred warriors to the Continental army in the

Revolution. Their burial ground, beyond the houses, has a tombstone commemorating Eunice Mauwee, "a Christian Indian princess," who died in 1860. Now continue back into Kent. From here return to Litchfield.

WHERE TO STAY AND EAT

One would think Connecticut would be full to the brim with great inns and restaurants, but it doesn't work that way. Certain areas—the western section and the shore area—do have attractive, good places to stay and eat, and in the New York commuting area in particular there are some very fine New York–type restaurants with New York–type prices, but in the Connecticut River Valley area north of the mouth of the river, arguably the most interesting area, with the richest history, in the entire state, great inns are nonexistent, as are great restaurants.

That doesn't mean you won't be comfortable or eat well in that region; it just means that there are no great finds. Therefore, if you do not wish to stay in Hartford or at a bed-and-breakfast, you can make the inns elsewhere in the state your base of operations from which to explore the valley, for distances, after all, are not great; Connecticut is only 55 miles from the northern border to the southern.

Where to Stay

Area code: 203

Hartford and the Central Connecticut River Valley

For this entire region, I can recommend only one hotel and four bed-and-breakfast inns as being acceptable. Please see other Connecticut sections for further recommendations.

Farmington

Barney House, 11 Mountain Spring Road, 06032
   An 1832 house with seven comfortable rooms. It is part of an

old estate that is now owned and operated by the University of Connecticut. The grounds are very pleasant, with gardens, tennis courts, and a heated pool. Open: All year. $$$. Telephone: 677-9735. Credit cards.

Glastonbury (convenient to Wethersfield)

Butternut Farm, 1654 Main Street, 06033

Glastonbury is a suburb of Hartford and near Wethersfield. The inn is attractive and very nicely furnished. It's quite small—two rooms, a suite, and an apartment attached to the barn—but pleasant and informal. Open: Year-round. $$$. Telephone: 633-6197. Credit cards.

Hartford

The Goodwin Hotel, 1 Haynes Street, 06103

As I mention in the text, making Hartford your home base for seeing this part of the state makes a good deal of sense, and one reason is this hotel, the only luxury facility in the city and definitely the nicest place to stay in the area. The 1881 Queen Anne–style building, restored on the outside, completely redone on the inside, is centrally located in Hartford next to the Civic Center and within easy walking distance of the Atheneum. No two rooms are alike, but those I have seen are comfortable and pleasantly furnished. Service is good and friendly, which is important after you come back from a day of touring. Open: All year. $$$$$. Telephone: 246-7500. Credit cards.

Wethersfield

Chester Bulkley House, 184 Main Street, 06109

This lovely old Greek Revival house (c. 1830) has the distinct advantage of being in the village, which is, as the text notes, one of the best-preserved villages in New England. Open: All year. There are three rooms with private bath, a suite, and two rooms with a shared bath. $$$–$$$$. Telephone: 563-4236. Credit cards.

THE CONNECTICUT SHORE AND THE LOWER CONNECTICUT
RIVER VALLEY

Essex

Griswold Inn, 36 Main Street, 06426

Probably the most famous of all the inns in this part of the
world. Located right in the center of this lovely town, this is the
place to stay if you want to be at the center of the action. The
inn, built in 1776, really is a charmer. One of its more attractive features is its collection of artworks, in particular the
Currier and Ives prints. Another is the taproom. Open: All
year. $$$–$$$$. Telephone: 767-1812. Credit cards.

Ivoryton

Copper Beech Inn, 46 Main Street, 06442

There are four rooms in the inn and nine in the carriage
house, where each has a Jacuzzi. Truly lovely grounds, includ-
ing an English-style garden and the splendid copper beech that
gave the inn its name. Attractively furnished and well run.
Open: All year. $$$$–$$$$$. Telephone: 767-0330. Credit
cards.

Mystic

Red Brook Inn, Gold Star Highway, P.O. Box 237, Old Mystic 06372

The eleven rooms in these two restored and attractively fur-
nished buildings feature canopied four posters and stenciled
floors. There are fireplaces in seven of the rooms. Open: All
year. $$$$–$$$$$. Telephone: 572-0349. Credit cards.

The Inn at Mystic, Route 27 and Route 1, 06335

Calling this an inn is pushing it a bit, for most of the accom-
modations are in what can only be called a motel, and a not
very attractive one at that. However, the 1904 main building
and gatehouse are quite attractive and offer good views over
the harbor. If you decide to stay here, be sure to specify the

older buildings. Open: All year. $$$$$. Telephone: 536-9604. Credit cards.

New London

Lighthouse Inn, 6 Guthrie Place, 06320
Housed in an old estate once known as Meadow Court, this really is more like a hotel than an inn because of its many rooms, both in the main building and in the carriage house— which is large enough to handle corporate meetings. Still, the service is friendly and efficient and the rooms comfortable, and in the main house the baths are furnished with whirlpool tubs. It is very convenient to Mystic. Open: All year. $$$$–$$$$$. Telephone: 443-8411. Credit cards.

Old Lyme

Bee and Thistle Inn, 100 Lyme Street, 06371
A 1756 building filled with fireplaces and attractively furnished. A little on the formal side, but there's nothing inherently wrong with that, and Old Lyme is such a lovely village. There is also a cottage with a bedroom, kitchen, bath, and two other rooms if you wish more elaborate accommodations. Open: All year except the first two weeks in January. $$$–$$$$. Telephone: 434-1667; reservations, 800-622-4946. Credit cards.

Old Lyme Inn, Box 787, 85 Lyme Street, 06371
Another attractive inn, slightly less formal. Open: All year except the first two weeks in January. $$$$. Telephone: 434-2600. Credit cards.

Old Saybrook

Saybrook Point Inn and Spa, 2 Bridge Street, 06475
This is part of a condominium complex and is quite luxurious. Most rooms have wonderful views over the Connecticut River and Long Island Sound, and many also have a balcony.

The rooms are spacious, and some have fireplaces. The inn has a health club, full-service spa, indoor and outdoor pools, and a marina. For this you pay. Open: All year. $$$$$. Telephone: In Connecticut, 395-2000; outside the state, 800-243-0212. Credit cards.

Westbrook

Water's Edge Inn, 1525 Boston Post Road, 06498
Another elaborate place to stay that really qualifies as a resort, with indoor and outdoor pools, occasional entertainment, tennis courts, platform tennis, and a spa. Again, there are lovely views of the Sound, and the rooms are comfortably luxurious. And again, for this you pay. Open: All year. $$$$$. Telephone: In Connecticut, 399-5901; outside the state, 800-222-5901. Credit cards.

THE LITCHFIELD HILLS AND THE HOUSATONIC RIVER VALLEY

Best in the Region: The Mayflower Inn, Washington

Lakeville

Interlaken Inn and Conference Center, 74 Interlaken Road (Route 112), 06039
Obviously not a cozy country inn, but if you want to stay at a resort offering a fitness center, sauna, lake swimming, tennis, golf, and boating, this is for you. Open: All year. $$$$$. Telephone: 800-222-2909, 435-9878. Credit cards.

Wake Robin Inn, Route 41, 06039
Originally built in 1896 as a school for girls, this Georgian Revival building has been an inn since 1913 and now has forty units. It is set on a hillside offering pretty views from the attractive and comfortable rooms, and there are fireplaces in the library and common room. Open: All year. $$$$$. Telephone: 435-2515. Credit cards.

Litchfield

Tollgate Hill Inn, Tollgate Road (Route 202), 06759
This 1745 inn is on the National Register of Historic Places. On the smallish side—there are twenty rooms, eight with fireplaces—this is my first choice of a place to stay in Litchfield. It also offers very good dining. (see Where to Eat). Open: All year. $$$$–$$$$$. Telephone: 800-445-3903, 567-4545. Credit cards.

The Litchfield Inn, 432 Bantam Road, 06759
The thirty-one units are comfortable, and the inn has both a restaurant and a pub and bar. Some of the rooms, by the way, are decorated around themes—Queen Victoria, for example. This, depending on your point of view, can be good news or bad news. Open: All year. $$$$–$$$$$. Telephone: 567-4503. Credit cards.

New Preston

Boulders Inn, Lakeshore Road (Route 45), 06777
On Lake Waramaug, this comfortable 1895 inn has some wonderful views of the lake and the surrounding woods. There are six rooms in the inn and three in the carriage house, and there are eight guesthouses with fireplaces. A quiet, pleasant place to stay, the inn also offers swimming, tennis, boating, and hiking trails. Open: All year. $$$$$. Telephone: 868-0541. Credit cards.

Hopkins Inn, 22 Hopkins Road (off Route 45), 06777
A good choice in this area for various reasons: The inn is located high above Lake Waramaug, the views are truly lovely, and in summer there's al fresco dining. I also like the fact that the inn has a trout tank that supplies the dining room (see Where to Eat). In addition, the 1847 Federal building is cheerful and welcoming, and the rates are reasonable. Add it all up, and you get a pleasant inn. Open: Late March–December. $$. Telephone: 868-7295. No credit cards.

The Inn on Lake Waramaug, North Shore Road (off Route 45), 06777

Another old (1790s) and lovely inn. Of the twenty-three rooms, sixteen have fireplaces. There is a heated swimming pool and a sauna, tennis, boating, and lake cruises—the inn has its own boat. Also see Where to Eat. Open: All year. $$$$$. Telephone: 800-LAKE-INN, 868-0563. Credit cards.

Ridgefield

Ridgefield, within sneezing distance of New York, is nonetheless a lovely New England town and is blessed with three excellent inns.

The Elms, 500 Main Street, 06877

Right in the heart of Ridgefield, this lovely building dates from 1760 and has been an inn since 1799. It also offers a good restaurant (see Where to Eat). Open: All year. $$$$$. Telephone: 438-2541. Credit cards.

Stonehenge, Route 7, 06877

This delightful inn overlooking a pond replaces the old inn, which burned down in 1988. The rooms are comfortable and pretty, the setting as bucolic as one could wish, and the food is first-rate (see Where to Eat). There also is a pool. Open: All year. $$$$$. Telephone: 438-6511. Credit cards.

West Lane Inn,   22 West Lane, 06877

This inn offers luxurious accommodations, some with fireplaces. Open: All year. $$$$$. Telephone: 438-7323. Credit cards.

Salisbury

Under Mountain Inn, 482 Under Mountain Road (Route 41), 06068

This eighteenth-century farmhouse has seven rooms and a good restaurant, but it is the setting and the surrounding countryside that, for me, make it a place to recommend. Open: All year. $$$. Telephone: 435-0242. No credit cards.

Washington

The Mayflower Inn, 118 Woodbury Road (Route 47), 06793
This originally was a school that opened in 1894. It began its life as an inn in 1920, slowly went downhill in the seventies and eighties, and has now been revivified as one of the most luxurious inns in the country by former Wall Street investment banker Robert Mnuchin and his wife, Adriana. Everything is perfect here, from the gardens to the twenty-five exquisitely decorated guest rooms to the selection of books on hand to the tennis courts and heated swimming pool. There is a fitness center and an excellent restaurant (see Where to Eat). In fact, everything may be just a teeny bit too perfect. Needless to say, this does not come cheap. Open: All year. $$$$$. Telephone: 868-9466. Credit cards.

Where to Eat

Area code: 203

HARTFORD AND THE CENTRAL CONNECTICUT RIVER VALLEY

Avon

This little town has three restaurants worthy of note, and two are quite good.

Avon Old Farms Inn, Junction of Routes 44 and 10. Open: Lunch, dinner. Reservations required. $$. Phone: 677-2818. Credit cards.
This was a stagecoach stop in the eighteenth century, and it's not only pretty but reasonably priced as well. At the same time, the food can be a bit on the pretentious side.

Jetstream's Café, 51 East Main Street. Open: Lunch, dinner. $$. Phone: 677-9026. Credit cards.
I wouldn't make a special trip to eat here, but I sure wouldn't pass it by, particularly in the summer, when the patio is open.

If you want plain old American food that will suit the entire family, and you don't want to empty your wallet, this is the place.

Max-A-Mia, 70 East Main Street (Fairway Shops). Open: Lunch, dinner. $$. Phone: 677-6299. Credit cards.

This is one of the best restaurants in the Hartford area and certainly is my candidate for the best Italian restaurant. The pastas are tops, and some dishes are prepared on the now practically obligatory wood-fired oven (but here they know how to use it). I love garlic, so you can imagine how I feel about the perfectly roasted bulbs they serve here. And on top of all that, the prices are moderate—particularly considering the quality.

Farmington

Apricot's, 1593 Farmington Ave. Open: Lunch, dinner. $$$. Phone: 673-5405. Credit cards.

It's worth making something of an effort to eat here because the setting, with a view of the Farmington River, is delightful, the food is quite good if a little on the expensive side, and the service first-rate.

Hartford

Capitol Fish House Restaurant, 391 Main Street. Open: Lunch, dinner. $$. Phone: 724-3370. Credit cards.

A perfectly good seafood restaurant in a pleasant setting. Service is friendly, and the prices reasonable.

Carabone's Ristorante, 588 Franklin Ave. Open: Lunch, dinner. $$. Phone: 296-9646. Credit cards.

If you crave good old-fashioned southern Italian food, rich with tomato sauce, this is the place for you. The veal parmigiana is particularly popular.

Chale Ipanema, 452 Wethersfield Ave. Open: Lunch, dinner. $$. Phone: 296-2120. Credit cards.

One of the interesting things about Hartford is the great variety of ethnic restaurants found there. This Brazilian-

Portuguese eatery has very good food at reasonable prices. The setting is modest, but if you like this kind of cooking, you will be pleased you came here.

Congress Rotisserie, 7 Maple Ave. Open: Lunch, dinner. $$. Phone: 560-1965. Credit cards.

Businessmen love this restaurant at lunchtime, and it's popular at dinner, too. Good news: The well-prepared, new American fare comes in large portions at moderate prices. Bad news: It's always crowded and it can be very noisy.

Costa del Sol, 901 Wethersfield Ave. (Monte Carlo Plaza). Open: Lunch, dinner. $$. Phone: 296-1714. Credit cards.

Another one of those ethnic restaurants that make Hartford an interesting place for dining out. Forget the unfortunate shopping-mall setting while enjoying the delicious tapas and other Spanish delights.

Gaetano's, 1 Civic Center Plaza. Open: Lunch, dinner. $$. Phone: 249-1629. Credit cards.

Another just plain good Italian restaurant, this one with a northern bias. Prices are moderate.

Hearthstone, 678 Maple Ave. Open: Lunch, dinner. $$–$$$. Phone: 246-8814. Credit cards.

This is an old-fashioned steakhouse in looks with an old-fashioned steakhouse menu. No more need be said, except that the steaks are good.

Hot Tomato's, 1 Union Place. Open: Lunch, dinner. $$–$$$. Phone: 249-5100. Credit cards.

Italian, trendy, and very good.

Max on Main, 205 Main Street. Open: Lunch, dinner. $$. Phone: 522-2530. Credit cards.

Under the same ownership as the restaurant in Avon (Max-A-Mia), this very good restaurant offers more experimental dishes and definitely should be at the top of the list of restaurants to visit in Hartford. The best surprise—the prices are extremely reasonable.

Truc Orient Express, 735 Wethersfield Ave. Open: Lunch, dinner. $$. Phone: 296-2818. Credit cards.

Why is it that once you get out of major cities, Asian restaurants so often are dreadful? This Vietnamese restaurant, though, is an exception to that rule and well worth a visit.

THE CONNECTICUT SHORE AND THE LOWER CONNECTICUT RIVER VALLEY

Centerbrook

Fine Bouche, 78 Main Street. Open: Dinner. $$–$$$. Phone: 767-1277. Credit cards.

If you're going to be attending a performance at the Goodspeed Opera House and need a very good place for dinner, search no farther than this charming French restaurant. You'll be very pleased.

Chester

Du Village, 59 Main Street. Open: Dinner, Wednesday–Sunday. $$–$$$. Phone: 526-5301. Credit cards.

Another good choice if you will be attending Goodspeed. The food is well-prepared country French, and the service is friendly and efficient.

Essex

The Griswold Inn, 36 Main Street. Open: Lunch, dinner. $$–$$$. Phone: 767-1776. Credit cards.

The Griz, as everybody calls it, is the best-known restaurant as well as inn in this area. It is particularly famous for its Sunday brunch. Now, I love this inn, and I love Essex, but the much-vaunted brunch is only so-so.

Ivoryton

Copper Beech Inn, 46 Main Street. Open: Dinner. $$$. Phone: 767-0330. Credit cards.

Another convenient and beautiful spot for dining before

going to the Goodspeed Opera House. It can be a little stuffy, and it isn't cheap, but the French menu offers generally good food.

New Haven

Frank Pepe Pizzeria, 157 Wooster Street. Open: Lunch, dinner. $–$$. Phone: 865-5762. No credit cards.

First-timers come here as to a shrine, for many consider this to be the best pizza in the world, let alone the United States. Made in coal-burning brick ovens, the pizza is indeed perfection. Eat your heart out, Harvard.

Leon's, 321 Washington Ave. Open: Lunch, dinner. $$. Phone: 777-5366.

Old-fashioned and quite good southern Italian food in a setting that is so dated it borders on camp. Portions are huge, service casual.

Louis's Lunch, 261 Crown Street. Open: Lunch, and dinner on Thursday, Friday, Saturday. $. Phone: 562-5507. No credit cards.

Louis serves hamburgers between two pieces of toast, the old-fashioned way, and they are delicious. I first started eating them when I was a student in New Haven, and I still think they're the most delicious burgers I've ever had.

Scoozi, 1104 Chapel Street. Open: Lunch, dinner. $$. Phone: 776-8268. Credit cards.

A pleasant, up-to-the-minute trattoria with up-to-the-minute food selections.

Old Lyme

Bee and Thistle Inn, 100 Lyme Street. Open: Breakfast, lunch, dinner. November–April, Monday, Wednesday, Thursday, High Tea, 3:30–5:00. $$$. Phone: 434-1667. Credit cards.

Quintessential New England setting, good food, lovely village. You won't go wrong here.

Old Lyme Inn, 85 Lyme Street. Open: Lunch, dinner. $$$.
Phone: 434-2600. Credit cards.

A choice between this and the Bee and Thistle is difficult; I
give a slight edge to the food here but prefer the setting of the
Bee and Thistle. Whichever you choose, you'll be happy.

Stonington

Noah's, 115 Water Street. Open: Breakfast, lunch, dinner.
$–$$. Phone: 535-3925. No credit cards.

The fancy restaurants in Stonington are Randall's Ordinary
and the Harbor View, both of which are perfectly acceptable,
but this one offers excellent American food and absolutely delicious breads and desserts. No tablecloths here—for something
more fancy, try one of the other two—but a real find.

THE LITCHFIELD HILLS AND THE HOUSATONIC RIVER VALLEY

Canaan

The Cannery Café, 85 Main Street. Open: Lunch, dinner. $$.
Phone: 824-7333. Credit cards.

The food (American-style) is good, the wine selection (also
American) is good, the service is good. Obviously, then, if you're
in the area, this is the place to go.

Kent

The Cobble Cookery, Kent Green Shopping Center. Open:
Lunch. $–$$. Phone: 927-3393. No credit cards for purchases
under $25.

Open only for lunch and tea, this makes a nice stopping place
if you're in Kent at lunchtime and want soup and a sandwich.
There's a gourmet shop here, too. Very pleasant.

Lakeville

The Woodland, 192 Sharon Road (Route 41). Open: Lunch,
dinner. $$. Phone: 435-0578. Credit cards.

The good news: The southwestern-style menu is reasonable, portions are large, and the food is good. The bad news: Consequently, it is popular and, because reservations for fewer than five people are not accepted, there can be a long wait for a table.

Litchfield

Tollgate Hill Inn, Tollgate Road (Route 202). Open: Lunch, dinner. $$–$$$. Phone: 567-4545. Credit cards.

The food here is another reason to stay in Litchfield. This is a very good contemporary American restaurant in a lovely setting. It is fairly expensive.

West Street Grill, 43 West Street. Open: Lunch, dinner. $$–$$$. Phone: 567-3885. Credit cards.

A little bit of chic Manhattan in the Litchfield Hills. If you want to get away from urban pretensions, don't come here. However, the food, again contemporary American, is very good, and prices are about the same as at the Tollgate Hill Inn. Reservations are recommended for dinner but are not accepted for lunch.

New Preston

Boulders Inn, Lakeshore Road (Route 45). Open: Lunch, dinner. $$$. Phone: 868-0541. Credit cards.

The setting, and the fact that you can dine al fresco in the summer, make this a lovely place to dine. As for the food . . . well, it's good if not memorable.

Doc's, 62 Flirtation Ave. (Route 45). Open: Lunch (Friday–Sunday), dinner (Wednesday–Sunday). $$. Phone: 868-9415. No credit cards.

Not in a beautiful setting such as the inns offer—in fact, *modest* is almost kind—but the northern Italian food served here makes up for the surroundings. And it's reasonably priced. Reservations are required, and if you want wine, bring your own bottle.

Hopkins Inn, 22 Hopkins Road (off Route 45). Open: Lunch, dinner. $$. Phone: 868-7295. No credit cards.

This is certainly one of the prettiest places to dine in New Preston, and that alone makes a meal here worthwhile. At the same time, the food is a bit on the heavy side—wiener schnitzel and duck à l'orange, for example—so be prepared.

Inn on Lake Waramaug, North Shore Road (off Route 45). Open: Lunch, dinner. $$$. Phone: 868-0563. No credit cards.

Another beautiful setting, but the contemporary American food here is only moderately good.

Ridgefield

The Elms, 500 Main Street. Open: Lunch, dinner. $$$. Phone: 438-2541. Credit cards.

As one moves closer to New York, prices rise in direct proportion. The Elms, then, is not cheap, but neither are the other two eateries listed below. The setting is country-inn-perfect, and the food is good.

Stonehenge, Route 7. Open: Dinner. $$$. Phone: 438-6511. Credit cards.

The best Ridgefield has to offer. The menu offers excellent food with a French bias, and the setting and service are hard to improve on.

The Inn at Ridgefield, 20 West Lane. Open: Lunch, dinner. $$$. Phone: 438-8282. Credit cards.

The slightly old-fashioned Continental menu offers good food, but it is the setting and service that make dining here truly worthwhile.

Salisbury

Ragamont Inn, 8 Main Street (Route 44). Open: Lunch (Saturday and Sunday), dinner. Closed November through April. $$$. Phone: 435-2372. No credit cards.

A lovely inn in a lovely village. There is dining on a terrace in summer, and two very attractive dining rooms for other seasons. The food, Continental with some Swiss specialties, is good, but it's the overall setting that you'll remember.

Under Mountain Inn, 482 Under Mountain Road (Route 41). Open: Dinner only, Friday and Saturday. $$$. Phone: 435-0242. Credit cards.

The chef-owner is a Brit, which has influenced the menu. Good food in a deep-country setting. Reservations are required.

The White Hart, Village Green (the conjunction of Routes 41 and 44). Open: Breakfast, lunch, dinner. $$$. Phone: 435-0030. Credit cards.

The very popular restaurant in this inn has a contemporary American menu offering food good enough to merit a visit just for the dining room. The prices are moderately expensive, and if price is a factor, eat in the excellent Tap Room for considerably less.

Washington

Mayflower Inn, 118 Woodbury Road (Route 47). Open: Lunch, dinner. $$$. Phone: 868-9466. Credit cards.

As with everything else at this inn, all is perfection. The setting can't be beat, the wine list is top-drawer, the American-food-based menu imaginative, the service quietly flawless. And it's expensive—but not out of sight.

West Cornwall

Freshfields, Route 128. Open: Lunch, dinner. $$$. Phone: 672-6601. Credit cards.

A country restaurant with city prices, but the contemporary American food served here is quite good, the country setting, including a porch and a dock, is very relaxing and, let's face it, you only live once.

INDEX

Acworth, N.H., 98
Adam, Robert, 108
Albert Schweitzer Center,
    Mass., 134
Allen, Ethan, 5
American Indian Museum,
    Mass., 186
America's Stonehenge, N.H.,
    104
Amherst, Mass., 172–73
Amherst College, 172, 173
Amoskeag Manufacturing
    Company, N.H., 100–101
Annabelle's, Portsmouth, N.H.,
    127
antiquing, 7, 70–71
Appledore Island, N.H., 114,
    115
Apricot's, Farmington, Conn.,
    263
Arethusa Falls, N.H., 82
Arrowhead, Pittsfield, Mass.,
    147–48
Asa Stebbins House, Mass.,
    168–69
Ashley, John, 136
Austin, A. Everett (Chick),
    206–8
Avon Old Farms Inn, Conn.,
    262
Avon Old Farms School, Conn.,
    213

Bacon, Henry, 156, 157
Baker Memorial Library, N.H.,
    83
Balsams, Dixville Notch, N.H.,
    119–20, 123

Barnard, Vt., 26
Barney House, Farmington,
    Conn., 255–56
Barrett House, N.H., 95–96
Barrows House, N.H., 43, 56,
    61
Bartholomew's Cobble, Mass.,
    137–38, 139
Bash Bish Falls, Mass.,
    138–39
Basketball Hall of Fame,
    Mass., 180–81
Bedford, N.H., 121–22, 125
Bedford Village Inn, 121–22,
    125
Bee and Thistle Inn, Old Lyme,
    Conn., 258, 266
Beinecke Rare Book and
    Manuscript Library,
    Conn., 241
Ben & Jerry's, Vt., 20–21
Bennington, Vt., 31–35, 61
Bennington Battle Monument,
    35
Bennington Museum, 31–34
Bennington Station, 61
Bentley's, Woodstock, Vt.,
    60–61
Berkshire Athenaeum, 143
Berkshire Botanical Garden,
    157–58
Berkshire County Courthouse,
    143
Berkshire Museum, 148
Berkshires, Mass., 133–67
    general information, 133–34
    Great Barrington area, 134–
    39

Berkshires, Mass., *(cont'd)*
  Lenox area, 139–43
  Mohawk Trail, 164–67
  Pittsfield area, 143–49
  special interest services, 134
  Stockbridge area, 150–59
  Tyringham Valley, 159–62
  where to eat, 192–95
  where to stay, 187–91
  Williamstown area, 162–64
Berkshire Scenic Railway
    Museum, 142–43
Berkshire Theater Festival,
    152
Bidwell House, Mass., 160
Billings Farm and Museum,
    Vt., 25–26
Bingham Falls, Vt., 20
Blantyre, Lenox, Mass., 187–
    88, 192–93
Blue Strawbery, Portsmouth,
    N.H., 126
Boswell Botany Trail, Vt., 47
Boulders Inn, New Preston,
    Conn., 260, 268
Brattleboro, Vt., 39
Brattleboro Museum and Art
    Center, 39
Bretton Woods, N.H., 81–82,
    119
Bridge of Flowers, Mass., 166
Brigham, Mary, 136–37
Bryant, William Cullen, 149
Bryant Homestead, Mass.,
    148–49, 174
Bryant House, Weston, Vt., 63
Bulfinch, Charles, 211
Burlington area, Vt., 8–16, 50,
    58
Butternut Farm, Glastonbury,
    Conn., 256
Buttolph-Williams House,
    Conn., 221–22

Café Buon Gustaio, Hanover,
    N.H., 124
Cannery Café, Canaan, Conn.,
    267

Cannon Mountain, N.H., 77
Canterbury Shaker Village,
    N.H., 98–100, 125
Canyon Ranch at
    Bellefontaine, Lenox,
    Mass., 188
Castle in the Clouds, N.H., 92
Castle Street Café, Great
    Barrington, Mass., 193
Cathedral of the Pines, N.H.,
    95
Center Sandwich, N.H., 92
Chantecleer, East Dorset, Vt.,
    62
Chapin Library, Williams
    College, Mass., 164
Charlestown, N.H., 89
Charlotte-Essex Ferry, Vt., 16
Charter Oak, 203–4
Cheese Factory, Plymouth, Vt.,
    30
Chester, Vt., 41
Chester Bulkley House,
    Wethersfield, Conn., 256
Chester-Hadlyme Ferry,
    Conn., 234–35
Chesterwood, Mass., 155–57
Children's Chimes Bell Tower,
    Mass., 151
Choate, Joseph Hodges, 152,
    154–55
Choate, Mabel, 152–53
Christmas Farm Inn, Jackson,
    N.H., 73, 118–19, 124
churches:
  Connecticut, 212, 219–20,
    222, 235, 238–39, 246
  Massachusetts, 135–36, 140,
    151, 171, 180
  New Hampshire, 90, 101,
    109
  Vermont, 17, 34
Church Street Café, Lenox,
    Mass., 193
Claremont, N.H., 89
Clark, Francine and Robert
    Sterling, 162–63
Clemens, Samuel, 209

Cobble Cookery, Kent, Conn., 267
Cold Hollow Cider Mill, Vt., 21
Colonel John Ashley House, Mass., 135–37
Colt, Samuel, 205
Concord, N.H., 93, 97–100
Connecticut, 199–270
  central Connecticut River Valley, 212–24, 255–56, 262–67
  drives, 248–50
  general facts, 201–2
  Hartford area, 204–11, 256, 263–65
  history, 202–4
  Housatonic Valley, 251–55, 259–62, 267–70
  information, 204
  lower Connecticut River Valley, 257–59, 265–67
  map, 130–31
  Old State House, 211
  shore, 225–44, 257–59, 265–67
  State Capitol, 211
  western, 244–55
  where to eat, 255, 262–70
  where to stay, 255–62
Connecticut River Museum, 233
Connecticut River Valley:
  Connecticut, 212–24, 255–56, 257–59, 262–67
  Massachusetts, 167–87, 191–92, 196–97
  New Hampshire, 82–90, 120–21, 124–25
  Vermont, 24–49, 54–58, 60–62
Connecticut Valley Historical Museum, Mass., 179–80
Cooley Gallery, Conn., 236
Coolidge, Calvin, 29–30, 175
Copper Beech Inn, Ivoryton, Conn., 257, 265
Cornish, N.H., 86–89
Cornwall Center, Conn., 253

Craftsbury Common, Vt., 21–22, 53–54, 59
Crane Museum, Mass., 148
Crawford Notch, N.H., 80–82
Creamery Restaurant, Canterbury, N.H., 100
Cresson, Margaret French, 156–57
Currier Gallery of Art, N.H., 101–4

Danby Four Corners, Vt., 48–49
D'Artagnan, Lyme, N.H., 124
Dartmouth College, N.H., 83–84
Davis, Alexander Jackson, 206
Deerfield, Mass., 167–71, 191, 196
Deerfield Inn, 191, 196
Dickinson, Emily, 172
Dinosaur State Park, Conn., 222
Dixville Notch, N.H., 119, 123
Doc's, New Preston, Conn., 268
Dog Team Tavern, Middlebury, Vt., 58
Dorset, Vt., 43–49, 56, 61–62
Dorset Inn, 43, 56, 62
Downing, Andrew Jackson, 224
drives:
  Center Sandwich, N.H., 92
  Concord region, N.H., 97–100
  Dorset-Manchester, Vt., 44–48
  Dorset-Peru, Vt., 48–49
  Grafton-Brattleboro, Vt., 37–39
  Grafton-Weston, Vt., 39–43
  Housatonic River Valley, 251–55
  Litchfield, Conn., 248–50
  Middlebury, Vt., 19
  Mohawk Trail, Mass., 164–67

drives *(cont'd)*
  Monadnock region, N.H.,
    93–97
  Northeast Kingdom, Vt.,
    21–23
  Woodstock, Vt., 26–28
Dublin, N.H., 94–95
Du Village, Chester, Conn.,
    265

Earl, Ralph, 31–32, 184, 246
East Haddam, Conn., 235
Eastside Grill, Northampton,
    Mass., 196
Edwards, Jonathan, 173–74
Egrement Inn, Mass., 188–89
Electra Havemeyer Webb
    Memorial Building, Vt.,
    12, 13–14
Ellsworth, Oliver, 223
Elms, Ridgefield, Conn., 261,
    269
Elm Street Café, Montpelier,
    Vt., 60
Emily Dickinson House,
    172–73
Enfield, N.H., 86
Equinox Inn, Manchester, Vt.,
    44, 57
Essex, Conn., 232–33, 257,
    265
Exeter, N.H., 116–17

Fair Haven, Vt., 51–52, 59
Farmington, Conn., 212–14,
    255–56, 263
Farrand, Beatrix Jones, 142,
    213, 250
Federal House, South Lee,
    Mass., 189, 193
Fenton, Christopher Webber,
    33
Field, Erastus Salisbury, 169,
    177–79
Fine Bouche, Centerbrook,
    Conn., 265
Fitzwilliam, N.H., 96–97
Flume, N.H., 76–77

Fly Fishing, American
    Museum of, 47–48
Four Chimneys, Bennington,
    Vt., 61
Four Columns Inn, Newfane,
    Vt., 38, 50, 57, 62
Franconia Notch, N.H., 75–77,
    120, 123
Frank L. Boyden Carriage
    Collection, Mass., 171
Franklin Pierce Homestead,
    N.H., 98
French, Daniel Chester, 97,
    151, 155–57
Freshfields, West Cornwall,
    Conn., 270
Frog Hollow, Vt., 17
Fruitlands Museums, Mass.,
    185–87

Gastonbury, Conn., 256
Gateways Inn, Lenox, Mass.,
    189, 193–94
George Walter Vincent Smith
    Art Museum, Mass., 179
Gillette Castle, Conn., 234–35
Gingerbread House, Mass.,
    161
Glen Ellis Falls, N.H., 78
Goodspeed Opera House,
    Conn., 235
Goodwin Hotel, Hartford,
    Conn., 256
Grafton, Vt., 35–43, 56–57, 62
Granby, Conn., 214
Green Mountain Inn, Stowe,
    Vt., 53, 59
Griswold Inn, Essex, Conn.,
    257, 265
Grove Street Cemetery, Conn.,
    244
Guilford, Conn., 236–37

Hampshire College, Mass., 172
Hancock, N.H., 93, 121, 125
Hancock Shaker Village,
    Mass., 143–47

Hanover, N.H., 83–84, 120, 124
Hanover area river villages, N.H., 84–90
Hanover Inn, N.H., 120, 124
Harriet Beecher Stowe House, Conn., 209–11
Harrisville, N.H., 93–94
Hartford, Conn., 204–11
  where to eat, 263–65
  where to stay, 256
Harvard Shaker Community, Mass., 185–86
Hassam, Childe, 115
Hatheway House, Conn., 218–19
Havemeyer, Henry Osborne and Louisine, 9–10
Haverhill Corner, N.H., 85–86
Hawthorne, Nathaniel, 139, 140–41
Helen Geier Flynt Textile Museum, Mass., 171
Henniker, N.H., 98
Henry Needham Flynt Silver and Metalware Collection, Mass., 171
Henry Whitfield Museum, Conn., 237
Hildene, Vt., 44–46
Hillsborough, N.H., 98
Hill-Stead Museum, Conn., 213
Hinsdale and Anna Williams House, Mass., 169–70
Holley-Williams House Museum, Conn., 252
Home Hill Inn, Plainfield, N.H., 121, 125
Hood Art Museum, N.H., 83–84
Hooker, Thomas, 202–3
Hopkins Inn, New Preston, Conn., 260, 269
Hopkinton, N.H., 98
Hoppin, Francis V. L., 141
Hotel Northampton, Mass., 191–92, 196

Housatonic Valley, Conn., 251–55, 259–62, 267–70
Hyland House, Conn., 237

Inn at Mill Falls, Meredith, N.H., 122, 125
Inn at Montpelier, Vt., 54–55, 60
Inn at Mystic, Conn., 257–58
Inn at Ridgefield, Conn., 269
Inn at Sawmill Farm, West Dover, Vt., 39, 50, 57–58, 63
Inn at Shelburne Farms, Vt., 50, 58
Inn at Weston, Vt., 63
Inn on Lake Waramaug, Conn., 260–61, 269
Inn on the Common, Craftsbury, Vt., 21–22, 53–54, 59
inns, pricing key, ix
Institute for American Indian Studies, Conn., 249
Interlaken Inn and Conference Center, Lakeville, Conn., 259
Isles of Shoals, N.H., 114–15
Ivoryton, Conn., 257, 265–66

Jackson, N.H., 118, 123
Jacob's Pillow Dance Festival, Mass., 161–62
Jaffrey, N.H., 95
Jekyll, Gertrude, 249–50
Jetstream's Café, Avon, Conn., 262–63
J. J. Hapgood country store, Vt., 49
Joe's Diner, Lee, Mass., 194
John Hancock Inn, Hancock, N.H., 93, 121–22, 125
Johnny Mack's General Store, Vt., 48
Jones Library, Mass., 173
Joseph Allen Skinner Museum, Mass., 176–77

Joseph Smith Memorial and
    Birthplace, Vt., 27
Joshua Hempsted House,
    Conn., 231

Kahn, Louis, 242
Kancamagus Highway, N.H.,
    73–75
Kedron Valley Inn, South
    Woodstock, Vt., 55, 61
Kensett, John F., 138
Kent, Conn., 254–55, 267
Kent Falls State Park, Conn.,
    253
King House Museum, Conn.,
    219
Kingsbury, John, 115
Kitson, Sir Henry Hudson, 161

LaFarge, John, 151
Lake Champlain area, Vt.,
    8–19
  Burlington area, 8–16
  drive, 19
  Middlebury, 17–19
  where to eat, 58–59
  where to stay, 50–52
Lakeville, Conn., 259, 267–68
Lake Waramaug, Conn., 248
Lake Willoughby, Vt., 22–23
Lake Winnipesaukee region,
    N.H., 90–92, 122–23,
    125–26
Lee, Mother Ann, 99, 143
Le Jardin, Williamstown,
    Mass., 189, 194
Lenox, Mass., 139–43
Lighthouse Inn, New London,
    Conn., 258
Lincoln, Robert Todd, 44–45
Litchfield, Conn., 244–48, 260,
    268
Litchfield Hills area, Conn.,
    244–55, 259–62, 267–70
Litchfield Inn, 260
Lord Jeffrey Inn, Amherst,
    Mass., 191, 196
Lost River Gorge, N.H., 77

Lyman Allyn Art Museum,
    Conn., 231–32
Lyme, N.H., 84, 120, 124
Lyme Inn, N.H., 120–21, 124
Lyon, Mary, 175–76

McKim, Charles F., 151
MacMonnies, Frederick W.,
    32–33
Manchester, N.H., 93,
    100–104
Manchester, Vt., 44–48, 57, 62
maps:
  Connecticut–Massachusetts,
    130–31
  New Hampshire, 66
  Vermont, 2
Mark Twain House, Conn.,
    209–11
Marlboro, Vt., 39
Massachusetts, 129–97
  Berkshires, 133–67, 187–91,
    192–95
  Connecticut River Valley,
    167–87, 191–92, 196–97
  drive: Mohawk Trail, 164–67
  map, 130–31
  where to eat, 187, 192–97
  where to stay, 187–92
MassMoCA, 165, 166
Max-A-Mia, Avon, Conn., 263
Mayflower Inn, Washington,
    Conn., 262, 270
Mead Art Museum, Mass., 173
Memorial Hall Museum,
    Mass., 171
Merck Forest Farmland
    Center, Vt., 48
Meredith, N.H., 92, 122, 125
Merwin House, Mass., 151
Middlebury, Vt., 16–19, 51, 58
Middlebury College, 17–18
Middlebury Inn, 51
Middletown, Conn., 214–16
Mills, Robert, 232
Mine Hill Preserve, Conn.,
    249
Mission House, Mass., 152–53

Monadnock region, N.H., 93–97
Montpelier, Vt., 28–29, 54–55, 60
Monument Mountain, Mass., 139
Moodus, Conn., 235
Morgan, Justin, 18, 25
Morgan Horse Farm, Vt., 18
Moses, Grandma, 33
Moultonborough, N.H., 92
Mount Chocorua, N.H., 74–75
Mount Greylock, Mass., 164–65
Mount Holyoke Art Museum, 176
Mount Holyoke College, Mass., 172, 175–76
Mount Mansfield, Vt., 19–20
Mount Monadnock, N.H., 93, 95
Mount, The, Mass., 141–42
Mount Washington, N.H., 78–80
Mount Washington Auto Road, 79, 80
Mount Washington Cog Railway, 79–80
Mount Washington Hotel at Bretton Woods, N.H., 81–82, 119
M/S Mount Washington, 91
Mystic, Conn., 257–58
Mystic Marinelife Aquarium, 230
Mystic Seaport Museum, 226–29

Naumkeag, Mass., 153–55
Nervi, Pier Luigi, 84
New Britain, Conn., 216–17
New Britain Museum of American Art, 216–17
New Castle, N.H., 116
New England Cruise Line, 235
Newfane, Vt., 37–39, 57, 62
Newfane Inn, 38

New Hampshire, 65–127
  antiquing, 70–71
  central and southern, 90–104, 121–22, 125
  drives, 92–100
  general facts, 67–68
  Historical Society and Library, 97–98
  history, 68–70
  Lake Winnepesaukee region, 90–92, 122–23, 125–26
  maps, 66, 71
  northern, 71–82, 118–20
  Portsmouth and seacoast area, 104–17, 122–23, 126–27
  special interest sources, 70–71
  State House, 97
  upper Connecticut River Valley, 82–90, 120–21, 124–25
  where to eat, 123–27
  where to stay, 117–23
  White Mountains, 71–82, 118–20, 123
New Haven, Conn., 237–44, 266
New Ipswich, N.H., 95–96
New London, Conn., 230–32, 258
New London, N.H., 121, 124
New London Inn, N.H., 121, 124–25
New Preston, Conn., 248, 260–61, 268–69
Noah's, Stonington, Conn., 267
Norfolk, Conn., 252
Norman Rockwell Museum, Mass., 158–59
North Adams, Mass., 165–66
Northampton, Mass., 173–75
North Conway, N.H., 75
Northeast Kingdom, Vt.:
  drives, 21–23
  St. Johnsbury, 23–24, 54, 60
  where to eat, 59–60
  where to stay, 53–54

North River Glass Studio,
    Mass., 166

Oar House, Portsmouth, N.H.,
    126
Old Lighthouse Museum,
    Conn., 225–26
Old Lyme, Conn., 235–36, 258,
    266
Old Lyme Inn, Conn., 258, 267
Old Man of the Mountain,
    N.H., 75–76
Old Mill, South Egremont,
    Mass., 194
Old Newfane Inn, Newfane,
    Vt., 62–63
Old New-Gate Prison and
    Copper Mine, 214
Old Saybrook, Conn., 258–59
Old Sturbridge Village, Mass.,
    181–84
Old Tavern, Grafton, Vt., 35,
    56–57, 62
Oliver Ellsworth Homestead,
    Conn., 223
Olmstead, Frederick Law, 14,
    216, 245
Orchards, Williamstown,
    Mass., 189, 194
Orford, N.H., 84–85
Orvis, Manchester, Vt., 48

Palladio, Andrea, 108
Palmer, May Suydam, 32–33
Parris, Alexander, 109
Passaconaway Historic Site,
    N.H., 74
Pawlet, Vt., 48
Peabody Museum of Natural
    History, Conn., 243–44
Peru, Vt., 49
Peterboro, N.H., 94
Phillips Exeter Academy, N.H.,
    117
Pinchot, Gifford, 14
Pinkham Notch, N.H., 78
Pittsfield, Mass., 143–49
Plainfield, N.H., 121, 124–25

Pleasant Valley Wildlife
    Sanctuary, Mass., 142
Plymouth Cheese Factory, Vt.,
    30
Plymouth Notch Historic
    District, Vt., 29–30
Portsmouth, N.H., 104–17
    architecture, 107–9
    Athenaeum, 109–10
    excursions from, 114–17
    historic houses, 110–11,
        112–14, 116
    history, 104–7
    Strawbery Banke, 106–7,
        110–12
    what to see and do, 109–14
    where to eat, 126–27
    where to stay, 122–23
Portsmouth Gaslight Co., 126
Potter, Edward Tuckerman,
    209–10
Pratt Museum of Natural
    History, Mass., 173
pricing keys, ix
Publick House, Sturbridge,
    Mass., 192, 196

Quechee, Vt., 27–28, 60–61
Quechee Gorge, 28
Quechee Inn, 55, 61

Rabbit Hill Inn, Lower
    Waterford, Vt., 54, 60
Ragamont Inn, Salisbury,
    Conn., 269–70
Rail 'n' River Trail, N.H., 74
Red Brook Inn, Mystic, Conn.,
    257
Red Lion Inn, Stockbridge,
    Mass., 151, 189–90,
        194–95
Reluctant Panther,
    Manchester, Vt., 44, 57,
        62
restaurants, pricing key, ix
Rhododendron State Park,
    N.H., 97

Richard Alsop IV House, Conn., 215
Richardson, H. H., 177, 232
Riddle, Theodate Pope, 213
Ridgefield, Conn., 261, 269
Rindge, N.H., 95
Robert Frost Library, Mass., 172
Robertson, Robert Henderson, 14
Rockingham Meeting House, Vt., 39–41
Rockwell, Norman, 158–59
Rocky Hill, Conn., 222
Roseland Cottage, Conn., 224
Rupert, Vt., 48
Rutland area, Vt., 51–52, 59

Saarinen, Eero, 241
Saarinen, Eliel, 140
Sabbaday Falls, N.H., 74
Saint-Gaudens, Augustus, 86–87, 155, 156, 177
Saint-Gaudens National Historic Site, N.H., 86–89
St. Johnsbury, Vt., 23–24, 54, 60
St. Johnsbury Athenaeum art gallery, 23–24
Salisbury, Conn., 261, 269–70
Samuel Russell House, Conn., 215
Saybrook Point Inn and Spa, Conn., 258–59
Scott Bridge, Vt., 37
Sears, Clara Endicott, 185–86
Sergeant, John, 150, 151–52
Shaker villages, 86, 98–100, 143–47, 185–86
Shakespeare and Company at the Mount, Mass., 142
Sharon, Conn., 253
Shaw-Perkins Mansion, Conn., 231
Sheffield, Mass., 135–38
Shelburne, Vt., 8–15, 50, 58
Shelburne Falls, Mass., 166

Shelburne Farms, Vt., 14–15, 50, 58
Shelburne Museum, Vt., 8–14
Sheraton Portsmouth, N.H., 123
Simon Pearce Restaurant, Quechee, Vt., 27, 60
Skyline Restaurant, Vt., 39
Sloane, Eric, 253–54
Sloane-Stanley Museum, Conn., 253–54
Smith College, Mass., 172, 174
Smith College Museum of Art, 174
Smugglers Notch, Vt., 20
South Egremont, Mass., 138
Southern Vermont Art Center, 46–47
South Hadley, Mass., 175–77
Spratt, William, 246
Springfield, Mass., 177–81
Springfield Library & Museums, 177–80
Stanley-Whitman House, Conn., 213–14
Star Island, N.H., 115
state capitols:
   Connecticut, 211
   New Hampshire, 97
   Vermont, 28
State Street Saloon, Portsmouth, N.H., 127
Sterling and Francine Clark Art Institute, Mass., 162–64
Stern, Robert A. M., 159
Stockbridge, Mass., 150–59
Stonehenge, America's, N.H., 104
Stonehenge Inn, Ridgefield, Conn., 261, 269
Stone Village, Vt., 41–42
Stonington, Conn., 225–26, 267
Stowe, Harriet Beecher, 209–10
Stowe, Vt., 19–21, 52–53, 59
Stowehof Inn, Vt., 59

Strong House Museum, Mass.,
    173
Sturbridge Village, Mass.,
    181–84
Suffield, Conn., 217–19
Sugar Hill Inn, Franconia,
    N.H., 120, 123
Swift House, Middlebury, Vt.,
    51, 58
Swift River Inn, Cummington,
    Mass., 192, 197

Talcott Arboretum, Mass., 176
Tanglewood, Mass., 140–41
Tapping Reeve House, Conn.,
    247
Ten Acres Lodge, Stowe, Vt.,
    53, 59
Thaxter, Celia, 115
Thomas Griswold House,
    Conn., 237
Tiffany window, Stockbridge,
    Mass., 151
Tilton, Edward L., 180
Tobacco Valley, Conn., 217–28
Tollgate Hill Inn, Litchfield,
    Conn., 260, 268
Topnotch, Stowe, Vt., 53, 59
Town, Ithiel, 206, 215, 253
Townshend, Vt., 37
Trapp Family Lodge, Stowe,
    Vt., 52
Travelers Tower, Conn., 205
Tubbs, Montpelier, Vt., 60
Tuckerman Ravine, N.H., 80
Tyringham Valley, Mass., 159–
    62

Under Mountain Inn,
    Salisbury, Conn., 261, 270
United States Coast Guard
    Academy, Conn., 232
Upjohn, Richard, 101, 211

Vermont, 1–63
    central, 24–30, 54–55,
    60–61

drives, 19, 21–23, 26–28,
    37–49
general facts, 3
general stores, 30, 38, 42–
    43, 48, 49
Historical Society, 28–29
history, 4–7
Lake Champlain area, 8–19,
    50–52, 58–59
maps, 2, 7
Northeast Kingdom, 21–24,
    53–54, 59–60
northern, 19–24, 52–53, 59
southern, 31–49, 56–58, 61–
    63
special interest sources, 7
State House, 28
Upper Connecticut River
    Valley, 24–49, 54–58,
    60–62
villages of, 3
where to eat, 50, 58–63
where to stay, 49–58
Vermont Country Store, 42–43
Vermont Marble Inn, Fair
    Haven, 51–52, 59
Vermont State Craft Center,
    17
Vermont Wildflower Farm,
    15–16
Village Inn, Lenox, Mass., 195

Wadsworth Atheneum, Conn.,
    205–9, 223, 242
Wake Robin Inn, Lakeville,
    Conn., 259
Walpole, N.H., 90
Washington, Conn., 249, 262,
    270
Washington, N.H., 98
Water's Edge Inn, Westbrook,
    Conn., 259
Waybury Inn, Middlebury, Vt.,
    51
Webb, Electra Havemeyer,
    8–10, 14
Webb-Deane-Stevens Museum,
    Conn., 220–21

Webb Gallery, 12–14
Wells, Joseph C., 224
Wentworth, John, 69–70, 83, 91
Wentworth, Benning, 4, 24, 69, 109
Wentworth-by-the-Sea, N.H., 116
Wesleyan University, Conn., 215–16
Westbrook, Conn., 259
West Cornwall, Conn., 270
West Dover, Vt., 39, 50, 57–58, 63
West Dummerston covered bridge, Vt., 39
Western Gateway Heritage State Park, Mass., 166
West Lane Inn, Ridgefield, Conn., 261
Weston, Vt., 42–43, 63
Weston Bowl Mill, Vt., 43
West Street Grill, Litchfield, Conn., 268
Wethersfield, Conn., 219–22, 256
Wharton, Edith, 141–42
Wheatleigh, Lenox, Mass., 190, 195
Whip Bar and Grill, Stowe, Vt., 59
Whistling Swan, Sturbridge, Mass., 196–97
White Flower Farm, Conn., 248
White Hart, Salisbury, Conn., 270
White Memorial Foundation and Conservation Center, Conn., 247–48

White Mountains, N.H., 71–82, 118–20, 123
Wildcat Mountain, N.H., 78
Williams College, Mass., 164
Williams College Museum of Art, 164
Williamstown, Mass., 162–64
Williamsville Inn, West Stockbridge, Mass., 190, 195
Windflower Inn, Great Barrington, Mass., 190–91, 195
Windsor, Conn., 222–23
Wolfeboro, N.H., 91, 122, 125–26
Wolfeboro Inn, 122, 126
Woodbury, Conn., 249–50
Woodland, Lakeville, Conn., 267–68
Woodstock, Conn., 224
Woodstock, Vt., 24–28, 55, 60–61
Woodstock Historical Society, Vt., 26
Woodstock Inn & Resort, Vt., 55
Worcester, Mass., 184
Worcester Art Museum, 184
Wright, Frank Lloyd, 103–4

Yale University, 240–44
    Art Gallery, 242–43
    Beinecke Rare Book and Manuscript Library, 241
    Center for British Art, 243

Zimmerman House, 101, 103

ABOUT THE AUTHOR

TIM MULLIGAN is the author of *The Hudson River Valley: A History & Guide* and *Virginia: A History & Guide.* He has been editor at several magazines and has written for *Travel & Leisure, Holiday,* and *New York,* among other publications. He is currently director of communications for the New York State Council on the Arts. He lives in New York City.

ABOUT THE TYPE

This book was set in Century Schoolbook, a member of the Century family of typefaces. It was designed in the 1890s by Theodore Low DeVinne of the American Type Founders Company, in collaboration with Linn Boyd Benton. It was one of the earliest types designed for a specific purpose, the *Century* magazine, because it was able to maintain the economies of a narrower typeface while using stronger serifs and thickened verticals.